# POLITICAL
# PHILOSOPHY

# Fundamentals of Philosophy

Series Editor: A. P. Martinich, University of Texas at Austin

Each volume in the Fundamentals of Philosophy series covers a key area of study in philosophy. Written with verve and clarity by leading philosophers, these authoritative volumes look to reveal the fundamental issues and core problems that drive interest in the field.

*Forthcoming*

# POLITICAL
# PHILOSOPHY
## THE FUNDAMENTALS

Thom Brooks

**WILEY** Blackwell

*Registered Offices*
John Wiley & Sons, Inc., 111 River Street, Hoboken, NJ 07030, USA
John Wiley & Sons Ltd, New Era House, 8 Oldlands Way, Bognor Regis, West Sussex, PO22 9NQ, UK

For details of our global editorial offices, customer services, and more information about Wiley products visit us at www.wiley.com.

The manufacturer's authorized representative according to the EU General Product Safety Regulation is Wiley-VCH GmbH, Boschstr. 12, 69469 Weinheim, Germany, e-mail: Product_Safety@wiley.com.

Wiley also publishes its books in a variety of electronic formats and by print-on-demand. Some content that appears in standard print versions of this book may not be available in other formats.

*Library of Congress Cataloging-in-Publication Data*
Names: Brooks, Thom, author.
Title: Political philosophy : the fundamentals / Thom Brooks.
Description: Hoboken, NJ : Wiley, 2025. | Series: Fundamentals of philosophy | Includes bibliographical references and index.
Identifiers: LCCN 2024039293 (print) | LCCN 2024039294 (ebook) | ISBN 9781405189378 (paperback) | ISBN 9781118609019 (adobe pdf) | ISBN 9781118609026 (epub)
Subjects: LCSH: Political science–Philosophy.
Classification: LCC JA71 .B7574 2025 (print) | LCC JA71 (ebook) | DDC 320.01–dc23/eng/20240829
LC record available at https://lccn.loc.gov/2024039293
LC ebook record available at https://lccn.loc.gov/2024039294

Cover Design: Wiley
Cover Image: © atribut/Shutterstock

Set in 10.5/13pt Sabon by Straive, Pondicherry, India
Printed and bound by CPI Group (UK) Ltd, Croydon, CR0 4YY

C9781405189378_150325

*For Martha C. Nussbaum*

# Contents

# Acknowledgments

Since my first class in political philosophy, I did not know that this area would become a focus for much of my future career. But I knew instantly that I was hooked. My early interests quickly gravitated toward the classic works in the history of political thought – a typical core of most introductory classes – and soon expanded to cover contemporary debates, as well as works in non-Western areas like Indian philosophy. Over the years, I have noticed a divided approach to most introductions to political philosophy. Many follow the traditional path of summarizing the views of key historical figures from roughly from Plato to Marx. An alternative approach has become common over the last few decades to focus instead exclusively on contemporary scholars, especially since John Rawls's work from the 1950s. There is usually little cross-over between the two paths, and this is unfortunate as both have important contributions to offer about how we understand political concepts like freedom, rights, equality, democracy, and more. Indeed, as Rawls notes, much of his work may be thought of as putting old wine in new bottles. We must understand the contributions from the history of political thought to best comprehend insights found in contemporary debates.

This is the kind of book that I had wanted to find long ago after consuming vast quantities of philosophical introductions, as part of my academic diet as a graduate student. Topics are designed to bring together insights old and new that contribute to our understanding. Political philosophy is a philosophy that is *political*, applied to institutions. This requires we take context seriously providing a coherent, or what I describe as a "coherentist," approach to comprehending political ideas within context and in the world. A political philosophy that is not or cannot be applied is at best impractical and undeveloped. It must address a world where disagreement and pluralism reigns. Otherwise, we design ideas for fairy tales, not for political reality. This book attempts to provide an introduction to a *political* variety of political philosophy for our living world.

Speaking of fanciful wishing, this book is many years in the making. I am enormously grateful to Wiley-Blackwell for their patience awaiting the book's completion much later than planned. Originally, I had approached Wiley-Blackwell with a proposal to publish a major anthology on global justice which was accepted and published as *The Global Justice Reader* in 2008. However, it was agreed that the *Reader* would be part of a four-book deal publishing the *Reader* (in 2008 and revised edition 2023), a collected edition on *Hegel's Philosophy of Right* (2012) and *Reader* companion monograph *Global Justice: An Introduction* (2023). The last of the four is the book in your hands concluding an enjoyable and stimulating journey at long last.

For all this, I owe thanks in particular to the late Nick Bellorini who commissioned these books from me. I will always remember our conversation at a small coffee shop around the corner from St Edmund Hall, Oxford. It started with plans for one book (e.g. *The Reader*) quickly expanding to four. His faith in me and belief in these projects have been invaluable source of support from the start of my career and I wish he was able to see them come to full fruition at long last. I am hugely grateful to Will Croft and Juhitha Manivannan for their patience and support in seeing these projects completed.

I am enormously privileged to work with so many inspiring students during my eight years at Newcastle University and thirteen years thus far at Durham University. I benefited further during a sabbatical after completing five long years as Dean of Durham Law School. This period of research leave was made all the more enjoyable by being able to spend time as a visitor at Yale Law School in my native New Haven, Connecticut. I remain enormously grateful to Dean Heather Gerken for the opportunity and support over many years. My time at Yale has made a significant impact on my thinking that has shaped my work since.

The chapters in this book have taken various forms originally as lectures for my students, who are a source of great pride. Many have shaped my thinking over the years, but special mention must be made of my first student, Luke Sullivan, who opened my eyes to how academic work can meaningfully contribute to real-world politics in ways that I had not imagined. Luke has taught me more than I ever attempted to teach him and I hope this runs deep throughout this book.

My views on political philosophy developed below were further shaped through discussions on my various public lectures, keynotes, conferences, and departmental seminars delivered at the Ashmolean Museum, the Café Philosophique in Newcastle upon Tyne, the Edinburgh Fringe Festival, Glasgow Sceptics, Institute for Public Policy Research (IPPR) – North, Royal Danish Society of Science and Letters plus the annual conferences of the American Philosophical Association – Eastern Division and Political Studies Association, the Society of Legal Scholars and the universities of Arizona State, Boston, Bowling Green State, Bristol, Cardiff, Chicago, City University of Hong Kong, CUNY, Durham, Edinburgh, Glasgow, Hull, Indian Institute of Technology, Leeds, Limerick, Lincoln, LUISS Guido Carli, Milan, Newcastle, O. P. Jindal, Open, Oxford, Quincy, Rijeka, Rotterdam, Sciences Po, St Andrews, Sheffield, Stirling, Suffolk, Tilburg, University College Dublin, Uppsala, Warwick, Yale, York and an insightful roundtable on the impact of political theory held in the House of Lords.

I owe many thanks to several friends and colleagues for various conversations helping to shape my views on political philosophy. I owe deep thanks to Steve Shalom for first introducing me to the field during my undergraduate studies and encouraging me to pursue an academic career. In graduate school, I was fortunate to learn from Terence Ball, Chris Bennett, Mark Bevir, Joy Chaudhuri, Jack Crittenden, Avital Simhony, Leif Wenar and the late Bob Stern. My thinking has developed further thanks to conversations and feedback about ideas discussed in this book from some of the most wonderful and supportive colleagues one could hope for, including Scott Aikin, Liz Ashford, Christian Barry, David Boucher, Gillian Brock, Vittorio Bufacchi, Simon Caney, Andrew Cohen, James Connolly, Rowan Cruft, Albert Dzur, Paul Franks, Fabian Freyenhagen, Carol Gould, Les Green, Nicole Hassoun, Iwao Hirose, Stephen Houlgate, Alison Jaggar, Peter Jones, Matthew Kramer, Cecile Laborde, Hélène Landemore, Melissa Lane, Brian Leiter, S. Matthew Liao, Kasper Lippert-Rasmussen, Raino Malnes, Jeff McMahan, Sandra Marshall, John Mason, Matt Matravers, David Miliband, David Miller, Michael Morrell, Tim Mulgan, Peter Nicholson, Michael Otsuka, Jon Quong, Philip Pettit, Henry Richardson, Michael Ridge, Julian Roberts, Michael Rosen, Jesper Ryberg, Ian Shapiro, Scott Shapiro, Samuel Scheffler, Peter Singer, John Skorupski, Steven Smith, Keir Starmer,

Sebastian Stein, Luke Sullivan, Robert Talisse, Kok-Chor Tan, Jens Timmerman, Colin Tyler, Laura Valentini, Jeremy Waldron, Krushil Watene, Albert Weale, Kit Wellman, Jo Wolff and Leo Zaibert, and several sadly no longer with us, including Jerry Cohen, John Gardner, Dudley Knowles, Jeffrie Murphy, Gerhard Øverland and Joseph Raz, amongst others (with apologies for friends mistakenly left out).

I owe very special thanks to my dearest friend Lord (Bhikhu) Parekh, who has been like a guru to me for about two decades. His contributions to both academic and public life have been an enormous inspiration to me and his influence on my thinking on political philosophy is profound. More political philosophers should engage in real world politics, as he has shown me.

I dedicate this book to Martha C. Nussbaum. My first contact was through inviting her to join the editorial board of a new academic journal that I hoped to launch as its founding editor. We had never met before and I am forever grateful to Martha for accepting an invitation from an unknown second-year PhD student in Britain for an ambitious new project. The journal was the *Journal of Moral Philosophy* that has now published over twenty volumes and has become one of the most internationally reputable in the field. Over the years, I have benefited in more ways that I can describe from her work, advice, and example. Anyone familiar with Martha's ground-breaking, often revolutionary, and prolific works should see her influence across every page below. Few have been as kind or supportive to me throughout my career, and this book is one minuscule effort to repay a lifelong debt of immense gratitude to her for all she has done for me.

Finally, I am enormously grateful to my wonderful family, most especially to Claire and Eve. They may not always understand why I am so passionate about my academic work, let alone political philosophy, and devote long hours constructing works like this. But I am more thankful than can be expressed in words for their patience, support, and love in my being able to pursue it.

Books are said to be products of love; yet this love is not only of the author for their work, but their family, friends, and colleagues who nurture, challenge, and support them along the way. My thanks to all family and friends for their support over many years.

*T.A.K.B.*                                                    *New Haven, Connecticut*

# Introduction

## I.1   What Is Philosophy?

Defining philosophy is no simple task. Any answer to the question – "what is philosophy?" – is bound to be philosophical itself. The word *philosophy* has Greek origins meaning "love of wisdom." This definition begs the question of "what is wisdom?" and this has been answered very many ways that could take several books to explain. Generally speaking, philosophy is about gaining wisdom about fundamental areas of human existence. These areas include the meaning of life, the nature of justice, and the possibilities of knowledge. Philosophy aims to provide us with a clearer understanding of these key issues.

One of the best-known ancient Greek philosophers is Socrates. As portrayed in the writings of Plato, Socrates saw philosophy in action as a form of dialogue where we continually, and methodically, question our views and understandings of some area and gain new insights from the answers this discussion can yield (Plato 1997: 971–1223). Philosophy does this by challenging our assumptions, clarifying our definitions, sharpening our concepts, and critically reflecting on their uses and applications. Through his discussions and engagement with others, Socrates challenged the commonly held views of his time and, in doing so, created new ways of thinking about the world and its meaning. His work has influenced philosophical debates ever since and for over two thousand years.

*Political Philosophy: The Fundamentals*, First Edition. Thom Brooks.
© 2025 John Wiley & Sons Ltd. Published 2025 by John Wiley & Sons Ltd.

In this book, I see philosophy as generally about our gaining a clearer understanding of our world. As Bernard Williams argued, the aim of philosophy "is to be clear" and so to remove obscurity (Williams 1985: viii). My approach adopts a similar *analytic* style that aims to scrutinize what is complex or obscure in order to render it more accessible and comprehensible. For example, as we will consider later in this book, there can be many very different views on how we should best understand the concepts like *freedom* or *justice*. An analytical approach seeks to clarify these concepts by examining different views in order to get a clearer view of what each is about and how each compares with others. We can – and will – do the same with other concepts like democracy, equality, and many more.

## I.2    What Is Political Philosophy?

Philosophy is applied. It can often be described in terms of being a *philosophy of* some area of knowledge. This can take various forms, including political philosophy.[1] The form here is a philosophy of *the political*.[2] This subject-matter has invited many different views about how or where a political concept might be applied and, of course, what is considered political. But what they all generally have in common is the view that the *political* is fundamentally about *power*, including power relations. Political philosophers often focus on the relation of values and principles to institutions, as this is connected to the exercise of power that links them.

As Bhikhu Parekh argues: "It is difficult to imagine a society or a civilisation without political thought . . .. To imagine a society or a civilization without some kind of political theory is to imagine a people happy to muddle through life with a bunch of heterogeneous and conflicting ideas and lacking the capacity for reflective thinking" (Parekh 2019: 1). Any political community must grasp why and how it is to be organized and function as it is and does. Political philosophy is essential to understanding who "we" are as a political community and the ways in which our collective lives are conducted through public debate and shared institutions.

---

[1] There are many other ways of applying philosophy as a *philosophy of*, such as the philosophy of art, philosophy of language, and philosophy of mind among many other forms.
[2] For Dudley Knowles, who was the external examiner of my PhD in 2004, it is claimed that "there is no such science; there is no 'first philosophy' of political life. Yet it is vital that political philosophy be a careful academic discipline precisely because it is never merely that." See Knowles (2001: xi).

Political philosophy is about *what* power is, *where* it is located, *who* might yield it, and *how* it might be used. While political philosophers may agree that they are engaged in a philosophical exploration into power, they may hold starkly different views about their preferred philosophical approach and how power is manifest in the world. In other words, political philosophers can disagree about the political, as well as their philosophical, methodology.

A key aim of this book is to make these complex disagreements accessible and comprehensible for readers who might never have picked up a philosophy book before or previously studied political thought. Likewise, for those who have some previous engagement with political philosophy, this book aspires to introduce the subject in a new way and from an explicitly *political* kind of political philosophy that is more closely aligned around the relation of our ideas to political institutions in ways that will now be explained.

There are essentially two broad camps in political philosophy. This is usually referred to as the applied morality view versus a more practice-oriented political realism. For my purposes here I prefer the simpler, and I think more accurate, distinction of *the moral view* versus *the institutional view*.[3]

The first way of thinking about political philosophy is as fundamentally *normative*, involving norms, values, and moral judgments (hence, *the moral view*).[4] Proponents of this view typically

---

[3] This distinction is made similarly by others, for example as "a political morality" and "a theory of institutions" presenting two differing views of what political theory is about. This can represent two different considerations: first, the justified use of coercive political power and, secondly, the authority of such power. In this work, we will consider how these different approaches might compatibly relate together when viewed in context. See Raz (1986: 3, 25–26).

[4] Most people think about "norms" and "morals" interchangeably. My emphasis on normativity, and not morality, expresses a view that I have that normativity and morality are conceptually different. While they both refer to ethical evaluations about what we ought to do, I understand *norms* as general reasons to do, or refrain from doing, some act that we can assess independently from other norms. In contrast, I understand *morals* as reasons to do, or refrain from doing, some act as part of a wider *morality*, such as a system of morality, that may be assessed as a part of a systematic collection of morals. Moral systems may be philosophical or religious whether Kantian, utilitarian, Christian or otherwise. Both norms and morals provide us with reasons to do or refrain from doing, but norms are mere reasons that might be considered singularly while moral reasons are part of some wider systematic moral view. For example, Aesop's famous *Fables* contain several different normative principles that do not add up to a coherent moral system, such as "might makes right" versus "persuasion is better than force" and "the battle is not always to the strong" (Aesop 2003: 35, 105, 130). This suggests that normative principles may fit within a larger, coherent moral system or they may not, while moral principles should always cohere within a moral system. There is a conceptual difference between a norm and morals. I think this is an important distinction to make and which may continue to get more traction in future debates.

describe political philosophy as a subfield of the larger area of ethics and moral philosophy, or sometimes as an applied moral theory.[5] For example, Robert Nozick said that "moral philosophy sets the background for, and boundaries of, political philosophy" (Nozick 1974: 6). This means that the space of the political assumes a moral framework. In other words, moral justification is key to justifying anything political. Our politics gains its legitimacy and justification from the strength of the moral view that is its life's blood. The political is inseparable from its moral framework. This position accepts the view of natural law theory, as it sees law and morality as inseparably linked: to ask "what *is* the law" is to ask "what *morally justifies* the law"? In other words, law *is* to the degree it *is morally justified*. For example, if we are convinced by a consequentialist moral theory based on maximizing outcomes, then political ideas will be justified by the view of political philosophy insofar as they promote consequentialism.

Many argue that political justice requires moral justification. As an illustration, Thomas Nagel claims that "moral harmony and not only civil peace is the right aim of politics" (Nagel 1986: 206). The idea is that moral philosophy creates a normative framework relevant to legitimizing political institutions or justifying the exercise of political power (Kymlicka 2002: 5). Morality and politics are inextricably interlinked akin to morality and law within natural law theory. Without moral justification, our political institutions lack normative support. Political justice is morally justified.

This moral view of political philosophy might seem compelling to most readers – and it is probably no surprise that it has a powerful

---

[5] I use the words *philosophy* and *theory* interchangeably throughout. I do not see any essential differences between *political philosophy* and *political theory* so view them the same way although others may disagree. The most common distinction made is that political philosophers (usually viewed as those working in philosophy departments) are more focused on contemporary issues and debates while political theorists (usually viewed as those working in political science departments) can be more focused on historical issues and debates. As someone who studied and worked in both kinds of departments, my experience is that any such claimed difference is more down to the particular research climate of the individual philosophy or political science department than to any essential distinction about what political philosophy or political theory is essentially about. Self-identified political philosophers in philosophy departments can be just as interested in historical debates as self-identified political theorists in political science departments are concerned with contemporary issues. (I should know!) Indeed, many scholars (including me) work in *both* contemporary *and* historical contexts. Whether one is a "philosopher" or "theorist" seems to me more an indication of whether one's home institution is a philosophy department or political science department and not any essential difference between "political philosophy" and "political theory" which are, and will be treated in this book, as interchangeably the same things.

grip on much of the field for a large part of its history. We may see the creation of just political institutions as a manifestation of their underlying moral principles. Indeed, we might go further and say political justice is about instituting a just ethical view of the world for our community.[6] If we are convinced by some moral view, then it may seem obvious (or implicitly assumed) that this view is vital for understanding what form political justice should take. After all, who would defend a view of politics that was *not* morally justified?

A famous example of a moral view of political philosophy is found in the work of Immanuel Kant. As we shall discuss later in this book, Kant defends the idea that there is a knowable, universal moral law that governs the ethical relations between every individual helping us discern what is right or wrong. Kant divides his work into a "doctrine of right" and a "doctrine of virtue." The doctrine of right is about the application of the moral law to the political sphere. It is concerned with our enforceable rights and punishable wrongs in the external world, for instance, which we might see as classic political theory. In contrast, Kant's doctrine of virtue is about the moral law's application to the sphere of virtue pertaining to our personal conscience where the state is severely limited in how it might govern it if at all, this might be seen as more the province of moral theory beyond the political. It is Kant's moral law that sets the horizon and possibilities for the political and legal system, as it provides the justificatory framework for it (Kant 1996b). Morality and politics are overlapping parts of a common project with the moral law at its heart.

The moral view of political philosophy assumes a convincing background morality. If we argue for a view consistent with Kant's moral

---

[6] I use "just ethical view" as often our view of what is ethical, moral or just is taken to be good, most valuable or preferential. Thus, to claim a position is ethical (or moral or just) on this view is to also claim it is good, most valuable or preferential in comparison to any relevant alternatives. This commonplace everyday use of "ethical" is in mind for simplicity. However, strictly speaking, an ethical view is a position justified in relation to some view about ethical values. Whether or not an ethical view is compelling as a preferred view will depend, at least in part, on its merits. Undoubtedly, good people with good intentions will come to defend different ethical positions. We might reject the devil's ethical claims (so to speak and whatever these might be) and find them completely unacceptable, but these claims might still constitute an "ethical view" even if in defense of values we might reject. Indeed, there is a difference between an ethical view generally and a compelling ethical view. Thus, my use of "just ethical view" is intended to distinguish ethical views justified as morally good from other such ethical conceptions. Much more might be said about this distinction about ethics and goodness, but this note should suffice to make clear there is such a distinction to be aware about.

law, it is necessary that we can say that this moral view is itself convincing *prior* to advocating it as a justificatory normative source behind our preferred political philosophy. Our background morality is like a well from which we draw our political theory's reasoning and its justificatory defense. This means that anyone defending a moral view of political philosophy must work out their morality conception to be applied first. One challenge is there can be deep disagreement about which moral view should be applied. Thus, some may be divided as much about which morality should underpin a political conception as they might be about the political conception in question to be underpinned.

But, of course, no state likely fits perfectly *any* position on morality, whichever moral view is defended. Nor is there any Kantian kingdom of ends on Earth.[7] The moral view of political philosophy is often about creating an ideal – or what John Rawls would call a "realistic utopia" (Rawls 2001: 4) – that sets out a moral standard for designing our political institutions and a measure that our moral progress might be judged against. The debate may be as much about whether the moral theory is *convincing* in principle as to whether its application in the political realm is *achievable* in practice.

Even if uninterested in the moral justification of the political, it could be argued that much of what we talk about when discussing political philosophy is fundamentally concerned with morality, too. Consider our use of *political language*. We use words like "good" and "bad" or "rights" and "wrongs" or "duty" and "punishment": these are all terms that can have moral content. We can speak of some action's goodness or badness, the duties that ground rights, and the need for punishment when there are wrongs. But these words are not inextricably moral – and may all be used in a distinctly non-moral way. For example, we may find the weather to be "good" or "bad" based on if it is (or is not) agreeable to us. This is a normative claim expressing a value – such as "good" weather is what is our preferred weather, like a pleasant and sunny day when we planned to have a picnic or go for an outdoor walk – but not necessarily a moral value, such as goodness or virtue. For another example, we might search for

---

[7] Kant describes a community governed by his moral law as a kingdom of ends. It is so described, in part, because individuals would ethically relate to each other as ends-in-themselves rather than as means to some consequentialist end. In this way, Kantian morality is deontological and opposed to consequentialism.

the "right" umbrella to use if the weather takes a "wrong" turn. We may "dutifully" nestle into a chair to read a book before bedtime and say it would be like "punishment" if we could not do so should poor weather lead to a blackout and prevent us reading it. Each statement contains words (such as "right" or "wrong") that do not have a normative meaning in these contexts, even if they might do so if the context were different, such as if we said that someone was "wrong" to inflict harm on an innocent bystander.

These illustrations highlight that we should *not* assume our use of various words, such as "rights" or "wrongs," is inextricably connected with any particular moral view. In fact, the meanings of these words can even shift within the same sentence, such as when we say that "Smith is good at football but a bad politician" (Mabbott 1966: 13, 14). While "good" is used in a non-moral sense in terms of possessing sport-related skill, the word "bad" may refer to wrongful conduct or decision-making of an elected leader. We should not assume that words that *can* have moral meanings always *do* have moral meanings in every specific context without close examination. For example, to say political philosophy is about "rights" and "justice" *can* have moral meanings if political philosophy is understood in a morally-specific way, but it might *not* do so if political philosophy is considered from a different non-moral standpoint. We should not make assumptions either way, but instead consider the context to make clear whether a concept is meant to be understood in some morally-specific way.

A second way of thinking about political philosophy is as fundamentally *institutional* (hence, I call it *the institutional view*). This view sees the political as essentially practical, and so not necessarily interlinked nor infused with morality. Politics and morality are separable as different kinds of projects that can be considered in isolation from each other. An institutional view of political philosophy is a perspective from the ground up that gives greater weight to practical matters in the world as having a bearing on the justification of political concepts, including freedom or rights. It gives greater attention to how political institutions and public authorities inform political justice. The institutional view claims that what we *ought* to do must be *possible* to do (Williams 1981: 120).

As an example, the *moral* view of political philosophy might begin with the application of a moral theory to politics. Our focus is on how our politics might better meet moral standards in order to justify our political ideas.[8] In contrast to this perspective, the institutional view of political philosophy may start with the fact that societies contain diverse moral (and cultural) views and that these non-moral facts about our world raise issues that are relevant to how we might justify a political philosophy that takes equality and inclusion seriously given these practical facts about everyday life.[9]

Of course, we view morality differently. As an example, it is a commonly held Western view that we have a right to self-defense when another attacks us unprovoked and that this is a right we are supported in exercising. However in other traditions, such as for Jainism and some forms of Buddhism, harm to others is always a wrong even if in self-defense (Brooks 2017a).[10] This shows that it is not obvious that there is a single moral (or cultural) perspective that all individuals accept. To claim a moral view is not enough; we must also set out how and why others should accept it, in light of the fact that there can be significant differences about what is morally good or preferable. The benefit of the institutional approach is that it does not need nor aspire to defend a comprehensive, or "thick," conception of the good.[11] Instead, it offers a more "realist" account of political philosophy, as it is understood and used practically in the world (Larmore 2020: 46–47).

For the institutional view, our political conceptions can be limited by practical constraints of how communities work or the way that individuals relate to each other. For the moral view, our political conception is limited by the constraints imposed by the limits of our moral theory. Broadly speaking, the institutionalists work up from the practical level whereas the moral view usually works down from some ideal moral standard.

---

[8] This is sometimes because the compellingness of a moral theory is assumed; but, of course, no such view should be assumed. Yet, if not assumed, much of the work of this variety of political philosophy is about defending the moral theory providing the foundation. Such endeavors can risk developing our knowledge of moral theory much more than political philosophy, as the latter can appear secondary to the moral context.

[9] The main text presents a difference between the moral view and the institutional view as a difference between the application of a moral theory to justifying political ideas versus the application of non-moral facts to justifying political ideas. I note that some who defend a moral view claim there are moral facts about the world, although this is strongly contested. So, another way of grasping the difference between *some* forms of the moral view versus the institutional view is the former *may* focus on the application of *moral facts,* and the latter focus on the application of *non-moral facts.* On moral facts and moral realism generally, see Geoff Sayre-McCord (1988).

[10] The idea that doing a wrong is always wrong even in self-defense is not alien to Western philosophy. See Plato (1997: 42).

[11] In other words, it can be sensitive to concerns about ethnocentric political theory where ideas are "uncritically generalized and appears in a universal form." See Parekh (2019: 4–5).

## I.3    Making Political Thought Coherent

It is unclear that the moral view and institutional view are, or should be, incompatible. And it would be desirable to account for features of both. For example, every moral view of political philosophy cannot escape the practical importance of institutions that play some essential role in our political lives. The way things are governed and how power is exercised can constrain the possibilities for how a just society can be constituted that best embodies moral principles. This is inescapable and must factor in how we understand the practical possibilities of the political. Political philosophy *is* practical to some degree by its nature (Miller 2023: 441). Institutions matter. After all, political philosophy is about political concepts and issues. Institutions matter for understanding the relation of our political ideas to practice.

Moreover, few would argue that ethical views, such as our normative approaches to thinking about justice, are completely irrelevant to how power is used. In other words, political philosophy is about more than how power might be exercised, but whether it should be exercised in certain ways that are *normatively* justifiable. Norms matter for evaluating the justifiability of our political ideas.

Any political philosophy ought to be *fact-dependent* and responsive to changing facts about practices and institutions as a *political* philosophy, but at the same time it should also be *norm-dependent* and responsive to the normative justifications that support any *philosophy* of the political. Political philosophy must be relevant to the world *and* relate to normative evaluation in some way. Institutions and norms are both essential. It isn't an either-or choice. Political philosophy must consider ideas in relation to how they make coherent sense practically *and* normatively. For this reason, the moral and institutional approaches intertwine.

Understanding ideas within their wider context is important because it helps us respond to disagreements. We differ about which view of freedom, rights, equality, and other political concepts is most compelling – and even if we share the same ideology or political party membership.[12] There is no problem *per se* that people disagree about fundamental issues about political ideas. After all, if we agreed on everything, there would be no point voting or doing political philosophy as we'd all accept the same views for the same reasons. Of course, we do not all share the same views. Disagreement is *normal* and

---

[12] See Williams (2005: 2, 3, 5, 7, 77).

political concepts are essentially contested. As people debate which views are most convincing, our understanding about freedom, rights, equality, and other political concepts changes over time – and it has – as will be made clear in the chapters below.

Political philosophy is essential to discerning what political ideas are most compelling, grasping their normative justification and practical application. It is through our philosophizing about political ideas that we engage with different views and progress our understanding (Brooks 2013b). This must happen taking ideas in context to help ensure we avoid an overly narrow approach that misses potential relevant factors.

My approach might be called *coherentist* and contextual, if some label was required.[13] I understand political philosophy as, in its essence, an interpretation about the justifiable exercise of power in the world. How we understand its exercise and the explanatory narrative we share to convince others about it must be shaped by the relevant facts and norms of our world where we seek to make best sense of how they fit together in context. In other words, political philosophy should seek to create some coherent framework for how relevant facts and norms relate to the world. This may not always be clear at first, but we can consider the opposite: a political philosophy that could not make coherent sense of how institutions and norms fit together would be impractical and, indeed, incoherent – thereby rendering the theory self-defeating, as it is unable to relate to the world in a meaningfully way. Political philosophy *makes sense* of power by providing a coherent view about how we see power and its exercise. My approach will become clearer in the chapters below.

## I.4   This Book

In this book, we will explore several key topics in political philosophy. Each is examined considering the important contributions from leading political philosophers from both the past and our present, in order to connect the history of political thought with contemporary debates. Chapters conclude with some further readings if readers wish to pursue a deeper study into various ideas discussed.

---

[13] For a critical overview of coherentism, see Olsson (2022).

The first chapter focuses on freedom. This is a fundamental topic in political philosophy, as much can turn on how we understand other topics depending on one's view. For example, a view about what freedom is can shape what view of rights we might defend, especially if we see rights as protecting our freedoms. This chapter discusses views about what freedom is about, how we might know we are free, and the different forms of freedom that philosophers have defended over time. We will explore questions of how we might know the existence of and limits to our freedom. Is freedom the absence of interference? Or is it the opportunity to achieve an important goal? The chapter's aim is to show the multiple ways that freedom has been understood, the differences between these views, and how they might be considered.

The second chapter examines rights. It begins with a historical perspective of its earlier origins in natural law and natural rights toward contemporary understandings of human rights. The chapter explores the different functions that rights are thought to possess and the importance of our rights as mutually recognized by others. This discussion reveals competing views about what makes rights valuable and how we can know what they are. We will ask what are rights? How do we know which rights we have and what purpose they might serve?

The third chapter considers equality. It explores different ways of understanding what equality is and why it is important. The chapter will also examine different ways of implementing equality assessing their merits. For example, should we level up or level down? Is equality the same as exactness? And what is the difference between legal and political equality? The chapter makes clear the diversity of views about the nature and application of equality far beyond what appears a deceptively simple concept.

The fourth chapter focuses on justice. It focuses primarily on the influential work by John Rawls. He developed an innovative approach, drawing on select key ideas from the history of political thought, creating a vision of a well-ordered society governed by principles of justice. Built on the equality of free individuals, Rawls provides a view about how people with different views of the good could create an overlapping consensus on contentious policy issues. This chapter explores these ideas and examines the alternative views of Rawls's critics, such as the capabilities approach and stakeholder theory, that develop different understandings about justice and its implementation.

The fifth chapter examines democracy. This looks at theories of democracy from ancient Greece to the present day. The chapter surveys the different forms of democratic government that have been defended over the years, including in its deliberative and republican forms. It will also review critiques of democracy since Plato and the important, but often overlooked, role that unelected officials, including the civil service, might have for any healthy, functioning democracy. It considers issues about whether democracies should allow the people to make every decision and what place there is, if any, for unelected experts in democratic governance.

The sixth chapter considers punishment. It surveys the various ways that the three main penal theories – retribution, deterrence, and rehabilitation – have been understood and the longstanding debates between them. The chapter also assesses attempts at joining these different positions together in hybrid theories, including my unified theory of punishment, and their relevance for modern sentencing. It considers the issues of what role, if any, should there be for desert, deterrence, and rehabilitation, and how proportionality should be set.

The seventh chapter focuses on global justice. This is one of the hottest topics in the field. A key issue is severe poverty, sadly too pervasive in our modern world. The chapter surveys three ways of understanding any duties of affluent states to those in desperate need, such as positive duties, negative duties, and remedial responsibilities – and the various challenges of attempting to implement these views and save lives.

The eighth, and final, chapter examines climate change. It considers the two broad diverse approaches to handling climate change – mitigation and adaptation – to assess whether they are adequate for the challenges ahead. The chapter looks at the need for a new theory of impermanent environmental sustainability to account for the endangered world that we live in – and the need for a new climate change ethics built around it for the future.

## I.5   Conclusion

The primary aim of this book is to introduce a reader to some of the leading ideas in political philosophy. It is not my aim to be neutral in discussing every debate in the field. However, it is intended that readers will be able to make up their own minds about where they stand on key issues and with some helpful guidance in what the debate is and why they hold one view instead of another. Political philosophy is not itself either left, right, or centrist by its nature. What matters is the quality of argument, not whether it is thought to fit with someone's individual views, no matter who they might be. Political philosophy is engaging so readers are encouraged to engage with it. The reader can judge for themselves which views are most persuasively argued. My aim here is not to tell readers *what* to think, but, instead, to support readers in *how* to think and meaningfully engage with political thought.[14]

Political philosophy is intrinsically and endlessly interesting. Through it, we can better understand our lived world and how we relate to others in it. Readers can also view political philosophy as a lifelong voyage of self-discovery, exploring more deeply the views you have about key issues in ways that might provide re-examination and a changed future outlook. Your voyage begins!

---

[14] Students regularly ask in class if there are "correct answers" in political philosophy. My view is that there are some, but only when specifically defined. For example, it is a fact that Rousseau is a social contract theorist, that Mill defends a harm principle, and that Rawls argues for a specific form of political liberalism. Any contrary view is mistaken. However, if we ask more normative questions such as which view of social contract theory is best, is the harm principle compelling, or how might it be applied, the reply can admit of better or worse answers. Our answer will differ depending on the quality of the argument made. Some replies may be more persuasive, but there is no single correct yes or no answer. There are facts about political philosophy even if not every, or even most, political philosophy is mostly a matter of fact rather than argument.

# 1

# Freedom

## 1.1 Introduction

Freedom, or liberty, is widely recognized as having huge importance.[1]
The American *Declaration of Independence* says that we are all "created equal" with inalienable rights to "life, liberty and the pursuit of
happiness" (United States 1776). Our freedoms are a foundation that
political authority is built upon. However, if we should ask others
what freedom is, there can be very different answers to questions
about how it is defined and why it is valuable. So, what then is freedom? When can we be said to be free or unfree? Is freedom about our
having options or in our achieving goals? How, if at all, can we justify
any limits on freedom? This chapter discusses these questions.

We will begin by considering the foundational issue of how we
might understand ourselves as "free." This is followed by examining
the relevance of having choice and options. The chapter then surveys
three broad theories of freedom: negative freedom, positive freedom,
and republican freedom. We next consider the possible importance of
our convictions about how we relate to others for any theory about
freedom. The chapter concludes considering the issue of paternalism
and how some claim we might justify constraints on freedom.

---

[1] I use the terms "freedom" and "liberty" interchangeably.

---

*Political Philosophy: The Fundamentals*, First Edition. Thom Brooks.
© 2025 John Wiley & Sons Ltd. Published 2025 by John Wiley & Sons Ltd.

It is worth noting that some of this discussion is abstract, or at least more so than later discussions on other topics in the following chapters. We will consider how we might know ourselves free and think about it using hypothetical examples that can seem anything but concrete at certain points. This book is aimed at students who are studying this topic for the first time. As we proceed, the process of thinking about freedom – as well as our other topics – will become easier as the reader becomes more familiar with the analytical approach taken. It goes without saying that if everything to know about freedom was obvious, there would be little point in having to explain different views that have been defended over the last few centuries. Indeed, it should be unsurprising that there is a diversity of views and longstanding debates over how we know we are free, what freedom is, and how it should be understood because the question of "what is freedom?" is essentially contested.

## 1.2   Knowing Freedom

When most students are asked about what freedom is, the issue of knowing whether *they* are free themselves is often overlooked. This is most likely because our freedom is presumed. The assumption is that we question *how* we are free, not *if* we are free, because we assume that we are. So, we rarely consider the matter of *if* we are free. So, let us start with this foundational issue.

Consider moving your hand or simply reading this sentence. How do you know that you are freely doing either action? Does it matter that you were asked to do it? Can you see these words and choose whether or not to understand them as they are read? Could you prove to somebody else that you, and only you, are choosing to freely move your hand – and that it was not predestined to happen nor under the control of nature nor a supernatural entity like God? Or are we under the control of our animal instincts? Is our freedom knowable, if it is possible?

These questions are abstract and difficult. Some might dismiss them as merely "academic" (in its usual pejorative sense) and claim the topic is unimportant because it lacks "real world" relevance. But, of course, it matters whether we are free or not in a practical sense. This is because our views on responsibility are often tied to our making free choices. If someone is not free to do something, we might not hold them responsible for whatever happens. It is important to know *that* we are free — and not only *how* we might be free.

The 18th-Century German philosopher Immanuel Kant addressed this issue. He was interested in understanding what the use of our reason could achieve and its limitations. Kant considered various thought experiments, including about the nature of freedom. His thought experiments are meant to show how we might best understand complex issues, such as whether or not we are free.

For example, Kant asks us to first consider the assumption that we are free. This is understood to mean the idea that we are *the cause* of our own activities.[2] This means that we are free when we act autonomously, such as when our hand moves because we intended to make it move in a particular way that we choose. Or that we walk briskly or stop and stand still depending on whichever way that we happen to choose to do it. In these ways, we are free where the choice is ours and we enable that choice to happen. We act freely when exercising our "free will" (O'Connor and Franklin 2022).

Imagine that you are playing soccer. A teammate passes you the ball. You rush forward towards the opposing team's net, kick the ball hard, and score a goal in the last minutes of the match. It is easy to imagine your teammates congratulating you for scoring. We can make sense of this if we understand that *you* are responsible for *your actions* and so acted freely. Your goal scoring is your achievement. It was not caused by anyone nor anything else. Assuming that you are free, it makes sense to congratulate you for what you did.

Now consider the same activity from a different point of view in comparison. Imagine that we are *not* the cause of our own activities. Instead, every action happens according to the laws of nature – or at the choosing of an all-powerful God.[3] When you receive the soccer ball, run down the pitch and kick it into the opposing net, it is your foot that touches the ball that scored the goal, but this was not caused by your free will; instead, it was predestined to happen, a natural reaction or the invisible hand of an almighty deity. Congratulating you for this event makes no sense in this context. You are instrumental to the goal – it was your foot that kicked the ball – but the cause was beyond you and, most importantly, *not* you. The goal is not an achievement of yours and so to celebrate you for making it happen would be to reward you for an achievement that was not yours.

---

[2] Kant (1998: 484 [A444, 446/B472, 474]). The citations in brackets are the commonly used format in referencing Kant's work and used for this and his other words references.
[3] Kant (1998: 485 [A445, 447/B473, 475]).

This is the problem of free will: namely, how might we know we are free, if we are free? Many students will say that to imagine we are not the cause of kicking a ball or even reading this sentence does not make sense either. But this is Kant's point. His argument is that it seems improbable that we can prove through rational argument alone that we are (or are not) free. The use of our "pure" reason can only get us so far. Consider another hypothetical example. If a mischievous wizard, in a magical cave many miles away, was secretly controlling your movements and influencing your thoughts, we act at the wizard's bemusement without knowing that he is the true cause of what we do; in other words, we are unfree. So, how could we ever conclusively prove with complete certainty that this secret control of our mind and body is impossible? Or if you do not like wizard examples, suppose it is an alien with these powers controlling you from a distant planet unknown to humanity. How could you rationally prove its impossibility?

We have a situation where we cannot prove with perfect certainty either one side (we are free) or the other (we are not free). Kant calls this an *antinomy of reason*.[4] This antinomy is an example, he argues, about where our reason alone cannot prove or disprove our actions are a cause of our freedom or a product of nature and unfree. Our use of reason alone brings us to a philosophical fork in the road. It may seem unclear which path we should take and why.[5] We might all accept the philosophical fork in the road and agree that there is only one road to take. When we imagine a world where we are generally free or unfree, Kant argues that only a world where we are understood to be free – and our freedom is thereby *assumed* – can we make the best *coherent* sense of our world. If we assume our freedom and consider individuals as free, then it makes the best sense for us to congratulate them for great achievements or blame them for terrible wrongs.

A world without freedom is a world without praise or blame. It is a world where life might not make much sense at all. If whatever happens to us is never our achievement, then it would not make sense to see any merit or demerit in the actions of others. Whether someone passes a test, gains a qualification, performs unsuccessfully at a job interview, or kills others unprovoked in cold blood would all lack ethical meaning.

---

[4] Kant (1998: 486, 489 [A448, 451/B476, 479]). An antinomy is a contradiction between two beliefs or conclusions that are themselves reasonable. In this case, the reasonable exercise of pure reason that I am free or that I am unfree creating a paradox.

[5] A similar antimony is described famously by the Chinese philosopher Zhuangzi. He said that he dreamt he was a butterfly fluttering about conscious only of his happiness as a butterfly. On awakening, he claims that he did not know whether he was a man who had dreamed about being a butterfly or now a butterfly dreaming about being a man.

These actions would be things that happen because they do; they just happen as mere happenings. There is no rationale to explain why.

Kant argues that we should assume *that* we are free to make best sense of our world.[6] We assume our freedom in praising others for achievements or blaming them for committing wrongs. We celebrate a goal scored because we see it as an action caused by the free choice of the goal scorer. Or we punish wrongdoers who deliberately harm others precisely because their harm can be understood as the outcome of their choices. These assumptions may make intuitive sense, but it might leave some readers perplexed by the idea that our freedom might only be assumed, but not proven.

But there is an alternative view. It says that we can know we are free when our freedom is mutually recognized as such, as acting freely – and so thereby not merely assumed. This position is defended by G. W. F. Hegel, a 19th-Century critic of Kant (Brooks 2013a, Hegel 1990: §15R).[7] Hegel takes a different view about how we might discern freedom. He describes his view as showing how "the free will wills the free will" (Hegel 1990: §27). This is the idea that we have a free will, but it is only free when it is freely willing some outcome.

The first step is to distinguish the making of a free choice from an arbitrary choice. The former is a product of reflection and thought. Our choice is, to some degree, controlled by us. The latter is we simply following wherever our desires or passions may take us. Hegel saw this distinction between free choice and arbitrariness as a defining difference between humans and animals, as animals were enslaved by their passions and how they feel at any given time. They eat when hungry, flee when scared, and sleep when tired. These activities are not free because they are arbitrary, as actions dictated to animals by whatever feeling that they happen to have at a particular moment.

We, as human beings, are different from the animal world. We have the ability to control our passions. We can reflect on what we do before choosing what to do, rather than merely follow wherever our desires take us whenever they happen to arise within us. For Hegel, this view of what makes us human also helps define us as free versus

---

[6] This view is called transcendental idealism because it makes a leap of faith in assuming our freedom.

[7] References to Hegel's work are to the section (§) and use common abbreviations of "R" for Remark and "A" for Additions to those sections. This is the standard referencing for his work. The "Additions" are from the notes of his students supplementing Hegel's texts from the students' notebooks. While Hegel is notoriously described by many as among the most complex and difficult of canonical Western philosophers, I can promise readers that a sustained engagement with his work is enormously rewarding and well worth the effort. Any reader wanting to know more should contact me.

animals as unfree because arbitrary decision-making is, for Hegel, a lack of freedom and not its exercise.

The second step is to see freedom as having an essentially *social* dimension. If only human beings have the capacity for freedom, then – for Hegel – only human beings have the ability to determine when decisions are free or not. We might each believe that we act freely in making a choice. However, this is only a subjective opinion by itself, or at least until we acquire a more objective view through the mutual recognition of our freedom by others. An object or decision is freely mine when recognized by others as mine. We achieve mutual recognition with others when we both recognize others as free and *vice versa*.

Hegel accepts that requiring such mutual recognition of others in society may be a "struggle" at times (Hegel 1990: §57R). Individuals may have different views. But, for Hegel, this is a difficulty we must face. If everyone did however and whatever they pleased, we could not distinguish what is freely chosen from what is arbitrary. Our behaviors might bear more resemblance to the animal kingdom than the reasonableness that defines human conduct. It is only through the recognition of our actions as free (or not) by others who share our capacity for freedom that provides a more objective view. We require others – and they require us – to discern, determine, and develop our freedom in social cooperation together.

The final step is to consider our freedom in context. Our choices are not made in a vacuum nor a utopia, but in the world. The conditions we find ourselves in are often nonideal to varying, sometimes extreme, degrees. For example, Hegel acknowledges that how we view rights and wrongs may change according to "the condition of civil society" (Hegel 1990: §218). We may judge similar events differently if the circumstances are different, but we seek to form a coherent view from what we have. Hegel illustrates this point by saying that we may punish crimes more harshly where our state is in civil unrest or at war and so "a penal code is therefore primarily a product of its time and of the current condition of civil society" (Hegel 1990: §218R). We will consider this view later when examining punishment in Chapter 6. But it is worth noting that if recognition by others is critical for providing some objective basis for determining whether we act freely or not in doing right or wrong, the context within which rights and wrongs are considered is significant and adds further complexity.

Critical readers may consider that group judgments are not always free from error, which of course is true. Just because most may believe something to be true does not make it true. Therefore, there remains an ongoing debate of interest about how we know we are free, whether we are persuaded more by Kant's or Hegel's approach, and how much we are convinced by their attempts at making coherent sense of freedom.

## 1.3    Contemporary Freedom

When we think of freedom, how do we think about it? The 18th-Century philosopher Benjamin Constant identified two different approaches. Constant called the first the *freedom of the ancients* (Constant 1988). This freedom refers to the time of ancient Greece and the Roman Empire about 2000 years ago. Constant claims that freedom was understood at that time in a distinctively non-individualistic way at that time two thousand years ago. Philosophers did not talk about *my* freedom, but instead of *our* freedom as a community, such as a city. Freedom was secured by groups, for groups, and as a group.

This view of the ancients is in contrast to what Constant calls the *freedom of the moderns* that we enjoy today. Constant's idea of modern freedom is understood as the freedom of only individuals, not collectives. We talk today about *individual* freedom for ourselves and no longer the freedom of some group.

Constant claims this distinction helps us think about freedom in at least two ways. First, we should be aware that philosophers have thought about freedom differently over history. When we see the word "freedom," it has not always been understood the same way over time: the ways in which classical thinkers conceived of freedom has changed to how we understand it today. We should therefore be sensitive to how the meaning of this concept has developed over time.

Second, Constant claims the shift from the seeing freedom as relating to the community toward it becoming related to individuals is an irreversible change. He claims that there is no going back from this individualistic view of freedom once it has taken hold. In this way, Constant captures the dominance of liberalism that emerged from his time with its emphasis on individual liberty. Wherever it has taken root, *how* we think about individual freedom may change, but not whether individual freedom has special importance. This is a lasting insight from Constant on an essential feature of modern liberty.

While there are many different views about what freedom is today that we will examine, they all have in common the view that being free requires *individual* autonomy (Raz 1986: 369–370). Thus, to be free is to be autonomous to some degree. The implication is that if we lack autonomy and the ability to control our lives, then we lack a capacity for exercising freedom. This is true for any view of freedom, an important contribution to how we understand contemporary theories about freedom thanks to Constant's insights.

## 1.4   Choices and Options

We have only discussed the abstract matter of whether I can be free and how I might know this – either through an assumption or mutual recognition. If I *can* be free, how *might* I be free? This is a question about knowing when freedom might be exercised, if I am free and autonomous. It is a matter of whether or not freedom requires our having a choice of options.

For example, it might be argued that freedom requires a choice. If I have only one option and no alternatives, it could be said that an individual had no choice but that one available option. We are free only where there are two or more options to choose from. To use our free will, we require the opportunity to exercise it. Let us examine this view.

So, what if you did have two options to choose from, but one of them is too awful to pick? Imagine you are at a bank waiting to withdraw money. A thief pulls out a gun and demands that you hand him your money or you will be shot dead. It might be argued that we had no choice but to agree to the thief's demands. Probably about all of us might say the same if in that situation. While we have the options to either hand over the money or refuse to comply with the armed thief, this second option of refusal might be thought to be too awful to pick because it could mean our instant and unlawful death. A choice of compliance or death is like a deal that we can hardly refuse, especially given the significant consequences for us if we did refuse.

In a famous passage from his *Leviathan*, Thomas Hobbes considers a hypothetical example of a sinking ship (Hobbes 1996: 146).[8] Imagine you are on a ship that is sinking fast and far out at sea. The only way for those on board to survive and avoid drowning is to throw the ship's precious cargo overboard however valuable it might be. Only if all such cargo were lost at sea might our ship avoid sinking and so make it safely to shore. Otherwise, all will drown. We might claim that we had no

---

[8] In my view, this passage is not famous enough and a great issue to discuss in philosophy seminars!

choice, or at least not a genuine choice worth making, as one of the options is too awful to pick: namely, to hold onto the cargo and go down with the ship. Our only choice is to save our own lives by ridding the ship of its cargo because otherwise all lives would be lost if we did not.

Perhaps surprisingly for most students, Hobbes disagrees with that view. He claims that we *are* free because there *is a choice*. For Hobbes, it does not matter that we like the choices we have so long as we do have options. The bare fact that we have *any* choice, even if the only alternative option is too awful for us to pick, is sufficient to make us responsible for whatever choice we select. It might be that everyone would dump the cargo overboard to save their lives if in the same position. That would not indicate we were unfree in Hobbes' view, but, instead, merely tell us that we are exercising our freedom in the same ways. We are likewise free to disobey the law even if, from the fear of punishment, we refrain from doing so. The fact that a choice is bad or repugnant is only relevant for thinking about how we exercise our freedom when choosing between alternatives, but the bare fact we have a choice means that we remain free either way. Hobbes' example of a sinking ship helps us reflect on whether mere options should be sufficient for freedom or whether options worth choosing are required.

Now consider a very different example. Would it matter that we had only one option if that is the only choice we want? Harry Frankfurt considers the following hypothetical scenario (Frankfurt 1971). Imagine there is a so-called happy addict. This person has an unbreakable dependence to highly addictive narcotics that must be supplied constantly. While the individual is unable to act differently and stop taking these drugs, suppose that they would continue to use them even if they could choose to do otherwise. The happy addict is someone who has only one option, but might still be thought free. Does it make sense to say they act freely despite having no other choice so long as the only choice that they have is the one they want?

One possible response might be to say that, while freedom may be about doing what we want in some sense, it is also about having the freedom of will to choose what we want. The happy addict lacks the capacity to choose otherwise and so is unable to make a free choice – irrespective of whether they might claim they would only choose a certain way. So, we might argue that we are free even where we have only a single option, but *only* so long as we have the *capacity* to consider how we might exercise freedom and if the option we have is what we would choose whether or not other options were available.

The happy addict is not free in this sense. While they might claim their only option of continually using narcotics is what they would choose, their actions are directed by their addiction and not a result of reflective choice as they do not have the capacity to consider other possibilities if they were could be options. On the contrary, suppose you are at a market and the only item for sale is the one object you want.[9] Would you think that you are any less free because you had less choice even if the option you do have is the only one you desire at all times? This raises the distinction between freedom-as-having-options versus freedom-as-option-preference. The first claims freedom is about the fact of available options whereas the second argues freedom is achieved where we have the option we would choose anyway, even if other possible alternatives are unavailable.

The key problem here is autonomy. If I am unable to make a choice, I lack the capacity for autonomous control and, by extension, I am unfree. Moreover, it is important for freedom that what I can choose is worth my choosing it (Raz 1986: 381). If my only options are what is required for bare survival, it is unclear that there is any autonomous choice (and, therefore, no freedom). This is true whether I am coerced by the threat of death from the wrongful conduct of another or natural causes.

Freedom requires our autonomy, even more than our options for expressing it. When our autonomy is constrained or coerced, our freedom is restricted or denied.

## 1.5   Theories of Freedom

The discussion thus far has been pitched at a very abstract level concerning the issues of *if* we are free and *how* we might know it. In this section, we consider the three broad theories of how freedom has been defined traditionally. These are negative freedom, positive freedom, and republican freedom. Each will be considered separately before turning to a challenging problem for all three views that is presented where individuals feel they lack freedom because they are

---

[9] The example is not a perfect analogy as you might not wish to purchase anything. But suppose you are incredibly hungry, perhaps at near risk of starvation, and suffer from having severe allergies so have very restrictive dietary requirements whereby eating the wrong foods can be potentially fatal. Imagine the one thing on sale at the market is not only a food that you have no allergic reaction to, but is your favorite of all foods. Consider whether in this situation are you free with only the one choice?

alienated from others. These different views about freedom offer a variety of ways to understand how our autonomy is relevant to freedom – whether as unconstrained (negative), as achievements (positive) or as non-domination (republican).

## 1.5.1    Negative Freedom

One way of defining freedom is as negative freedom. A classic definition is by Thomas Hobbes, who says (in 17th-Century English): "liberty . . . consisteth in this, that he finds no stop, in doing what he has the will, desire, or inclination to do" (Hobbes 1996: 146). In other words, freedom consists in our *not* being constrained by others to do whatever we want to do. Notice how freedom is understood in a generally *negative* way: freedom is defined by an absence of interferences, where we are *not* being encumbered or otherwise constrained. Where the laws do not prohibit us, Hobbes says that every individual may act "according to his discretion" (Hobbes 1996: 152). If we are not interfered with, we are free to do as we like. Freedom is being free from such constraints.

A broadly similar way of defining negative freedom in more contemporary language is found in Isaiah Berlin's famous essay "Two Concepts of Liberty." He argues:

> I am normally said to be free to the degree to which no man or body of men interferes with my activity. Political liberty in this sense is simply the area within which a man can act unobstructed by others . . . You lack political liberty or freedom only if you are prevented from attaining a goal by human beings (Berlin 1969: 122).

Berlin defends freedom negatively as our *not* being prevented by others from pursuing some end. We lack freedom when we are unable to do as we like by other people. The key to unlocking whether or not we are free is whether others prevent our desired pursuits, and not whether our chosen goals are worth pursuing. Whether or not our goals are valuable or not in some objective sense is irrelevant – they need only be goals that we wish to pursue. In short, it is not what we do, but whether we are restricted from doing it that matters when determining if we are free.

Negative freedom has been a very popular way of understanding freedom, in part, because it appeals to a powerful intuition that being free is being unconstrained. Negative freedom's advocates can say that someone handcuffed or tied to a tree is unfree because another person has interfered with their movement and constrained them. They would only become free if not handcuffed or untied and so unfettered. Being free is being free from interference.

But this intuition runs into some possible difficulties. One is where we are prevented from doing something, but not because another individual is blocking us. For example, suppose you are walking through a park and seek to cross over a hill. However, the winds sweeping across the park are so strong that you are unable to climb up the hill. You are prevented from pursuing a goal and there is an obstruction, the wind, blocking your path. So, are you unfree to continue walking through the park? It might seem so as you cannot go past the hill in front of you. But negative freedom only counts constraints on your liberty where it is imposed by another person. According to Berlin's view, interference is defined as something others do to you. So, for Berlin, you would appear free to walk through the park despite your being unable to actually move forward in it – which seems intuitively implausible.[10]

Or imagine that you wish to attend a school to be educated. However, the school requires its pupils to pay upfront and this amount is more than you can afford. Nobody is directly preventing you from attending the school: if you had the money, you could start immediately. You are not interfered with. Or suppose the school is a distance away that is too far to reach and attend each day. Nobody is stopping you from attending – and further suppose there are no school fees so there is no cost. In both cases, you cannot pursue a goal because barriers are faced, either financial or geographical. It may seem odd to say that you are free to attend either school despite being unable to actually do so in reality because of affordability or distance. In these cases, there are obstacles which block you from receiving an education, but you are not interfered with by others. Should we say you are free to do what you cannot achieve, as a negative freedom proponent might claim? This seems counterintuitive.

## 1.5.2   Positive Freedom

A second way of defining freedom is positive freedom. This is the idea that we are free when we achieve some goal or end worth achieving. Positive freedom defines freedom *positively* in terms of what you can or may *do* or *achieve*. We are free insofar as we accomplish some goal or end.

---

[10] Our intuitions can play an important role in helping us weigh arguments. What do your intuitions in this example highlight for you about whether someone is free or unfree?

The classic definition of positive freedom is by the 19th-Century philosopher T. H. Green. He says freedom is "a positive power or capacity of doing or enjoying something worth doing or enjoying" (Green 1986: 199). This entails two important caveats. First, freedom is about what we can do. If we seek to walk across a park or wish to receive an education, we are only free if we can do it. If strong winds or prohibitive costs prevent us from achieving these goals, then we are not free – and whether or not anybody is trying to stop us. Our focus is not on who, if anyone, is setting obstacles like negative freedom does; but, instead, we focus on whether we are able to achieve our goals. Positive freedom emphasizes outcomes.

The second important caveat is that positive freedom is about the achievement of outcomes "worth doing or enjoying" only (Green 1986: 199). It matters which goals we choose. We might argue that worthy goals include the pursuit of a good education, for example. For Green, this means that the state must support conditions that allow us to exercise this freedom, if we wanted to do so.[11] This does not entail that the state must deliver education or that all schools must be state run. But it does mean that the state is required to support our pursuing goals worth doing or enjoying, and this could involve delivering some services as a public good, as it would promote our freedom. So, positive freedom is not about our ability to do anything, only the ability to do things worth doing.

What is potentially counterintuitive for some critics is that a consequence of positive freedom is that the state may play a necessary role in promoting our freedom. If true, then this would be very different from negative freedom where the actions of others may be viewed as obstructions to freedom. Often we might think of ourselves as free when not constrained by state action (like under negative freedom) rather than free when this is enabled by state action (under positive freedom). However, it is unclear that the state must be large and active in our lives in a negative way. For instance, Green was himself famously a liberal whose ideal of a community of rights prioritized individual pursuit of the common good instead of an activist state (Simhony 2003).

In addition, if we can identify suitably worthy goals, such as education, that positive freedom should promote, it raises questions about whether we are really free to choose to pursue it – or whether we lack

---

[11] For important discussions about Green's theory of freedom, see Dimova-Cookson (2003) and Simhony (1991).

the choice to choose valuable goals for ourselves. For example, if education is "worth doing or enjoying," it might appear to create an obligation on us to pursue it.

This raises the further question of who decides which ends are valuable for pursuing? Positive freedom is about worthy goals that our state or community must facilitate our ability to achieve. So, who is it that chooses what is a worthy goal that will be facilitated for us? This concern echoes the perhaps ironic comment from Jean-Jacques Rousseau that individuals might be "forced to be free" (Rousseau 2011: 167; see Brooks 2005; Orwell 1954: 6). As Constant argued above, the freedom of the moderns is the freedom of individuals. This would appear to entail that it is for individuals, not collectives, to choose their own goals for what individuals within a community might seek to achieve as most of positive freedom's proponents claim.

A further criticism of this view is raised by Berlin against Green's positive freedom. Berlin says: "everything is what it is: liberty is liberty, not equality or fairness or justice or culture, or human happiness or a quiet conscience" (Berlin 1969: 125). Berlin's argument is that when positive freedom advocates argue that all should be able to pursue some particular "worthy" goal, this confuses the concept of freedom with other concepts like equality. Berlin claims there may be good reason for the state to ensure all can achieve certain goals, such as education, but this is not about fostering freedom but rather the promotion of other values like equality. There is nothing unique about values coming into conflict: it may be that requiring all to be educated is a restriction on freedom, insofar as not everyone may want it. For Berlin, a problem with positive freedom is its inability to make such a distinction by confusing freedom with the pursuit of equality.[12]

### 1.5.3 Republican Freedom

A third way of defining freedom is republican freedom. This view is "republican" named about a view of freedom found originally in ancient Rome. It is not the republicanism of any contemporary political

---

[12] It is worth noting that it is not always clear where the lines should be drawn. For example, in the next chapter we will consider rights, which some conceive as protecting freedoms. If true, perhaps not every freedom is protected by rights, but in many cases it may be difficult to distinguish between violating the freedom of another from violating the rights of another.

party like the Republican Party in the United States – and they should not be confused with each other.

Republican freedom is defined by Philip Pettit quoting the *Letters of Cato*: "Liberty is, to live upon one's own Terms; Slavery is, to live at the mere Mercy of another" (Pettit 1999: 33). Republicans define freedom as non-domination. Its classical opposite was tyranny. The tyrannical dictator exercises domination over others by enforcing laws over others at any time and in any way, in a manner that may appear alien and arbitrary to those under the tyrant's rule. The people have no say over how they are governed and their domination defines their unfreedom. Republican theories understand freedom as being free from domination.

Republicanism can be seen as occupying a space somewhat in between negative and positive freedom. Republican freedom agrees with negative freedom that to be free is to be uncoerced by others – our lives are to be lived on our own terms. However, republican freedom is also different because coercive measures can be acceptable if we agree to them and so still live on our own terms. For example, all countries criminalize murder backed by severe penalties, including life imprisonment or even capital punishment. The state coerces us to avoid criminality, but does this mean that this kind of coercion must restrict our freedom? For republicans, it does not. The issue is not whether the state coerces *per se*, but whether the state coerces in a way that dominates. Provided that the state's coercive power does not arbitrarily impact on me, then its power does not limit my freedom. Instead, it helps mark out recognized limits of my freedom.

In this light, republican freedom also agrees with positive freedom that to be free is to achieve certain goals. But there is a difference. Whereas positive freedom advocates defend the achievement of goals as ends, such as access to education, republican advocates defend the achievement of goals *as a process*. This process is inclusive community deliberation over our public affairs. For example, Pettit claims we must each share discursive control over decisions that may have an impact on us (Pettit 2001: 65–103). We participate in discursive control by being a part of the public conversation, such as engaging in how the community is governed. When we can take part and help shape our laws, for example, they are not arbitrary constraints on the exercise of our freedom. Instead, they demarcate the recognized boundaries between what we are free and not free to do. Republican freedom as non-domination is not the absence of law or governments, but where law and government are shaped by the governed. In other words, the people determine the laws that they co-create and not *vice versa.*

Sometimes it is claimed that republican freedom is indistinctive from other theories. For example, negative freedom is based on non-interference while republicanism is grounded on non-domination. It may be true that when I am not interfered with by others that I am also not dominated by others. Both theories may appear to justify the same position. Republicans reject this view claiming that I am not necessarily free if not interfered with. For instance, if others do not constrain me physically, they may dictate my future politically or economically by denying me a voice or a vote. Therefore, I can be dominated even if not interfered with and so, for republicans, their theory is different.

Republicanism might also be accused of being very close to positive freedom. Positive freedom advocates the achievement of certain goods, such as being able to obtain an education or access to health care. It could be argued that non-domination is compatible with being able to secure valuable ends like education or access to health care. The difference that republicans might point out is that positive freedom is about the *end* to be achieved whereas republicanism is about the *process* used to achieve ends. Non-domination features in *how* we engage with others deliberating about our democratic future. It does not set out *what* should be secured after a deliberative process, suffice to say it that the non-domination within a well-run process is thought to help legitimate whatever is agreed. But the focus is on how we come to a view rather than, as per positive freedom, what that view should be.

A further concern is with regard to republicanism and children (Brooks 2025b). Republicans claim that domination is an evil to be avoided and contrary to freedom. Yet, parents exercise authority over their children determining when and what they might eat, how they are educated and more. It would appear that republicans would find children unfree and, indeed, republicans in ancient Rome thought exactly that. If true of contemporary republican thought, it would undermine their claim to oppose domination in all forms.

However, republicans demanding discursive control are clear that there need not be interaction every time. The importance of deliberation is that such opportunities exist and that I can effectively participate in them, not that I must always participate at every such available opportunity. In this way, republicans might argue that so long as parental authority over children is normatively restrictive with a goal of supporting autonomous development and where these restrictions increase further over time as children transition to teenagers and young adults, there are not dominated but enabled to become civic republicans. Such a perspective on freedom and children may relate to other views of freedom, too. For example, negative freedom advocates opposed to interference do not claim it is *never* justified to interfere with the freedom of another in any situation, such as where there is an imminent danger and risk to life. In these cases, parents may justifiably raise children without denying their freedom, but rather enabling it (Brooks 2025b). Noticeably, there is importance placed on the development of an individual's autonomy for freedom in both cases suggesting common ground between different conceptions about freedom, at least in some areas.

## 1.6    Are Different Theories About Freedom Compatible?

These three views about freedom – negative, positive, and republican – dominate discussions in political philosophy today. It is easy to see why as each seems to focus on something about how we think about freedom and its value. Negative freedom seems to get right the idea that our being *free* to do something requires our ability *to do* that something. If we are constrained by another, then we lack the ability to act. This may limit our exercise of freedom. However, nobody thinks that we are free to do *anything*.[13] There are necessary limits where others may rightfully constrain us from doing something. For example, it is often claimed that our causing harm to others (or even harming ourselves) creates a limit on how we might exercise freedom. This creates a difference between being able to murder or steal, but not being *free* to murder or steal, as this would wrongfully cause harm to others.

Our freedom to do something is limited by obvious constraints of reasonable feasibility. For instance, we are not free to run faster than any car or travel unaided across the galaxy, as such activities are unreasonable and unfeasible. Strictly speaking, we are no more free

---

[13] When a student might suggest in my philosophy seminars that freedom is about being able to do whatever you want, I would raise the issue of vampires: if someone believed that they were a vampire, would they be free to bite strangers along the high street? Students never see such an example coming! While an absurd hypothetical case, it can get students out of their dogmatic comfort zones and engage with not only which theory of freedom they find most plausible, but also its normative limits.

than what we might be free to do or not do some activity. Some activities might be beyond our reach, such as to access adequate health care or obtain an education for various reasons, such as our having a lack of resources. In such cases, our freedom to obtain an education might be reasonable and feasible if resources are available to us and we are treated equally by the state. Some, like Berlin, as we have seen, might view this as more of a case about the balance between freedom and equality or social justice – and not about freedom alone. But a freedom that only allowed a choice beyond our possible reach seems to miss something valuable about freedom: namely, that the value of freedom is, in part, the value of what freedom may realize. Positive freedom's defenders seem to get right that freedom is not about being free to do anything at all and freedom involves a kind of achievement, even if different philosophers might understand freedom's realization in different ways.

It might be noted that an authoritarian state could also achieve these goods (Brooks 2002c). Lacking freedom to choose unhealthy foods could help ensure that we live longer and compulsory education through earning a qualification at university might create a better-educated public. The only hitch is no one would have a say about their health or how they were educated. Republican freedom theorists seem to get right that freedom requires our not being dominated by the decisions of others and so ensure that we have opportunities to contribute to help determining public policy outcomes. Freedom is about being free to do some things, but not anything: *freedom is a pursuit of what has value, that we are autonomously free to do and what is possible to achieve.*[14] Our

---

[14] I note a more radical conception of freedom along these lines that can be traced to the French existentialist Jean-Paul Sartre that may interest readers. For Sartre, "not only is man what he conceives himself to be, but he is also only what he wills himself to be . . . Man is nothing else but what he makes of himself. Such is the first principle of existentialism" (Sartre 1957:15). I am free when I autonomously choose for myself. This helps renders my choices as valuable because they are chosen by me. It may be obvious that how and what I choose in a world of scarcity will be constrained by the activities by others. Sartre claims this constraint is more wide reaching as simply being in the gaze of another can constrain my freedom to be. For example, I may conceive of myself as wise, funny and good natured; but this may not match the perceptions held by others over which I cannot control and, in turn, they restrict my freedom to be especially where others hold a contrary view (Sartre 1989). For Sartre, "man is condemned to be free" as we have no choice but to create ourselves. However, in his view, this logically requires there is no God or all-knowing deity as if there was we would exist under a constant gaze rendering us unfree (Sartre 1957: 22–23). While there is much to unpack, Sartre highlights how our perspective of an autonomously exercised free will can be restricted from the perspective of another.

autonomy is of primary importance for our freedom. But what this view of freedom shows is that having choices in pursuit of what is valuable can make the three different approaches to freedom compatible under the umbrella of autonomous choice along a horizon of future possibilities. Any coherent account of freedom must account for our autonomy and the possible realization of our freedom.[15]

As we have seen, each of these parts is heavily contested. We recognize that no one is free to do anything, but it is not always clear where the line should be drawn, although it is usually to avoid harm to others and oneself may play a key role in drawing this line. We acknowledge that freedom is valuable and allows us to pursue what we find valuable. Nonetheless, we may view value differently and have contrasting positions on what makes freedom valuable. Finally, we must see freedom as *our* choices that are possible to realize, but how this might manifest itself within political institutions is also contested, as we shall see in Chapter 5 on democracy.

Nonetheless, these three different parts do work together. For example, we argue that we are free to pursue goals valuable individually to ourselves provided that we do not cause unjustified harm to others. This view accepts our freedom is constrained so we avoid harming and pursue what is of valuable, and that this is a choice we are able to exercise. Of course, I have not said what these goals might be only that they cannot cause unjustified harm to others. Nor have I set out when harm might be justified, such as in self-defense. A *unified* theory of freedom that brought these parts together would need to do so. But the example suffices to illustrate that this unity is possible.

In sum, there are three main theories about freedom that are usually presented as rivals to each other. This is because each sees freedom in a different way: a negative freedom *from* constraint, a positive freedom *to* achieve some end, or a republican freedom *without* coercion. It is not obvious that these three different ways of understanding freedom are incompatible. Instead of three different theories about freedom, my comments are meant to indicate that elements from each might be unified together.

---

[15] My account of freedom emphasizes *possibility* and not *probability*. It is not essential that my autonomously chosen pursuit will probably lead to a desired achievement for it to be free. For instance, I may be free to learn Latin where I can access suitable instruction, but its lessons might not become learned and my desired goal not achieved. My pursuit of learning a language was possible in this case and that is enough, no matter how probable it would be achieved.

### 1.6.1    Alienation

There is a missing part to our discussion about freedom thus far. Is it enough to say you are free when you can get an education, but nevertheless choose not to? Or are you free when the community shapes its laws, but you choose not to take part in the community's deliberations?

This missing part is the problem of alienation, where individuals have a conviction about themselves as essentially separated from others. Hegel says:

> When a large mass of people sinks below the level of a certain standard of living . . . that feeling of right, integrity and honour which comes from supporting oneself by one's own activity and work is lost. This leads to the creation of a rabble (Hegel 1990: §244).

Hegel's rabble refers to individuals who are alienated from their community. This is sometimes thought to be a situation only arising from economic poverty, as Hegel describes the rabble as falling "below . . . a certain standard of living" (Hegel 1990: §244). But he is clear that anyone rich or poor can become a rabble as their extremes of wealth or poverty can fuel a disconnection of themselves from others (Brooks 2020a).

Alienation is a concern for any theory of freedom. These theories posit that we are free if unconstrained by others or able to achieve goals or have opportunities to shape how we are governed. The alienated see themselves as essentially removed from their community. They have a conviction that their say does not matter, that no matter how loud their voice they will not be heard nor will it make any difference. The ways in which they are governed are perceived as like being ruled by a foreign despot where rules are seen as drawn up and imposed by others on them. While they may live side-by-side with others, the alienated see their neighbors as part of a separate world that excludes them. Their world is not their own; it is an other to them.

Alienation is a problem because when we say that someone is free to achieve a goal or to take part in deliberating about how they are governed this is supposed to mark out something of importance. But if someone does not recognize such goals or identify with the community and its deliberative ends, the value of their freedom seems lost. For example, republicans can say that we are free where everyone can take part in a deliberative democracy. However, this assumes most, if not all, of us will wish to take part and co-create our laws and public policies.

When many do not or see this process as not inclusive, the outcomes of deliberation may well appear like an arbitrary imposition on them and contrary to being free. Republicanism assumes that the ability to participate is enough to secure freedom. However, it neglects those that see this option as illusory or inauthentic: where taking part is meaningful as a fellow member in a shared enterprise. The problem is that not every citizen feels like they are a part of the community in some essential way. Too often "the community" is seen as a separate entity to which the alienated individual lacks any substantive standing within. And too often they are overlooked by political philosophers, too.

Hegel thought the problem of alienation was one of the greatest threats to civil society and without any easy solution. He was right. So much of how our society works runs on shared understandings and trust (Brooks 2022d). Where this trust breaks down, so too can social cohesion weaken – and make finding freedom with others more elusive. Changing convictions towards improved inclusion is easier said than done. We might start with the idea that integration of people within a community is a two-way street with obligations cutting both ways: there must be effort by individuals to connect with other and a community that supports and facilitates this coming together – or we risk communities continuing to grow further apart. Such work seems critical if most theories about freedom are to have relevance for those they apply to: we must possess freedom *and* a conviction of ourselves as free. Having one without the other will simply not work.

This is why alienation poses a threat to our autonomy. Where we are separated from others, alienated individuals may lack the ability to self-govern themselves without that valuable connection with others; the alienated become disconnected to the point it might inhibit their autonomous decision-making as they act in isolation. But this does not mean that alienation makes us unfree, only that it threatens our ability to be free. If we want freedom, then we must protect ourselves and others from alienation.

## 1.7  Paternalism

Paternalism is about justified interferences with our freedom. It is often claimed that with freedom comes responsibility and that all freedoms have limits. A freedom of speech is not a right to shout "fire" in a crowded theater which may create a panic leading to serious injuries. Nor is a freedom to possess arms a right for any individual to own and use any kind of weapon, like nuclear weapons. Freedoms have limits. The question is where to draw the line between what we are free or unfree to do.

The best-known and most influential view of paternalism is John Stuart Mill's *harm principle*. He says:

> The object of this essay is to assert one very simple principle . . . That principle is that the sole end for which mankind are warranted, individually or collectively, in interfering with the liberty of action of any of their number is self-protection. That the only purpose for which power can be rightfully exercised over any member of a civilised community, against his will, is to prevent harm to others. His own good, either physical or moral, is not a sufficient warrant (Mill 1989: 13).

Mill's principle appears simple. We are free to do whatever we like if what we do does not cause harm to others. This principle can restrict freedom in several areas where we might want limits. For example, actions like violent crimes are obvious harms to others and so no one is free to do them according to the harm principle. Likewise, actions like theft also harm others in terms of their property rights or livelihoods and so also disallowed.

If someone seeks to do harm to others in these or other ways, they are not free to do so. This means, for Mill, that we are justified in such instances to interfere with that individual's liberty of action. When someone has no right to harm, we have a right to constrain them. This is the only instance where we may justifiably interfere with another's freedom. Freedom has limits and the harm principle helps show where these limits are drawn.

The harm principle is more complicated than it may appear. Consider contact sports like soccer or American football. The object of these games is not to hurt others, but players may hurt others however unintentionally in playing these games. Mill's harm principle might be amended to say that where any such harm is consented to in advance and unintentional it may be that players may consent to a risk of harm. Now consider a sport like boxing where the object does involve harming others, such as knowing out an opponent to win a match. It might be said similarly that participants can consent to boxing if the risks were known in advance. But there seem very clear limits to what might be consented to. Suppose there was a likely or certain risk of being seriously maimed or killed, like in the fictional television series *Squid Game*. The likely risks and more serious harms may well be too much for the state to allow others to consent to it.

Readers will notice that the harms referred to are harms to others. Philosophers sometimes refer to these as *other-regarding harms*, as harms regarding other people. But we might ask: what of *self-regarding harms*? These are instances where what we do causes harm to ourselves. Examples might include the use of illicit drugs where the only one harmed, at least directly, is ourselves. Mill's harm principle does not explicitly speak to such cases, but we can work out how it might apply.

There are three ways of thinking about the harm principle might, or might not, apply to self-regarding harms. The first might be to say that Mill's original definition is correct and that we should only restrict freedom where we might cause harm to others, no matter what our actions might be. The second way is to say that Mill's definition applies because we reject the idea that any harm is only self-regarding. For example, the families of those harmed through prolonged drug use may suffer in trying to support their loved ones. In some sense, none of us lives isolated from others and it might be argued that all harms impact others either directly or indirectly. A third way of thinking about the harm principle is that it can apply to self-regarding harms too – even if not envisaged in Mill's original definition. So, we might be thought free to do whatever we like as long as we do not damage ourselves in some substantial way.

No matter which view we agree with, the main issue is what exactly constitutes *harm*? It is probably uncontroversial to say that harms which include unconsented violence like assault and murder should be banned by *any* version of the harm principle. Other kinds of harms like breaches of the property rights of others through crimes such as theft, burglary or fraud would also be included. But where else to draw the line? Some activities where harm may arise, such as through boxing or contact sports, might be justified on the grounds of consent to reasonable risks. But it is not obvious that consent is always sufficient nor what counts as a tolerable risk of harm. Moreover, others may raise concerns about a harm to other things – such as to social cohesion or harm to public morality.

These examples show that the harm principle is deceptively complex. It is not that one cannot do any form of harm, as some kinds of harm may be justified or excusable. Contact sports or acting in self-defense are commonly used examples of permissible harmful activities.

We need to know which kinds of harms should be forbidden, the possible role of consent and where the relevant limits should be drawn.

## 1.8    Conclusion

This chapter has examined the topic of freedom. We started with abstract questions of whether we are free and how we can know it, whether it is assumed or through a social process of mutual recognition. We have considered whether freedom consists in having a choice of options or whether the only important factor is if our preferred option is available, even if there were no alternatives. We then looked at the three main definitions of freedom as negative, positive, and republican examining their attractiveness, limitations and possibility compatibility. On the latter, we observed the importance of possibility; that any conception of freedom must relate to freedom that might be realized. No one is free to do what they cannot achieve under any circumstances. An omnipotent God is free to do anything, not human beings like you and me.

Everyone may think they know what freedom is about, while often taking for granted they know that they are free. Philosophers have debated these issues for centuries and this chapter is only a first glance at a fascinating, as well as complex, area. Readers should reflect on which view of freedom seems most coherent and compelling and why to grasp better how they see themselves fitting into these wider discussions.

## Further Reading

Berlin, Isaiah. 1969. *Four Essays on Liberty*. Oxford: Oxford University Press.

Carter, Ian, Mathew Kramer and Hillel Steiner (eds). 2006. *Freedom: A Philosophical Anthology*. Oxford: Blackwell.

Mill, John Stuart. 1989. *On Liberty and Other Writings*. Cambridge: Cambridge University Press.

Miller, David. 2006. *The Liberty Reader*. London: Paradigm.

# 2

# Rights

## 2.1 Introduction

We might all agree that rights have significant importance that require protection and propagation, but disagree about much else. Philosophers are divided about which rights we have and why. What makes rights important? What, if anything, is the difference between human rights versus rights more generally? How do we know which rights we have? And what to do if our rights might clash or pull us in different directions?

This chapter surveys some of the main arguments behind these key questions. It will begin by examining the historical roots of human rights as natural rights and how they are understood today. The chapter will distinguish between our *mere* rights from our *human* rights. It will then consider defining rights and their taxonomy, including how rights and duties connect. Much of this discussion will focus on individual rights as the subject of most interest and attention. However, we will also consider the issue of group rights. While there is virtually no disagreement that we have rights, there is much debate about which are accepted, how many there are, and how they work – and which this chapter will explain.

*Political Philosophy: The Fundamentals*, First Edition. Thom Brooks.
© 2025 John Wiley & Sons Ltd. Published 2025 by John Wiley & Sons Ltd.

## 2.2    The Divine Right of Kings

It can be easily overlooked that it has not always been the case that most believed that everyone had rights. For example, an early view of rights is *the divine right of kings*. Its defenders argued that kings derived their authority from God. Only the king was empowered to have rights. The divine right of kings also holds that the king alone may choose to grant rights to others, but only at his pure discretion: any right he recognizes could cease without notice nor cause. Thus, the king is a divinely sanctioned source from which all rights are derived. In other words, individuals might not have rights unless the king chooses to recognize them.

The divine right of kings is most famously defended in Sir Robert Filmer's *Patriarcha*. Filmer argued that "the greatest liberty in the world . . . is for people to live under a monarch" (Filmer 2008: 4). The king's divine right to rule is a right he inherits from Adam, the first man according to the *Bible*. Filmer says that, through God, Adam possessed "lordship . . . by creation . . . over the whole world" and his divine right to rule is held by "lineal succession" by kings over the centuries since Adam (Filmer 2008: 4). Kings are the descendants of Adam and possess his "lordship" over the world by inheritance. The king is believed to rule his people like a father rules his family (Filmer 2008: 12).

This divine right of kings is a divine right of absolute monarchy, or absolutism. Filmer claims that "there is not in scripture mention . . . of any other form of government" (Filmer 2008: 24). Any alternative form of government, including democracy, is not only unjustified on this view but it contradicts the will of God itself. Therefore, to support democracy is to oppose God's intention. Since there is, for Filmer, a divine right of kings, it is a right for only the king to determine what, if any, rights he recognizes for others. It is a right held at the king's pleasure to be granted or removed at the king's discretion. Filmer claims that such a view of rights best safeguards the liberty of all. This is because if individuals, all lacking divine authority to determine rights for themselves, had the right to recognize rights, it would lead to division and factions leading to chaos as disagreements would be difficult to manage.

Today, there are few, if any, who would agree with Filmer's views on the divine right of kings. The idea that individuals have rights is pervasive, even if there remains disagreement about which rights we have and why. The divine right of kings view is mostly only of historical interest now.

But rather than simply dismiss this view (as tempting as this might be), it is worth considering some of the important critiques leveled at this view of rights – as we should not take its rejection for granted because it does not meet with our contemporary political sensibilities.

One of the most powerful challenges is made by the 18th-Century English philosopher John Locke. While many political theorists focus mostly on his *Second Treatise of Government* setting out his defense of natural rights, it is in his *First Treatise of Government* that Locke rejects Filmer's arguments and with devastating effect.[1]

Locke does not merely repudiate Filmer's arguments but Locke shows how his claims are utterly nonsensical. For example, Filmer claims that God granted Adam dominion over the world and that, as monarchs are Adam's descendants, kings have inherited from Adam his divine right to rule over others. Locke points out that Adam, as the first man, is the father of literally *everybody*, of both you and me and princes and paupers alike. If all of Adam's ancestors inherit his nobility, then we all have it today ourselves and so it is not the exclusive possession of any king. Additionally, Filmer claims, God's command to honor one's father and mother is what helps ground divine rule as Adam is the father of us all. However, Locke highlights that this only makes *every* father a king and *every* mother a queen, and this is not the sole position of any single individual (Locke 1988: 188). We all inherit Adam's divine right as we are all his descendants, in addition to the king.

There is also my favorite of Locke's criticisms of Filmer's views that must be mentioned. (Shouldn't we all have a favorite such criticism?) Locke draws attention again to Filmer's claim that kings have a divine right to rule inherited from God's granting Adam dominion over the world. Locke notes that, if this is right, then Filmer must go further and claim "that Princes might eat their subjects, too, since God gave as full power to Noah and his heirs to eat *every living thing that moveth*, as he did to Adam to have dominion over them" which is

---

[1] A brief note on Locke's *Two Treatises*. Readers might assume that Locke wrote the *First Treatise* before he produced the *Second Treatise*, but he actually set out the *Second* before he wrote the *First*. They were originally published together at the same time. The two books work together. The *First* focuses on a critique of the then common view of the divine right of kings to show that it is unjustified and unmerited. This then begs the question of what might take its place – and this is what Locke seeks to do in the *Second Treatise*. The *First* plays an important role for setting the stage for why we need a new theory of rights to replace the divine right of kings. In my view, the importance of the *First* Treatise is too often overlooked and underappreciated. See Locke (1988).

obviously patent nonsense (Locke 1988: 160). And, so thus, Filmer's analogy does not work and his claimed view of rights is unjustified, as well as illogical and absurd on its own terms. There has been no serious defense of Filmer's views since Locke's critique.

## 2.3   Natural Rights

Arising from the ashes of the divine right of kings is the view of *natural rights*. This is the view that individuals possess rights *naturally*, and they have it from birth. Rights are a part and parcel of who and what we are – they are a part of our DNA. We do not require the approval of a king to have them. Rights are naturally a part of every one of us.

The idea of natural rights raises important issues. The first is that natural rights are *natural*; they are an integral part of our world. That we have rights from birth is as much a part of the world as fish can be found swimming in the sea or birds seen flying overhead. Our rights are a part of our *naturally given* world, in other words an intrinsic part of the world as it is. Originally, many defenders of natural rights claimed that these rights were God-given and so divinely sanctioned because God had created the world and all within it, including our rights. While this religious perspective on rights plays a much less prominent role in contemporary discussions today, it is important to note the historical origins of this idea. Natural rights proponents disagree with those who defend the divine right of kings, but both have their origins in the idea that each view was part of a divine plan.

The second important issue about natural rights is the idea that our rights are naturally a part of "us," that is, of everyone everywhere. Natural rights are the rights of every human being and we possess them precisely because we are human. Where we live, whatever our citizenship or ruling king has no bearing on whether we have natural rights. Our natural rights are held *equally* by each of us. Nobody has more natural rights than anybody else.

A third issue is that our natural rights are inalienable. They are an inextricable part of us that we cannot remove nor amend. As a necessary part of who we are, natural rights have a pre-political existence. This is because we have these rights at our birth whether or not we find ourselves born in any political state. In other words, natural rights are ours to keep and not for anyone, even a king or president, to take away. Natural rights provide a constraint on any justifiable use of political authority as the government should respect, not refuse, recognition of the natural rights of that political state's citizens.

Natural rights proponents broadly agree on those three issues. The other substantive issue is what these universally held, inalienable rights possessed by all since birth are – and whether we each possess more than one natural right. This is where there is deep disagreement.

For example, Thomas Hobbes argued that individuals all have a single natural right: a right to self-preservation (Hobbes 1996: 91). He argues that human societies were originally in an anarchic *state of nature* where individuals live among each other but without any government or political authority. Each individual was free to do as they pleased but without any legitimate means of resolving disputes or disagreements should they arise. Life in this hypothetical state is described as being "poore, nasty, brutish and short" because individuals live in a war of one against all to survive and get by, but without any authority to regulate or organize their interactions (Hobbes 1996: 89). Hobbes claimed individuals in a state of nature would endeavor toward peace and seek to leave the anarchic chaos behind. He argued that, if we could imagine ourselves in that position again, we would agree to give up our "rights to all things" surrendering our liberty to do as we like in the state of nature in order to join with others in forming a sovereign state (Hobbes 1996: 92).

It might seem odd to consider giving up any of our liberty so we might form a sovereign state. Hobbes's point is that we have the liberty to do anything in a state of nature, but our freedom is highly constrained and insecure as we lack any institutional means to safeguard our liberties nor even our livelihoods. However, if we surrendered a part of our liberty, the freedom we have that remains can be made more secure because it would have institutional protections made possible by our creating a political state. In agreeing to create a state whereby we restrict our freedom, we secure our one natural right to self-preservation.

Natural rights defenders generally agree there is a natural right to life. But they disagree on whether there are other natural rights and what those rights might be. One influential account is supported by John Locke. He claims that we have three natural rights. These rights are to "life, liberty and property" (Locke 1988: 271). Famously, Locke's view on natural rights inspired the American founding fathers who relabeled these rights as about "life, liberty and the pursuit of happiness" (United States 1776).

Locke argued that our right to life (or self-preservation) was as important as our liberty or ability to own property. This is because each needs
the others. A right to life is a right to a life with liberty and have property
rights. Something fundamental is missing when any one of these three
natural rights is not enjoyed. Having a life requires the right to be free.

Natural rights theorists – like Hobbes and Locke – disagree about
what natural rights we are each claimed to have. They both claim that
through the use of our reason, we can discern what natural rights we
all possess. A usual exercise for my students is to reflect on what
rights they believe are held by everyone universally and how they
might convince others who disagree, as a means of better understanding the project that figures like Hobbes and Locke were engaged in.

Natural rights views have come in for criticism. One criticism is
that natural rights theorists do not agree among themselves about
what natural rights we have or how many natural rights we each possess, as has been seen above.

A second criticism of natural rights theories concerns the idea of
natural rights as "natural." For example, Peter Jones says:

> Trees, bees and buttercups are all parts of nature, so, on this view it
> would seem, are rights. We cannot doubt the existence of trees, bees
> and buttercups, nor, it would seem, can we doubt the existence of
> rights. Yet rights clearly do not "exist" in the same manifest way as
> these other things ... Not unreasonably, therefore, natural rights theo-
> rists have been accused of trying to pass off a highly questionable moral
> notion as though its presence in the universe were a matter of fact
> (Jones 1994: 79).

This criticism is that natural rights have a question begging nature.
The claim that a right to life, liberty, or other goods exists *because it
is natural* makes several assumptions. First, it assumes that rights exist
naturally in the same way that trees or bees exist. Yet, trees or bees
have a physical presence we might perceive directly while our rights
have a *metaphysical* presence where we grasp them, if at all, in a
different way.

A second assumption is that by claiming natural rights are naturally part of the world that they are necessarily a good thing. However,
not everything that is "natural" is a positive entity to be protected or
promoted all the time. Examples abound of naturally bad things, not
least including cancer, COVID-19, and being allergic to poison ivy.

The fact that something exists in nature does not require we render it as positive or benign. It must be argued why any such natural rights are worth having and defending. We cannot assume they are worth having and defending because it is claimed they exist naturally and so necessarily good in themselves.

Natural rights theorists disagree about what are our natural rights. And if not obviously natural or good, it raises the question of how might we identify a right when we see one – and how might be justified on some different ground?

## 2.4   What Are Rights?

A common view of rights today is that *rights protect the interests of a rights-holder against interference by others.* Rights have sometimes been seen as "trumps" where having a right is like having a trump card that provides an extra reason to prioritize a protected interest over other less significant considerations (Dworkin 1978: xi). Our rights set out boundaries protecting specific interests, should they clash with other factors. We may have a right to free speech even if what we say is unpopular or controversial according to others. In having a right, others are duty-bound to protect a rights-holder's interest. In other words, we might defend the right of another to express their free speech even if we disagree with what is said (Raz 1986: 44). This view of rights is individualistic: rights are the rights of individuals, often as a defense against coercion of the individual by the state.

Joseph Raz famously defines rights like this:

> "X has a right" if and only if X can have rights, and, other things being equal, an aspect of X's well-being (his interest) is a sufficient reason for holding some other person(s) to be under a duty (Raz 1986: 166).

Rights are about protecting interests, but not an interest to do anything without limits. For example, Raz is clear that our interests are grounded in well-being.[2] We might argue that we have rights to life,

---

[2] I will refer to *substantive interests* as a shorthand for the kinds of interests relevant to the promotion of our well-being that could serve as a subject for rights (rights-subject). Rights theorists disagree over many things but broadly agree that only some interests, namely the more substantive, and not others, such as more trivial or otherwise unimportant, have relevance for well-being and can serve as a protected right.

liberty, and the pursuit of happiness. These rights can each be said to center on the promotion of what is in our substantive interests and, therefore, may serve as the protected subject of our rights (which we might call *rights-subjects*). Moreover, our rights establish duties on others to comply so that our interests can be exercised, within specified boundaries and balanced against the interests of others and given protection. This approach to rights is called the *interest theory* of rights and it is the most dominant in the field (Kramer 2013).

First, we must establish who is a rights-holder. The interest theory of rights builds off of the widely shared view that human beings have rights because we have valuable interests that demand protection, such as to life, health, and the possession of property (Raz 1986: 191). These interests have special importance for the well-being of any rights-holder and this gives them value. Thus, the value of rights is in their providing "a protective shield" against any infringement of these interests (Raz 1986: 250). Not all rights have equal weight, nor do all interests share the same value. The more important the interest, the greater the value of its corresponding right (Raz 1986: 262). So, the right to life is weightier than a right to property as, without life, we cannot enjoy property. All rights protect important interests, but some rights have greater importance in relation to the relevant weight of the specific corresponding interest that it promulgates and protects.

It is commonly argued that only individuals can be rights-subjects, and thus rights-holders, because only individuals can have such interests. For example, we all have an interest in our own lives. Therefore, this interest should be protected as a right to life to safeguard ourselves from being arbitrarily killed. Our individual interests are an essential part of what justifies rights, which provide protection for our interests (Raz 1986: 181).

One contested issue is whether we only possess rights when we are alive. On the interest theory, rights serve to protect interests and these might be thought to expire with death.[3] In response, interest theorists might argue that my interests might reasonable live on in some way after I die, such as when I write a will for how my possessions might be divided on my death. The fact that I have died does not mean that my will should be ignored because I am not alive to pursue its

---

[3] For discussion on this and related topics, see Kramer (2001) and Nussbaum (2004: 154–156).

enforcement. My interest is manifest in agreeing to set out the terms of the will and it is that living interest that is relevant.

A second contested issue is whether non-human animals might possess the same right to life as we do. Some may argue that it is *speciesist* to claim that only humans can be rights-holders, as this might be thought to give our own species priority simply by discriminating against all others. However, nobody thinks that all living organisms have the same (or any) rights like human beings even if all non-human species shared similar interests in their continuing survival, whether or not they understand that they do. For example, no one claims that bacteria or viruses harmful to humans have any right to life: for instance, if we can eradicate polio forever, we should do so. Of course, the mere fact that nobody argues for a view does not necessarily entail that such a view must be false. While the traditional view that human rights are only held by humans appears like a tautology, it does seem to capture an important truth that the full set of rights that we believe *we* have are different (and more) than whatever rights we might claim for any non-human species. We must specify why the substantive interests, if any, of some non-human species might count as rights, but not others if seeking to extend the range of rights-holders beyond human beings.[4] Only then might we clarify what rights, if any, non-human species might possess.

After we establish who is a rights-holder for a theory about rights, we need to consider what kinds of substantive interests could be a subject for rights that are protected. This can be a matter of both identifying which substantive interests should count, as well as discerning their boundary limits. For example, consider free speech. It can be argued that we have a substantive interest in protecting free speech as an important interest generally, and as essential to the proper functioning of any democratic system. If this right was left unprotected, then only one political party might have a voice and this would deny the public any possibility of a viable alternative to consider at elections rendering the exercise pointless. But such a right to free speech is not unlimited. We cannot defame others through spreading false rumors intended to cause harm as this would violate their substantive interests in being protected from such smears and associated harm. Likewise, we cannot knowingly and falsely shout "fire!" in

---

[4] I discuss the possibility of rights for animals toward this chapter's end.

a crowded room knowing that we unjustifiably risk causing harm to those attempting to flee after hearing us shout.

Rights are protections of our substantive interests that create "grounds of duties in others" (Raz 1986: 44, 167). So, we must establish what duties our rights establish and how they might be enforced. My having a right to life does not require everyone else to constantly monitor my well-being and undertake every action that might potentially extend my life for as long as possible (Raz 1986: 171, 183, 249). But it does impose a duty on others not to harm me and this can be enforced. Crucial to this view is that the protected interest is of value and so worthy of protection. For instance, I do not have a right to see a butterfly flutter past my window as I type these words, as pleasing as this sight might be to perceive.[5] This is because I neither have any such substantive interest that it does happen nor could I enforce such a happening even if I did.

A criticism of the interest theory of rights is that it extends rights too far, including third party beneficiaries. This is shown as follows. Suppose Mike promised his brother Bill to pay his sister Betsy $100.[6] It could be argued that there is now a duty on Mike to pay Betsy, but *in addition* a duty might be said to be owed to Bill, too, who also benefits from the knowledge she received $100. If Betsy plans to spend this $100 on her daughter Stella, then Mike also has a duty to her and so on (Sreenivasan 2005: 262). This example is thought to illustrate the problem that ascribing rights to anyone and everyone who might benefit extends claims far too wide and implausibly.

Interest theorists reject the claim that their theory justifies such an overextension of claims like this (Kramer et al. 1998: 66–68, 80–81). One problem with the example is it takes *any* claim to ground a right with the *same* status. Mike is thought to owe duties to Bill, Betsy, Stella and perhaps others. Yet, these claims are not equally weighty. Mike has made no promise or offer to Stella nor any other third party. His offer of money is only to Betsy. If Mike does not honor his promise, Bill may be aggrieved at Mike's dishonesty but it is unclear that any wrong done to him is of equal weight to Betsy's sense of wrong.

A second issue is the example is unpersuasive. Consider two versions where Mike promises Bill he will give Betsy $100. In the first scenario,

---

[5] For any reader that might be interested in the actual weather conditions outside my window right now, there is a downpour outside and alas no butterfly.
[6] While I have added names to the example, my outline of the criticism follows the example used in Sreenivasan (2005).

Mike finds $100. He tells Bill that Betsy will be given the $100. Later that day, Mike's boss Cindy imposes a paid parking system at their work that costs $100 annually. Mike pays his boss $100 with the money that he found, and so can no longer give it to Betsy. It is unclear how significantly either Bill or Betsy is wronged by Mike's breaking his promise. They might both be disappointed or even upset, but intuitively we would not say Mike should be fined or worse. In a second scenario, Mike owes Betsy $100 because she fixed his car for him. Mike tells Bill he will pay Betsy $100. If Mike breaks his promise, Bill may be disappointed and have difficulty trusting Mike. However, the aggrieved party is Betsy whose claim is not only that she is owed a gift, but a service. How the case plays out changes significantly when some contextual content is added. Context shapes our assessment. Such examples sharpen further when we reflect what legal consequences ought to flow. Betsy has a stronger claim in the second scenario as the promise to pay her arises from a contractual relationship relating to services of a different nature than an offering of a gift later rescinded.[7]

The main alternative view is the *will theory* of rights. This view holds that rights are where we have what H. L. A. Hart called a "measure of control" over a duty comprised of powers to waive a duty or not, to enforce someone's duty or not given a breach and a power to waive any duty to compensate for a breach (Hart 1982: 183–184). Will theory is thought to suffer from two problems. The first is it conceives of rights as essentially alienable. I have powers to waive my rights. A standard objection is that the will theory would permit someone to not exercise a right against enslavement. Some rights are inalienable and provided important protections that the will theory does not support. The second problem is that the will theory requires the ability to exercise power. However, individuals with cognitive impairments may be unable to do so and, as a result, the will theory would deny recognizing these individuals are rights holders – and, it is argued, this would be a repugnant conclusion that shows the will theory is unsuccessful as a theory of rights.

There is something substantive in these debates. One view is that rights are about the promulgation and protection of interests; the second view is that rights are about our having control in the exercise of

---

[7] When reflecting on rights, it can be helpful to reflect on what consequences ought to follow from any breach of a right to signpost those with a potential claim and to assess their relative weights.

specified powers. These are different conceptions of rights for sure. Nevertheless, some claim that what is it at stake is not so much interests or powers, but rather the reasons – whatever these may be – that count and compel us to support one view instead of its alternatives (Bedi 2009: 1). Of courses, the weight of reasons that support one view over another is crucial. Nonetheless, we seek not reasons in general, but reasons that support a compelling narrative about the rights we have.

## 2.5    A Taxonomy of Rights

A useful way forward is to consider what kinds of things we might *claim* as rights. When we reflect on the kinds of things we believe to be rights, it can help us understand how the word "rights" in our rights-talk can fulfill different purposes. In plain English, not all rights may work in the way. An examination of how we understand rights generally can expose that we see different kinds of rights – and that they can function differently.

We think about rights in different ways. One such way is that we might claim a right to be *exempt* from general duties holding on us all normally. For example, we cannot break into the home of another to restrain them. However, we recognize the right of police officers to do just that when pursuing suspects in order to make an arrest. The fact that police officers have this right does not require them to exercise it. They have discretion – a *privilege* – about whether or not to use their right to an exemption. Similarly, consider how we cannot drive a car without having a driver's license. Possessing a license to drive gives an exemption and so a right to drive a car that those without a license do not possess. Likewise, having a driver's license does not require the driver to use a car. They have discretion on when they can exercise their exemption from general duties.

A second way we think about rights is as a kind of *claim*. An example is where we claim a right to not be physically harmed by somebody else. This claimed right is a source of protection for me against possible injury from others. Another example is where an employee claims a right to their pay from an employer. In this case, my claimed right is a demand for others to perform a specific action.

There is a third way to think about rights. This is as a *power*. A power is a kind of right about changing our exemptions or claims, as well as the power to ensure our exemptions and claims are not changed by others (Wenar 2005: 230–231). Suppose Alex owns a large fortune worth several million dollars. She is under no duty to share one penny of it. Nor does anybody else have a right to it either. If Alex decides to promise her fortune to Brian in her will, Alex creates a new claim for Brian on her fortune. This is one way that rights might alter claims as a power.

Or consider a judge who must decide the punishment for a convicted criminal (Wenar 2005: 231). The judge has a right to punish convicted criminals. This right to punish is a power that changes the exemptions or claims of the criminals who, for example, may become imprisoned and lose their freedoms as a result. Moreover, this power can be exercised with discretion where a judge can decide against imposing imprisonment and, instead, impose a community sentence.

A fourth, and final, way to think about rights is as a kind of *immunity*. The US Constitution protects the right to free speech. This right is an immunity from the government or others violating this right. Or, for another example, the Universal Declaration of Human Rights provides an immunity for most citizens to overly severe or unnecessary punishment (Brooks 2025a). In these ways, our rights can protect individuals from government interference on what might be said or how much they might be punished.

In summary, we understand rights not as one kind of thing, but, instead, as an umbrella term covering different kinds of rights, including rights as privileges, rights as claims, rights as powers, or rights as immunities. These kinds of rights are sometimes referred to as "Hohfeldian incidents" named for Wesley Hohfeld who originally developed this taxonomy of rights (Hohfeld 1919).[8] Each kind of right has one or more functions, such as an exemption, discretion, protection, or performance. In his insightful study of Hohfeld's framework, Leif Wenar argues that it shows us that rights are of more than one kind and that they can have multiple functions (Wenar 2005: 246).

---

[8] I describe Hohfeld's approach to my students as follows. His analysis considers the wide range of rights that are recognized. His project is to identify the features of the various rights we endorse and then attempt to reveal how the given legal rights can be described in a taxonomical way that shows us the ways incidents and functions interact. This taxonomy is a structure providing us with a lens through which we might identify and apply the rights we have, but also provide us with tools for future scenarios in discerning if and how further rights might be identified according to his theoretical framework.

On this Hohfeldian view, we identify the rights we have when we can link a kind of right with one or more of its functions. Rights are all one of the four different varieties identified, but not where they lack a function of rights. Consider the case of university students. No university has the power to grant citizenship to its students. It might be said that students would have an immunity against receiving citizenship from their university since it cannot be done. But this would be a mistake. Students have no right to their university's inability to grant them citizenship because it fulfills no appropriate function. For example, university students cannot claim any immunity from gaining citizenship providing them with a protection. However, when it comes to the state having the ability to grant citizenship this does create claims that provide protections, such as citizenship rights to live in a state permanently with full rights of political participation, for instance. Individuals gain rights where the state grants them citizenship because one of the kinds of rights connects with one of the functions of rights.

Before moving to the next section, I should note the following. In my experience, students come to lectures with different ideas about rights. While most agree about most of the rights they have, students come prepared to debate over particular individual rights and the consequences of supporting or rejecting different approaches to justifying rights. These discussions are often well informed and focused around key substantive issues, such as at the beginning or end of life. I suspect students expect, and come prepared, to consider the *ethical* and *political* complexity of rights. What I do not think they anticipate is the *taxonomical* complexity behind picking out how we know what could be a right from what cannot that lies behind these ethical and political considerations – such as the taxonomy offered by Hohfeld.

## 2.6  Human Rights

We speak about some rights as "human rights." This raises the question of what, if anything, is the difference between "human rights" and other kinds of rights generally? After all, aren't all rights "human rights" insofar as they are rights belonging to individuals? Or not?

There are some features about human rights that are worth clarifying. Human rights are a special variety of rights held by all human beings. All human rights are part of the rights that we have, although not every right is a human right. One difference between rights and human rights is that *every* human right is a right that every human has, but not all rights are possessed by everyone. For example, we might have certain rights in relation to our social or political roles. An employer has rights to hire to fire employees that may not be held by others, such as non-employees including the unemployed. Or a political leader, like a President or Prime Minister, may have the right to choose who might serve in their Cabinet, but not the rest of us. We might seek to persuade a President about who should be nominated for appointment to a specific role, but only the President can make he nomination and this need not take account of our views.

We might call these rights *mere rights*. A mere right is a right that not all of us might possess all the time. This is often true for rights relating to our social or political roles. If we run a company, we might have rights over who is a part of it with us. These kinds of rights we possess only when in that role. Sometimes these mere rights can be especially significant. No one can deny that the right of a political leader to choose Cabinet members is a very important right. But it is a right that not everyone has. Mere rights are rights that we do not all have all the time.

In contrast, a *human right* is a right that all of us possess all of the time. It is a permanent feature of each one of us. This raises the question of how to distinguish between the kinds of rights we must have all the time (human rights) from the kinds of rights we might only have some of the time, if ever (mere rights).

The primary way that human rights are understood is their having greater fundamental importance for every one of us generally. This might be understood as concerning our most basic needs. For example, Locke claims we all have rights to life, liberty, and property. These rights offer essential protections over our basic physical and social well-being.

Others have described these protections as best defined in terms of our *basic needs*. These form a "global minimum" that must be secured for everybody and that impose obligations on every government (Miller 2007: 166). The idea of human rights as basic needs is meant to highlight what is essential, as opposed to what is merely optional, that signifies its greater moral urgency and more "substantive moral view" (Miller 2007: 122). There is a greater wrong and injustice done to us whenever we are deprived of any basic need (Miller 2007: 181). The idea of basic needs is meant to focus on our real, universal human rights. The concern is that some claim ever-expanding lists for the terms "rights" and "human rights" especially relating to evolving cultural norms and social justice that weaken the genuine universality meant to underpin human rights (Miller 2007: 182–183). Thinking about human rights as essentially our basic needs is intended to refocus our attention on the true universality of human rights for all.

However, when do we know a basic need when we see one? Miller admits that it is essential to determine what is required to lead decent lives where we live and not merely "what people in those cultures may believe is necessary" from a non-objective point of view (Miller 2007: 184). So, it may be very difficult to discern whether basic needs that seem essentially required to us in *our* country are truly basic needs that are essentially required for anyone *everywhere*. This reveals a concern about the universality of basic needs across cultures globally.

For example, some, like Miller, distinguish *societal needs* relating to social justice within a community from basic needs that relate to all communities. But which needs are one or the other, either basic needs or societal needs? Not every community is a democracy, for instance. So, is democratic self-government only a societal need for some, but not a basic need for all?

We could reply that basic needs are understood and justified on their merits. If basic needs are justified but not in place somewhere, this is a way in which basic needs help us understand whether everyone everywhere has the protection of their essential needs to live decent lives. So, where we might believe democratic self-government is a basic need, then we might look to the world to identify which political community does satisfy this basic need – and identify those communities that do not.

If we only identified basic needs from what *is* practiced, then we could not pick out what *should* be practiced: there is a crucial difference between *what is* from *what should be* (and from *what should never be*) that any normative analysis should never lose sight of. Democracy is not everywhere. Whether or not it should be needs to be argued and defended, such as if it protects a basic need for all and including communities where it is not practiced.

To summarize, basic needs aim to provide a clearer focus for thinking about human rights, namely, as covering our most basic needs. But this does not alter the fundamental task of discerning what are our most important universal rights. This task remains the same.

We might ask: so, what are our basic needs? One way of thinking about this is to consider what are our central *interests*. We might argue that we all have a fundamental interest in being able to live our own lives, for example. Yet, while we might agree we should be able to exercise some degree of freedom as an essential right, we have seen in the last chapter that there are multiple ways of thinking about what freedom is – and how it should be protected.

Moreover, we would need to show that, despite the real possibility that different people might claim different interests, there are some interests that *everyone* possesses, perhaps even if they are unaware or unconvinced – otherwise, our interest is not universal, which it must be to ground a universal human right. So, even if we can agree that we have a central interest in being free and, so, we agree that we have human rights to fundamental essentials like freedom, this is only the beginning of the argument for what kind of human right this might be.

The idea of human rights is not purely philosophical. There are identifiable and widely recognized human rights that can be found in international law. Human rights have what we might call a concrete *materiality* as acknowledged rights shared and enforced across most countries. A prime example is the *Universal Declaration of Human Rights* (UDHR) adopted by the United Nations General Assembly in 1948. It is an international consensus – as its name suggests as a "universal declaration" – that sets out the minimum standards that all governments must respect. The UDHR affirms that there are human rights to everyone being born free and equal, a right to "life, liberty and security of person," a right to free education, the prohibitions of slavery, of cruel and unusual punishment, and of torture to name only a few.

The UDHR is a broad, international agreement on universal human rights that sets out the minimum standards that all governments must respect. It shows that we can forge global agreement about what universal rights we all possess. But, of course, the UDHR is a list that various countries do agree about. It does not include views on rights that countries disagree about, such as whether university education should be free or whether everyone is entitled to free national health care. This highlights a distinction between the universality of human rights versus the non-universality of mere rights. The list of the former is noticeably shorter than that of the latter.

But it is not clear that less universally accepted views about rights mean that those rights are somehow less important. Consider that not everywhere will recognize a right to free health care for all. There is no such recognized human right in international law. Yet, it might be argued that this is a right that should be acknowledged for all as it underpins a basic need for protecting public health. Or consider how not everyone in every country has a right to stand for elected office. Whether or not the rights recognized in one or more countries should be recognized universally is a matter where we debate and hope to convince others. But it makes clear a difference between universal human rights that are universally recognized and may be part of international law versus universal human rights that are not, or at least not yet, universally recognized and which may only be enforced in domestic law.

So, a human right is a right we claim applies universally to all human beings and that it is of some fundamental importance that everyone should enjoy beyond any mere right that is not as essential or universal – an important theoretical distinction not always easily drawn. We must always distinguish our conception of human rights from whatever human rights are part of international law as this allows us to use the former to help us assess the latter. Of course, this works both ways. We should not assume that our task is only to see how all recognized human rights should be *expanded*, but we should also reflect on whether all recognized human rights should remain recognized. What rights should have fundamental importance for all? Does having such a right protect some universally-held essential interest? Does this claimed right fit into one of the four kinds of rights (e.g., privileges, claims, powers, or immunities)? These are some of the questions we must ask ourselves when considering what should count as a human right.

## 2.7   Capabilities and Human Rights

The capabilities approach is an important and influential alternative to the view of human rights as basic needs. It may also help us consider how we should understand the content of human rights and its enforceability.

Capabilities are about our ability "to do or be" (Nussbaum 2003). It is concerned with fundamental freedom to do or be in certain ways. One popular view of capability is by Amartya Sen, who conceives of capability along a continuum where we may have either more or less. We each have capability to a degree, some more than others. He defends capability as a superior way of measuring progress in human development. Traditionally, the development of different societies is measured in terms of the per capita Gross Domestic Product. The higher a community's average income, the more it is believed to have developmentally advanced. Development policy should aim at continually raising the average income of communities in order to help promote their growth on that view.

Sen's critique is that this model is badly flawed. One reason is that counting average wealth masks deep inequalities. Imagine a community of 100 people where each earns an equal income of $10,000 each. Average earnings are $10,000 and the same for all. Compare this with a second group of 100 people where one earns an income of $1,000,000 and the others receive only $1000 each. The second group's average earnings are $10,990. The traditional model of assessing average wealth would find the second group better off than the first group overall. But, in fact, all but one in the second group is materially much worse off than everyone in the first group. Assessing average wealth can fail to be attentive to significant inequalities in a community, and so it can prove to be a poor measure of development.

Sen's second criticism is that what matters for improved development is not necessarily monetary gain, but an increase in human flourishing. Sen argues that we should look to human development indicators, such as infant mortality, literacy rates in the society, and longevity, to get a more accurate view of developmental advancement. His view is that progress is measured in terms of these indicators. When a community has lower infant mortality, has improved literacy rates, and lives longer, these indicators are a better sign that a community is enjoying better development than merely showing average income has improved.

This is because, as Sen has been at pains to show, a community with more average wealth than another might not score better on these capability indicators. As a result, Sen argues we need to redirect attention to improving flourishing through securing capability to do or be so we can improve development (Sen 1999). While this will take resources, it is not by resources alone that gains can be made.

Sen's *capability approach* is developed philosophically in several ways by Martha C. Nussbaum's *capabilities approach*.[9] Nussbaum argues that there is not one continuum of capability, but 10 different capabilities. She lists these capabilities as life; bodily health; bodily integrity; senses, imagination, and thought; emotions; practical reason; affiliation; other species; play; and control over one's environment (Nussbaum 2011: 33–34). We might think of these 10 capabilities falling within three groups centered around the body (achieving capabilities of life and bodily health), the mind (achieving capabilities of senses, imagination, thought, emotions, and practical reason), and our boundaries with others (achieving capabilities of bodily integrity, affiliation, other species, play, and control over one's environment).[10]

Nussbaum's capabilities approach has several key features. First, we only have justice for all when each and every capability can be enjoyed above a threshold by all of us, if we chose to exercise them. This does not require that we *must* exercise each capability, only that we *can* if want to. For example, we may have access to a satisfactory level of health care and yet choose an unhealthy lifestyle, or perhaps simply refuse to receive medical support for whatever reason. Capability is about a freedom to do or be. So long as we have the opportunity to exercise our capabilities, there is no injustice if we should choose against it. But there is injustice if we cannot choose.

Second, Nussbaum argues that each capability has equal importance and weight to all other capabilities. Therefore, no capability is more valuable than another. Moreover, we cannot make up being below a sufficient threshold of satisfying one capability by being far above any such threshold for another capability. All must be accessible and available without any exceptions. Otherwise, we are unable to enjoy a minimally decent life.

Thirdly, Nussbaum claims that her list is subject to possible future revision. Her argument is that her list of capabilities are the full range

---

[9] Too often commentators speak of the "Sen and Nussbaum's capabilities approach" but it is important to highlight that they take dissimilar approaches. Sen's *capability* continuum and Nussbaum's list of 10 *capabilities* is one notable difference.

[10] Elsewhere, I describe these as concentric circles of "Body," "Brain," and "Boundaries" where the first is required for the second and their combination is required for the third. This view does not see the capabilities as being equal, but where some have greater importance for the exercise of some capabilities than others. For example, we require satisfaction of Body-related capabilities like life and health in order to be able to fully exercise capabilities relating to our minds. To enjoy affiliation, we need to secure capabilities to life and practical reasoning. See Brooks (2020c: 199–213, especially 204–205).

we should recognize. However, this list is not set in stone forever. Nussbaum claims it is "open-ended and humble" and "can always be contested and remade" (Nussbaum 2000: 77).

An important, but often overlooked, point is that ensuring all can exercise capabilities does not require the state must intervene. The capability for bodily health needs to guarantee that each of us is "able to have good health" above a satisfactory minimum (Nussbaum 2011: 78). This might be achieved by launching a well-functioning National Health Service maintained by the state and free for citizens to use. Or it could be enabled through alternative means and led by the private sector. Nussbaum's capabilities approach is flexibly open to *how* a community is able to secure our all being able to exercise our capabilities. What matters is that we have the freedom to – and not an overly interventionist state. In fact, some capabilities might require little or no intervention, such as our being able to make friends through social interaction as part of a capability to Affiliation (Nussbaum 2011: 79). Governments can play important, even decisive, roles in protecting capabilities, but the point is that capabilities need not require the state intervenes.

Fourthly, Nussbaum argues there is "a very close relationship" between capabilities and human rights (Nussbaum 2011: 97). She says: "The right to political participation, the right to religious free exercise, the right of free speech – these and others are all best thought of as capacities to function" (Nussbaum 2011: 98). Securing rights is a project about ensuring we can exercise our capabilities. This is a view of rights as protections of our fundamental interests that we must be able to pursue.

But what is interesting is how Nussbaum powerfully challenges our everyday thinking about human rights. Human rights are universal. This might tempt us into thinking that if everyone has the same set of human rights that they must be applied in the same way for every community in a one-size-fits-all model. Such thinking is mistaken. For example, we might all accept a right to democratic political decision-making, but also recognize that this right can be realized in different forms, such as in presidential or parliamentary democratic models. Thus, the same rights can be realized in full but in different ways. The capabilities approach understands that our fundamental human right to capabilities can be guaranteed for all, however in different ways.

A common criticism of capabilities concerns the issue of whether we must exercise them. For Nussbaum, it is only necessary that we have the choice to exercise any or all capabilities at or above a minimal threshold. Her claim is that if this choice is *possible* then we can live a full life with human dignity.

One concern is that if enjoying capabilities is necessary for a decent life and securing our human rights, why is it satisfactory if we chose *not* to exercise our capabilities? In other words, if capabilities are highly valuable to choose, it seems important that we *do* choose to use them and a problem when we *do not*. For example, consider a community where everyone decides that no one will seek to exercise any of their capabilities. Suppose this decision is freely chosen and uncoerced. Compare this scenario with a second community that ensures all of its citizens can and do enjoy all of their capabilities individually. It is difficult to see why we might see these two communities as equal when only one protects and enjoys the full range of capabilities while the other does not. Having and enjoying capabilities should matter – and not only whether or not we wish to exercise them (Brooks 2014a).

This raises a related concern about capabilities. If it is *possible* that we can choose and exercise any and all capabilities above a threshold, then justice is secured. However, it also seems important that it is *probable* that we might routinely choose to exercise most, if not all, capabilities most, if not all, the time. Otherwise, if it made no difference that we did enjoy capabilities above a threshold (and that doing so over a threshold is essential to justice), the substantive importance of having capabilities and their link to our human rights might appear to lose some of its force.

A way of resolving this concern is to claim that it must be *both* possible *and* probable that we can *and* do exercise capabilities most, if not all, the time. This allows us to retain the importance of free choice about whether or not to exercise a capability at some particular time while making it clear that having and enjoying capabilities is important for justice.

## 2.8  Group Rights and Mutual Recognition

The idea that there are group rights may seem very controversial. As former British Prime Minister Margaret Thatcher famously once said "There is no such thing as society," only individuals. We have considered *individual* rights so far. But what of *groups*? Do we, as individuals, have rights arising from our membership in a group?

Group rights are defined as rights that individuals *only* possess because of their group membership. These rights are typically claimed for groups, such as a state or nation, commercial corporations, religious organizations, and other bodies. Group rights theorists typically distinguish between what we might call mere collectivities (often called the *collective* conception of groups) and groups capable of possessing rights (called the *corporate* conception of groups) (Jones 1994: 182–187). A mere collectivity would make a collection of people bound together in a way that lacks some fundamental valuable connection, such as, a collection of people interested in collecting baseball cards or supporters of a baseball team. They are connected to each other through a love of a game, pastime, or hobby – and it is not denied that the enjoyment of such has value for those who cherish it.

However, group rights theorists typically claim that the kind of groups that can give rise to group rights are those that have some fundamental valuable connection, such as self-identifying as common members of a political and/or religious community. This *corporate* conception is of individuals incorporated together in a shared body. Groups like these may share a common history, a shared language, and/or a system of belief.

The bonds that connect individuals are more than a product of chance: while initial membership may be arbitrary from birth (and so individuals may not have originally chosen their group), the group's self-development is not entirely arbitrary but may be a product of debate and popular decision-making. For example, states are believed to have rights to self-determination precisely for these reasons and group membership can create responsibilities – or associative duties – between group members. An illustration is it is my group membership, say as an American or British citizen, that gives rise to my right to vote in American or British elections. Non-citizens usually have no such associative duties as non-group members. This is not to say they might not have rights to political participation in other states, but only that group membership can create rights among group members like this.

What may be of interest when we consider the possibility of group rights is the possible relevance of the sociality of justifying rights. In other words, while some may argue that the justification of individual rights stems purely from *individual circumstances* (such as whether individuals have human rights by virtue of their humanity), the conception of group rights and associative duties arising from group membership provides a different kind of justification of individual rights stemming from their *community relations*.

A major contribution to this social understanding of rights comes from Hegel, whose work was discussed in the previous chapter. Hegel argues that we understand rights through mutual recognition of our rights (Hegel 1990: 73–114). The idea is that our rights have a social and contextual nature. We have rights as members of our community. However, if every individual could choose for themselves what they had rights to, we would have anarchy and lack any way of resolving whose claim to a right succeeds or fails. It is through the recognition by others of my rights that my rights possess a more stable and secure basis. This is consistent with the view that I possess something when others can affirm that I do, such as that my right is enforceable and may be acknowledged by a court of law.

It may seem obvious that the practical application of rights requires the recognition of others. When no one is convinced that you have a right to do or possess something, practically speaking the right is not recognized. Mutual recognition by others seems essential and inescapable. It may also seem obvious that the specific rights of any individual can differ from one country to another as a part of their group membership. Our membership, such as citizenship, matters to what rights are recognized in our everyday lives.

What is somewhat less obvious is whether our rights are justified through some social means of mutual recognition or whether our rights are justified independently of others – where recognition by others serves a mere practical purpose, not a justificatory purpose. Readers might consider issues such as whether someone living alone marooned on a tropical island has rights and what that means in comparison to someone in an urban community. If rights impose duties, do we require another or are duties to oneself enough? If I have rights insofar as I am human, should it matter if I am alone or with others to have rights, even if I may struggle to exercise them on my own? Or if I have rights as a citizen of a state, should these rights be the same for any citizen in any state – or not?

These important questions have contested conclusions and leading philosophers disagree. So, I will not make any definitive claim for either side, as this would take the rest of the book (or, indeed, a second book!) to do. One point to consider is there is the *justification* of a right and there is the *practical application* of a right. Conceptually, these are clearly separable. We can speak of rights and of their application separately. It might be argued that the fact that it is practically difficult, if not impossible, to exercise a right does not show that a right is unjustified. A usual example is war crimes or torture. An individual or group may be murdered and this would clearly be a denial of any human right against being murdered, for example. However, the denial of a right in these circumstances is also clearly a serious wrong.

At the same time, a second point to consider in a more everyday sense whether one can have rights that cannot be enjoyed, or only rarely. Does it make sense to claim I have a right to an education that is unaffordable for me – or where the school is too far away for me to attend? In these circumstances, having a right means having achieved some exercise of a right – and it might be argued that while the justification of right may be conceptually separate from consideration of its application that, in fact, the two are inseparably linked. After all, rights are protections in a world of practical institutions where practical matters have relevance. *Context and coherence matters*. Such a view of justification as linked with practice can still limit what kinds of practices are permissible so that rights are enjoyed and such social justifications of political rights should not be ignored.

## 2.9   Animal Rights

This chapter has considered rights for human beings. However, some argue that animals (or *non-human species*) have rights, too.[11] In this last section, it is important to reflect on how this might be understood, if at all.

We might think the answer to the question – so, do animals have rights? – is both yes and no. On the one hand, few believe that we can do whatever we might like to animals, including those used for food. For example, there is widespread agreement that some species are at risk of extinction and so worthy of special protections against harm. Most accept there are and should be laws against engaging in animal cruelty, in order to protect the substantive interests that animals may have in avoiding such ill-treatment. This is a further sign that most people agree that animals can and do have rights.

On the other hand, animals clearly do not have rights like human beings do. Animals do not and cannot vote, run for office, or negotiate

---

[11] I will use the terms *animal* and *non-human species* interchangeably.

contractual terms. While it is clear that animals enjoy varied rights protections, it is also clear that the way that they might be thought to enjoy rights is very different from how we, as human beings, enjoy rights. So, how to explain this difference?

The first point to make is the need for finding some rationale. Peter Singer argues that in addition to guarding against racism or sexism, we must be mindful of what he calls *speciesism* (Singer 1979). Singer claims that if we treat animals differently from human beings merely on account of their being a different species from us then we are discriminating against animals. If we are to treat the rights, if any, of animals differently from our rights, then we must find some basis for justifying this difference other than that animals are a different species.

The second point to make is that animals are clearly unable to exercise any rights that they do have in the same kinds of ways that we can. Suppose you came across a crime being committed – whether it was an assault, a theft, or criminal damage. What could you do? You might call for help or ring the police. Anyone caught might be prosecuted and have an opportunity to explain their actions. If found guilty, the individual would potentially be punished through prison or a fine. Notice in this hypothetical scenario the central role given to agency – to act in calling for help, contacting the police, giving evidence in court, and so on. None of this applies to animals. While they might alert others by making noise or becoming agitated, they cannot communicate like humans so are unable to contact the police, give evidence, or negotiate contractual terms when buying a property. Non-human species play a more passive role in exercising their rights as opposed to the active agency enjoyed by us.

This difference is sometimes understood in terms of we as *agents* and non-human species as *patients*. We can play a more active role in maintaining and protecting the rights of ourselves and non-human species. We can better understand what these rights are and how they are enforced. Non-human species cannot act to protect their or our rights, but we can act to protect theirs. For this reason, the support for any animal rights requires active support by us.

With these two preliminary points in mind, it is controversial among those that argue non-human species should have rights what is the ground for doing so. One common justification is sentience. The possession of cognitive capacities and some degree of rationality has often been seen as what has helped distinguish humans from non-humans. However, the view of all non-human species as akin to mere things has changed enormously over time. For example, the 18th-Century philosopher Jeremy Bentham observed that the key question is not whether animals could talk or reason, but "can they suffer?" (Gruen 2017). When an animal expresses pain, it offers a reason to change its condition (Korsgaard 1996: 153). We can feel an animal's distress in such situations – and this may well help explain why we have animal rights protections against cruelty and maltreatment.

But should we only show compassion toward non-human species that express themselves in ways we easily perceive? Should we enforce rights protections more stringently for species that express pain in ways that we can connect with? It is not uncommon to view primates like chimpanzees as different from crustaceans like a clam. The former emote in ways that we can more readily recognize whereas there is some debate over whether clams can feel pain at all. Perhaps they do, but we have not yet found a way to confirm it. One study found that plants make high-pitched noises that ramp up when distressed or in need of watering, albeit inaudibly to our human ears (Knapton 2023). However, few argue that all plants must be undisturbed. Whether we can sympathetically connect with a non-human species seems to make a difference about whether we recognize it has rights to be protected.

A second argument about animal rights is that they have rights against being eaten by us. A common defense is that animals are thinking and feeling beings like us. We are not required to consume them to survive, as we are capable of choosing against eating animals and can be perfectly nourished without doing so. Removing meat from our diet has various health benefits to us, but it also greatly reduces suffering and harm to non-human species. And so we should have meat-free diets.

A common criticism of this view is that animals need not – and do not – have any such obligation. As Cicero remarks, animals merely respond to the world without awareness of the past or future whereas only we can comprehend the consequences of our actions (Cicero 1991: 6). Carnivores can and do consume other creatures. If they can do so, it is argued, then it is inconsistent to say that only we humans should not do so. If the point is that we are sufficiently similar in rights-relevant ways, then we should be able to eat meat since carnivorous animals eat meat.

The reply to this criticism is to reiterate that humans can make a choice against eating meat – and that we stand in an active agent-like position to the passive patient-like position of non-human species.

Rights protection is an obligation for us to deliver and so there are special duties on us.

Sometimes it is said that no meat should be consumed because we should refrain from killing non-human species. But it is implausible to make a blanket one-size-fits-all rule applying to all non-human species. Many of us would have no problem killing a mosquito that was biting our arm or swatting a fly buzzing around our kitchen. Some living organisms may be seen as bad, such as ringworm or a virus. The idea that we should allow *any* living thing to roam freely without harm is implausible. Moreover, if the main issue is prohibiting killing non-human species for food, we might seek to adopt ways of continuing to eat meat without killing, such as only eating animals that have died like vultures or artificially growing meat in laboratories for human consumption (see Brooks 2017a).

But this only compels us to think more carefully about *why* we justify rights protections for non-human species, *what kinds* of rights we ascribe to animals, and *the different kinds* of rights we assign to some but not all. In other words, the idea of animal rights is often not that all (or any) animals have the same rights as us. Nor is it the idea that non-human species all have the same rights, whatever species they are. No, the idea of non-human species rights is about the differentiation of rights among different species that helps explain why some non-human species should enjoy more rights protections than other non-human species – while some non-human species may enjoy little or none.[12]

## 2.10   Conclusion

This chapter has examined the idea of rights. This idea has evolved from a divine right of kings to natural rights to human rights. Each attempt to express what makes a right worthy of respect and moral urgency whether understood within a state or as a part of international law. I have surveyed some of the leading ideas about what

---

[12] I encourage readers to reflect on whether they believe a human, a chimpanzee, a clam, and any parasite have rights and, if so, what might justify differences in what rights, if any, some might be thought to have – and whether they accept that not all non-human species have rights (even if some others do). Readers are encouraged to examine Martha Nussbaum's discussion of *the species norm* that might help us discern different ways we might understand rights in relation to different species. See Nussbaum (2006: 364–366).

rights are by some of the most influential contributors. Theories of rights is an area with much complexity. It is hoped that this survey has provided readers with a clear glimpse of what the main ideas and debates about rights, human rights, group rights, and animal rights.

Everyone says that rights matter, but everyone says different justifications apply and even offers different lists of which rights we have. Readers are encouraged to reflect on why rights have importance for them, what justifies them best in their eyes, and to reflect on what this means more broadly for others and non-human species from within our lived context and make coherent sense of what you find compelling in our social and political context.

## Further Reading

Hobbes, Thomas. 1996. *Leviathan*, ed. Richard Tuck. Cambridge: Cambridge University Press.

Jones, Peter. 1994. *Rights*. Basingstoke: Palgrave.

Nussbaum, Martha C. 2000. *Women and Human Development: The Capabilities Approach*. Cambridge: Cambridge University Press.

Wenar, Leif. 2020. "Rights." *Stanford Encyclopedia of Philosophy*. https:// plato.stanford.edu/entries/rights.

# 3

# Equality

## 3.1 Introduction

Equality has become so popular an idea that it might be thought to have become a ubiquitous value. Who *isn't* for equality? It is commonly demanded across many areas of life at work, home, study, in music, the arts and more. To not receive equal treatment like others is to have been wronged. Concerns about inequality are everywhere, including gender pay gaps, discrimination in recruitment and elsewhere. Equality matters.

However, equality is understood in *very* different ways. For example, sometimes the demand for equality is a claim for better treatment, such as ending unjustifiable differences with others. Or the demand for equality might be a want that the advantages enjoyed by some are made available to all. Additionally, it may take shape as a desire for some to become worse off to reduce an unjustifiable gap between their advantages and the relative position of others.

Of course, not everyone wants greater equality. Providing equal opportunities for all might allow greater competition that could risk making the privileged lose their unfair advantage. While demanding equal pay can ensure those who are wrongly underpaid receive fair wages, those already enjoying the advantages of higher wages may worry that greater equality will put downward pressure on their own position. These scenarios assume a zero-sum context where the least advantaged are winners and the most advantaged become losers.

*Political Philosophy: The Fundamentals*, First Edition. Thom Brooks.
© 2025 John Wiley & Sons Ltd. Published 2025 by John Wiley & Sons Ltd.

Delivering equality might make things fairer overall, but this does not necessarily require that all are necessarily made better off.

These are just a few of the different ways that people think about equality and its effects. Talking about equality might also focus not only on equal treatment *today*, but how it might look like in the *future*. This could be because we are so far removed from achieving equality in many areas; thus, to speak of equality today is to speak about equality for the future.

Important as these questions are, we have not yet touched on the issue of *what is equality* and what, if any, amount or effort is required to achieve it? Is equality about achieving or possessing the exact same as others? Does what count as "equality" change over time? Is equality about having equal opportunities or is it achieved instead by an equality of outcomes? Is equality inconsistent with merit? Can any inequalities be justified? How might we choose in a context of equality? These are all serious questions about what equality is and how theories of egalitarian justice based on some view of equality might operate.

This chapter examines the different ways in which equality matters. It begins considering formal equality and equal treatment before the law before turning to political equality. The chapter concludes considering the meanings of economic equality and how we might understand it. Throughout, we will discuss equality in a *domestic* context between individuals living in the same community or within the same political state. We will consider equality in an *international* context between individuals living in different countries later in Chapter 7 when we consider the topic of global justice. This is an important caveat to keep in mind although many of the same issues arising between individuals within a state may arise globally between people inhabiting different states.

## 3.2   Formal Equality

Let us begin with the idea of a *formal equality*. This is where all individuals are treated generally equally according to some rule or measure. Most people may think that such a definition accurately captures the essence of equality. After all, is not equal treatment what equality is about?

This simple picture is question begging in some fundamental ways. For instance, the idea that all people are equally human is useful for highlighting our common humanity, if still a tautological argument that does not say anything substantive about what equality is or how it should be applied.

To better understand equality, we should first ask about the *equality of what* that defines our being equals. If we are all treated equally, then does this refer to our having equal wealth, equal welfare, equal opportunity – or equal poverty, equal squalor, or equal domination? This must be determined. As Raz argues: "There is no reason to care about inequalities in the distribution of grains of sand, unless there is some other reason to wish to have or to avoid sand" (Raz 1986: 235). The importance of equality is *the measure of what is valued* that an egalitarian principle aims to regulate. Raz is making the point that equality is about an equality of something valued, such as freedom, wealth or rights, but not trivial matters like grains of sand. This explains why we normally understand equality in terms of whether there is equal freedom, equal pay or equal rights rather than insignificant concerns. So, equality is about a measure of something we value.

A second issue we must address is *equality for who*. Equality is relational. We consider how one thing is equal *in relation to* another. Equality is about how one relates to others about something that we value. Suppose there is a shipwreck with a lone survivor, who finds safety on a nearby deserted island. It does not make sense to ask if the survivor is "equal" on the island as there is nobody else on the island to relate to in comparison. But we might consider whether the survivor living alone on an uninhabited island enjoys equal well-being, for example, in relation to people living elsewhere beyond this island. This might make sense because we relate the individual to others (such as, people in other lands) and in relation to something we value (such as, well-being).

As relational, equality is a measure of either *more, the same* or *less* between two or more individuals or groups. For instance, to examine equality of wealth is to consider how two or more relate along a shared continuum of wealth. They can be said to have more, the same or less than others. Similarly, when we consider the relative equality of two or more it is along a shared continuum of something valued.[1]

---

[1] In his *Second Discourse*, Jean-Jacques Rousseau claims that the relational aspect of equality informs our judgments about moral and political progress. He argues that what is once novel can become habitual over time to the point of becoming one of our "true needs" despite having been unknown to previous generations, and, thus, soon "it became much more cruel to be deprived of them than to possess them was sweet, and men were unhappy to lose them without being happy to possess them." Our reliance (overreliance?) on using smartphones is a good example. I can recall when phones were plugged directly into a landline and used only to make calls. The ever-impressive array of functions from texts and emails to maps and apps has made what was a novel showpiece into a burdensome must-have always nearby. And to be without a handy smartphone (or simply without a charged battery) is to be experiencing loss of a kind unknown two decades ago. Thus, what was once a novel innovation we once lived without has transformed into something that, if unavailable, we would feel aggrieved without it. See Rousseau (1997a: 164–165).

In the rest of this chapter, we shall apply these ideas to the most common areas where equality has been a focus. These areas include the law, the political and social world and economic wealth.


## 3.3   Legal Equality

On July 4, 1776, the United States *Declaration of Independence* said that "all men are created equal" (United States 1776). As every student of American history knows, the United States did not, in fact, treat all men (nor women) equally in 1776. In fact, part of the population was enslaved and many of those who were not were also denied the right to vote. All might be created equally, but there was no legal equality for all at America's beginning.

Nor was this problem short-lived. The Preamble of the United States Constitution refers to "We the People" which might suggest equality of individuals within a collective "We," yet there was no such equality in place (United States 1789). This painful, and shameful, fact about America's early past is not unique. Legal *inequality* was a normal practice in the past globally and, sadly, too often found today as well.

Legal equality is fundamentally about all individuals possessing equal standing before the law. This is central to the idea of a rule of law, or rule by law, where the activities of all are regulated by a legal system that applies in the same way (Bingham 2011). The "rule of law" is held in contrast to a "rule of people" whereby an individual or group is held to above the law and so the system's laws apply to others but not them.

The equal standing of all individuals is affirmed in treaties, such as Article Seven of the Universal Declaration of Human Rights (UDHR) (United Nations 1948). This makes equality before the law an equal right for everyone everywhere. It is right that the law must apply to each of us in the same way. One consequence is that no one can be above the law, as otherwise, the law would apply differently to different people.

A second consequence is that equal treatment before the law does not mean every application must have the same effect. Legal equality is about a process applying equally that may lead to different outcomes. This begs the question of how we might apply the same legal standing and arrive at dissimilar conclusions. For instance, if we cannot justify different outcomes, then we may be at risk of wrongful discrimination that denies legal equality. And if we cannot, we might risk being unable to justify treating the Good Samaritan differently from a thief. So, how might we make sense of treating all equally, but allowing for different treatment without being discriminatory and arbitrary?

In his book *Politics*, Aristotle says: "justice is thought by them to be, and is, equality – not, however, for all, but only for equals. And inequality is thought to be, and is, justice: neither is this for all, but only for unequals."[2] In other words, equality is concerned about treating like things alike: the old adage of comparing apples with apples, not apples with bananas (or widgets). If there are relevant factors that can justify applying equality differently to different groups of people, then equal treatment is about how we apply it to those groups in relevant ways. For Aristotle, we must treat each other equally, but equally in a justified relevant way. Legal equality can mean different treatment. We might call this view *equality as equity* as it seeks equitable treatment.

Readers will notice the importance of "relevant factors" for justifying any differences – and which begs the question: so what kinds of factors might justify relevant different treatment in a non-discriminatory way?

The first kind of factors is our protected characteristics. These include our age, disability, race, religion, sex, and sexual orientation among others. Each is an important part of who we are and shape our individual identity. They can often be features about us that we are given to at birth.[3] But the key feature of these factors is they are characteristics that are legally protected.[4]

As protections, they either allow or deny where relevant. We consider whether a relevant protection is justified and, if so, this can warrant different treatment. For example, there might be laws that require shortlisting any disabled candidate for a job if they meet all necessary requirements. The aim of such laws is to help disabled

---

[2] Aristotle (1984: 1280n11–1280n12). The numbers in parentheses refer to the standard referencing system used for Aristotle's work. This is repeated in references to his work elsewhere.

[3] It may be possible to change protected characteristics over a life, such as converting to a new religion among other ways. Any such new characteristic demands the same protection as any other.

[4] It will be observed that, while we might change our protected characteristics, these may be features of our identity from birth. In that sense, it might be argued that morally arbitrary features about who we are should not justify morally arbitrary discrimination against us for having those features. But, if so, features we choose might be protected differently and they are not. This is because these characteristics are protected for what they are – important aspects of our human identity – not for when we got them.

individuals get qualified paid work by assisting them getting considered at the interview stage. Applicants with a disability are treated the same insofar as they are assessed against the job specifications and, if met, they are short-listed. Job applicants without a disability are all treated the same way as their own group, but differently from those with a disability, as those without it need not be automatically short-listed even if meeting other formal requirements for the same role. Equality as equity treats like cases alike while treating unlike cases differently, but not on a morally arbitrary basis.

The second kind of factors relates to our ability and desert. These are characteristics where we may have a degree of control over our having them. Their relevant importance depends on what we are considering. Suppose we were selecting swimmers for a national Olympic team. We might think a relevant factor is ability to swim fast and so choose the quickest swimmers for our squad. We might apply the same standard to all assessing how fast individuals swim to make our decision. Notably, this kind of factor is proportionate and by degrees. Thus, all might swim, but the issue is some can swim much faster than others. So, this kind of factor does not serve a gatekeeper-like role as seen with protected characteristics. We consider how much or how well someone merits, not if they should be considered at all.

Desert can also be relevant to treating people differently. For example, we might justify treating individuals differently if they are convicted of a crime (Dworkin 2000: 11). Treating like cases alike here means treating the law-abiding differently from the convicted, and treating those convicted for more serious crimes more severely than those who were convicted for lesser crimes. Each receives just deserts in proportion. Equal treatment need not justify the same outcomes in cases like these.

Ronald Dworkin argues that we should consider our equal standing before the law as a general principle of "equal concern and respect" (Dworkin 2000: 1). He claims this is "the sovereign virtue of political community" as a government would descend into some form of tyranny without it no matter how prosperous or well-organized otherwise (Dworkin 2000: 1). For Dworkin, individuals are treated with equal concern and respect if, for example, the legal system applies to each the same even if it might impact them differently. We apply the same criminal law to all, but only those who infringe it might be punished. Legal equality requires equal application of the law but with respect for relevant factors – such as desert or protected characteristics – that could justify different treatment.

There are possibilities where a group might *want* to be treated differently than another. One example is where there may be a difference justified in relation to religious beliefs. For instance, an observant Sikh might claim an exemption from requirements that all motorcyclists wear helmets, as otherwise, he might be unable to comply given his religious commitments. This exemption from requiring Sikhs to wear motorcycle helmets on the grounds of religious freedom is commonly made. Or where those with especially important religious holidays having a right to celebrate those events instead of being required to attend work is similarly common.

Bhikhu Parekh describes this multicultural view as an *equality of differences* (Parekh 2006: 243–249). The idea is we might identify each different cultural and/or religious belief system integral to our identities. Parekh understands these beliefs as including "our values and commitments" and the communities with which we identify.[5] These may make demands on us, such as how we dress, what we eat, how we worship and so on in order to exercize these beliefs.

The consequence is that individuals with different beliefs may be bound by different demands relating to their beliefs. If we required the same demands from everyone, the concern is that this might forbid us from practicing our relevant beliefs if they were incompatible with the demands of the dominant group. For example, if the majority is in power and insists that no one may work on Sundays in keeping with the majority's belief system, this could impact minorities with beliefs about not working on a different day. Parekh's equality of differences claims we should treat such differences equally making exceptions where relevant, but aiming to treat the different cultural beliefs on a broadly equal basis.

A leading critic of this view is Susan Moller Okin. She argues that we should restrict any exceptions made for cultural differences where these might undermine gender equality (Okin 1999). Okin claims that many cultural practices do just this, such as practices like female genital mutilation, dress-related requirements like the wearing of a burqa or hijab, or rights relating to marriage or divorce that are different

---

[5] Parekh is clear that our cultural identities may be relatively stable, but that they are not written in stone and subject to change and evolution over time. While I do not have the space to consider the complexity of cultural identity and diversity, my thinking is heavily informed and influenced by Parekh's *Rethinking Multiculturalism*. It is one of the finest treatises in political theory I have read and I recommend it to all readers as the paramount analysis of multicultural political theory, as I do to my undergraduate and graduate students taking degrees in law, philosophy, and political science. See Parekh (2008: 29).

and less favorable for women than men. A common response to this objection is that it is not obvious that any differences in requirements for men and women are problematic, especially where a woman freely chooses to accept it. For example, it might be a relevant practice for someone's cultural group that women wear a burqa or hijab. This could be objected, along the lines suggested by Okin, for treating women differently than men and that in requiring such dress it entails women are treated less well than men. The counterargument is that it is unclear why a woman should be prevented from wearing such dress if she consents to it. People accept less well-paid jobs or less powerful social positions than they might have otherwise have enjoyed. This does not mean accepting such a position is always problematic. If such differences are avoidable but a product of choice, then we might accept that this difference is permissible.[6]

A second critic is Brian Barry. He claims that there should be a "single status of uniform citizenship" applicable to everyone else (Barry 2001: 11). If we admit exceptions based on multicultural differences, this "'politics of difference' is a formula for manufacturing conflict" as different rules apply to different people (Barry 2001: 21). Instead, we should depoliticize such differences, such as leaving it to individuals to bear the burdens for their beliefs instead of receiving exceptions, based on their cultural or religious beliefs, to the requirements directed at all (Barry 2001: 29, Jones 2006). Or if some exemption(s) to a general rule might make good sense, Barry recommends we see if we might simply abolish the rule to retain general legal consistency applied to everyone (Barry 2001: 53).

A response to Barry's position is that he wrongly sees the issue as a choice that must be made for culture or equality, but not both. Every society has members with different belief systems. To demand the disadvantaged to bear the burdens of their different beliefs is to disadvantage them further. Moreover, to claim that some general system of regulation is culturally-neutral is itself culturally-informed. Perhaps a key illustration is that Barry sees uniform citizenship as "the achievement

---

[6] I simply note the point that this counterargument to Okin might be convincing in relation to a woman agreeing to wear a hijab, but not in relation to what might be perceived as more extreme inequalities, such as female genital mutilation, where it is both unclear anyone would consent without coercion and that, even if they could, it is a difference too far. I share this view that there are limits to the cultural differences that might be permitted but recommend interested readers to examine the wider literature, starting with Parekh's *Rethinking Multiculturalism*, to develop your own insights into this complex issue.

of the Enlightenment," a culturally-informed notion relating to a specific cultural development in history (Barry 2001: 11). So, if our views of self and other are culturally-informed and if our community is composed of culturally diverse members, then we may find common ground on many, perhaps even most, issues. (Note that there are multiple "ifs" required!) At the same time, we might still seek to find equality in how we regulate, through consensus, any differences arising from our relevant beliefs as defended by Parekh.

Finally, we return to Dworkin's general principle of "equal concern and respect." There is a difference between some like Barry and Okin who see equal concern and respect as requiring an equality of rights and overall treatment, viewing any suggested exceptions as undermining equal respect for all individuals, and others like Parekh who see the equality of concern and respect for citizens as requiring equal concern and respect for their different beliefs. Which side we take depends on whether we see equality requiring the same requirements for all or whether equality is viewed as a shared standard that might be applied differently, where justified in relation to relevant beliefs. In other words, it is a choice between the inflexible and the flexible. In such circumstances, flexibility might be preferred as it allows the option of accounting for any relevant contextual factors, such as the value and importance of our cultural differences in contemporary society – underlining the importance of an equal concern and respect for what we value notwithstanding disagreements about it.[7]

## 3.4   Political and Social Equality

In the history of political thought, it is common to find justifications for the state built on a rejection of a pre-political, perhaps even mythical, time where all individuals lived in a *state of nature*. The idea is that our *natural* state of affairs is where there are individuals without any social or political institutions. Such an environment is anarchy in the classic sense of the word of no social hierarchy as there is no society: a state of nature is not a community, but a mere presence or what I would describe as a "collectivity."[8]

---

[7] Note the importance on the interests of individuals and what they value. This is what makes cultural beliefs relevant and important, and only insofar as they continue to receive support from our individual interests.

[8] It may conjure reference to the Biblical story of Adam and Eve who began life in a Garden of Eden surrounded by nature but without any social or political institutions. See Genesis 2:4–6.

This natural state is also seen as a problem. In the eyes of Hobbes, it is a situation where individuals are constantly in conflict with one another without any authority offering justice or protection, as we are each left to fend for ourselves against any intrusion into our interests. He claims our lives are left "nasty, brutish and short" that cry out for the need to create political institutions providing greater safety and security for all (Hobbes 1996: 89).

Another example is found in Locke's *Second Treatise on Government*. He argues that the state of nature is a "state also of equality" where no one has any greater power than any other (Locke 1988: 269). Individuals have only formal equality which can fuel inequalities in terms of our well-being. For instance, Locke's concern is that while we are equally free to make a living, we might not be equal in our abilities to do so – nor have an equal ability to defend what is rightfully ours from thieves (Locke 1988: 271–272). If someone were to attempt to steal our property, we could only prevent them through our own efforts as there are no laws nor police in a state of nature. Thieves who might outwit or outrun us (or both) can undermine our natural equality creating advantages for those who might seek to gain from infringing the rights of others. A political state is required, in Locke's view, to regulate the activities of community members in order to protect our individual rights and, in so doing, secure political equality between us (Locke 1988: 276).

The state not only helps protect our political equality but it is thought justified by each of us consenting to leave behind a state of nature and form a new social contract that creates political rights and responsibilities for all who accept it. Hobbes, Locke and other social contract theorists like Rousseau argue that we are each equal signatories to a social contract (Rousseau 1997b). Thus, for Rousseau, this "fundamental pact" of a social contract does not destroy "natural equality, on the contrary substitutes a moral and legitimate equality for whatever physical inequalities nature may have placed between men, and that while they may be unequal in force or in genius, they all become equal by convention and by right" (Rousseau 1997b: 56). The contract they envisage is not a historical document (although it has inspired the use of written constitutions), but a philosophical device that claims the justification of the state is built on the consent of the governed. In forming a social contract with others, we sacrifice our ability to act as we please in a natural state and accept restrictions on our actions that better protect and secure our freedoms and rights within a political state.

Whether or not there has been a state of nature, the idea that we are bound by a social contract created from our equal consent has become a very popular approach to political justification (and explored in the next chapter). The common criticisms are of two kinds. The first is that the social contract is a philosophical fiction (Hume 1994: 186–201). If it matters that there is a social contract to create rights and responsibilities, then it is relevant that the contract seems no more than a hypothetical thought experiment that never happened. Defenders of social contract theories might accept the criticism, but also claim that a contract of some form exists insofar as we can and do consent today to political institutions. However, an opponent of social contract theories might reply that this remains too elusive as, without some concrete terms for agreement, individuals who are thought bound by a hypothetical social contract might each have different views about its terms and applications.

A second common criticism of social contracts is that they are underinclusive and leave people out who should be accounted for. If a social contract is a product of consent, the concern is it could leave out those unable to consent because of having disabilities (Nussbaum 2006: 9–154). Instead of treating individuals equally, it could omit the most disadvantaged. Furthermore, if our rights arise from consenting to a social contract, there may be a concern for some critics that non-human species will lack rights protections as the natural world is not a party to the contract (Nussbaum 2006: 325–407). Of course, it could be said that any rights for non-human species arise from the need to protect their interests, irrespective of consent, if they do, in fact, have such rights, a position that some might contest. The same might be said more broadly about individuals: namely, that we possess rights because of the importance of the interests protected and not whether we happen to choose to have certain rights – although these positions are not mutually exclusive allowing us to support an interest theory view of rights and a social contract theory of the state.

Our equality in consenting to membership within a political state is no guarantee that we will have equal political power within it. We should first recognize that legal equality is not political equality. While we might each have the same citizenship rights to participate in democratic decision-making, some might exercise greater political influence over outcomes. This could be because they have greater resources or opportunities to do so, or because they can rely on more supporters to back their political views.

The example draws on a distinction between two kinds of political equality. The first might be called *formal* political equality. This is akin to legal equality whereby individuals have the same set of rights and responsibilities within some political institution, such as the state. Formal political equality is a strict form of equality – we might refer to this strict form as an *equality as exactness* – whereby individuals each share the exact same citizenship rights. There is formal political *inequality* where one has more or less participatory rights than another, for example.

Our formal political equality is important. It helps create a connection between other formally political equals that can foster a sense of solidarity and build social bonds. As noted in his famous *Fables*, Aesop says that "Equals make the best friends" (Aesop 2003: 119).[9] Formal equality of power provides a foundation for such relationships.

The second distinction is what we might call *informal* political equality. This refers to the ways in which two individuals may have equal citizenship in deciding democratic decisions, but not equal levels of influence over decision outcomes. There are many examples of this. One example is to consider a government or legislature that has a small governing majority. Each legislator has the same formal political equality as representatives elected in the same way and where each has an equal vote on any tabled legislation. Suppose if only one legislator opposed the government's vote, this could prevent legislation from being passed. While all legislators share formal political equality in this hypothetical scenario, informally they do not as the few that could switch sides may have more influence in gaining concessions given their wavering support is more crucial to passing a vote than the others who back the government more solidly.

A second example is to consider voters. Each voter has an equal vote and so formal political equality. Suppose there is the same number of young adults as there are retirees. It is likely that political candidates will pitch policies that benefit the retirees more than young adults in these circumstances. This is because retirees are usually far more likely to vote. If an election is close, retirees will have more informal power because their greater likelihood of voting makes an election result hinge more on their choices than the young adults who

---

[9] In my view, every political theory student should read Aesop's *Fables*. If you have not yet, I strongly recommend doing so. You may find that many of its maxims are familiar, but the arguments for how these are presented is not and sometimes in interesting ways.

are less likely to vote. Formal political equality does not mean informal political equality.

A final example is to consider political participation. While any citizen can run for president or aspire to become prime minister, elected representatives tend not to be fully representative of the state's demographics overall. Political candidates are less likely to have come from poverty and more likely to be university-educated. Those who have the resources and opportunities to pursue political office and direct influence over public policy have informal political inequality over those who do not.

These examples might inspire us to rethink the regulation of formal political equality, such as measures to help ensure people from underrepresented backgrounds have equal opportunities. But even if we did, some may exude greater expertise and persuasion skills than others allowing them to influence more over policy decisions than those who do not. Nor is this surprising as we might expect top scientists and academic leaders to help inform policy decisions relating to their fields. My point is only to note this as another case of informal political inequality among citizens otherwise formally politically equal.

Political equality is often considered an important achievement. When citizens are recognized as political equals, it might be described as "just" or "righteous" (Tsai 2019: 13). This is because political equality is defended as a goal in itself – regardless of whether it supports alternative goals like efficiency.

This begs the question: if equality is a worthy goal in itself, does it matter how equality is shared equally? For example, as Raz observes: "If all have a right to food, accommodation, education, etc. then their rights are the same regardless of whether they have no food, education etc." (Raz 1986: 226). His point is that equality must be about something more than having the same. An equal education does not mean it is a satisfactory education.[10] Instead, equality must be an achievement worth having. In other words, equality's importance is found in both its form and content; that is, having the form of being equal and the content of some achievement that makes achieving equality valuable. Having similarly to others matters where what we have matters.

Political equality is sometimes defended as ensuring everyone has equal opportunities. The claim is that the state should enable *fair*

---

[10] For example, if students only received one day's education a year, this would be equal - they would all have the same experience – but clearly unsatisfactory.

*equality of opportunity* for all. While this might appear straightforward, it also raises a number of challenges that we should explore (Swift 2014: 107).

The first challenge for fair equality of opportunities is understanding the importance of options. Consider communism. Friedrich Engels and Karl Marx claim the history of the world is a "history of class struggles" (Marx and Engels 1967: 79). Communism will see an end to such political inequalities found in class divisions. They say that their theory "may be summed up in the single sentence: abolition of private property" (Marx and Engels 1967: 96). The idea is that our capitalist "social conditions" can determine what we are taught, our access to power and overall social standing (Marx and Engels 1967: 100). Our social status is reaffirmed through our wage labor: our earnings do not only allow us to meet our needs, but they provide us with social status that fuels inequalities of wealth and power. Communism, as envisaged by Engels and Marx, aims to create equality between citizens by removing differences of class, social status, and wealth. Of course, one criticism that might be raised is whether their plans for transforming society would work, in addition to various attempts at doing so.

Instead, we might consider a simpler hypothetical communist state. Suppose it ensured that every individual had the exact same. Everyone lived in the same kind of home. All had the same opportunity to do the same kind of job earning the same income as part of the same class. This admittedly contrived communist state ensures all have formal equality of opportunity as they all have the exact same.

This model might be rejected. The main problem is that to have an opportunity is to have options. Opportunity is defined as a choice. Suppose Betsy has an opportunity to see her daughter play softball, perhaps thanks to someone offering her a lift to the game. Betsy might use the opportunity to watch her daughter. Or perhaps not, if she instead chooses to help her son with a project at home. Whenever there is an opportunity, there are the options of (a) the opportunity and (b) the non-opportunity (or status quo). For another example, Cindy is a keen runner and plans to jog home. Before leaving her apartment, she is offered an opportunity to join Joe for dinner instead. Cindy has a choice to do as she originally planned or go to dinner. Opportunities necessarily entail *choice* because the opportunity is, in essence, a *change* from what might otherwise transpire. The upshot is that we cannot have fair equality of opportunity where all have only one option to choose. Therefore, the example of the contrived communist state might demand that all its members are politically equal, but they lack opportunity where there is no choice.

A second concern is that equality as exactness can be deeply problematic. Does treating everyone exactly the same mean that they are treated equally? The answer is (mostly) no. Consider a factory that makes bowling pins. All pins are the exact same size, made from the same material, and painted identically. Let us imagine that we produce 10 pins for one bowling alley and another 10 pins for a second bowling alley. In this scenario, it does not matter which 10 pins I select to use for the first alley and those used for the second. I can select pins in any way that I want. I can treat every pin as interchangeable with any other pin because each is exactly the same. I can use bowling pins exactly equally.

Now suppose I come across 20 individuals. They might have differences in age, gender, sex, religion, disability or other factors. But, for the sake of this hypothetical thought experiment, imagine that they are all the same age. In this context, they are not perfectly interchangeable. They will have differences between them, such as their sex, abilities or any disabilities. But even if these were all the same, there could be one combination of individuals that might collectively make for a better soccer team or a second combination that together performs theater better. Individuals have different beliefs, tastes, and talents. (And, sadly, we do not all live for the exact same amount of time: some of us will become ill or die while others enjoy good health and live longer.) These will not be exactly the same and, so, equality as exactness does not treat all individuals in an equal way.

This is because to recognize our equality is to acknowledge our differences. Equal concern and respect require that we account for individual concerns with respect in an equal way. This takes us back to Parekh's defense of equality as an equality of differences. Fair equality of opportunity must be about options that are available to all, but must likely provide a range of possibilities to account for the diversity of interests that individuals have.

But now we are faced with a new question: must opportunity options be chosen? If having a fair equality of opportunity requires us to have options to choose from, we have not yet explored the issue of whether or how often options need be taken. Logically speaking, we might be satisfied by the bare fact of having options even if they were never chosen: if opportunities require options and we have two or more to choose, then this is enough.

The problem is this is a political issue and so our attention must turn to the potential exercise of power, which makes the practical *use* of options relevant. Consider an example about education. All boys and girls have opportunities to choose studying science from early years through to university-level to give everyone the chance to become a scientist. Suppose few, if any, girls take science classes and so few choose a career in this field. This could be because of encouragement from parents to opt for a different career or societal pressure favoring boys. Whatever the cause, it does not look like fair equality of opportunity applies where, for whatever reason, we find groups of people, such as women and girls, choosing among the same options as men and boys with significant disparities in outcomes. If opportunities are used much less by one group than another, it should make us question whether the opportunity is fairly available to all.

This is not to mandate that individuals must have an equal likelihood of choosing the same outcomes among available options. Not all options may necessarily be of equal merit; sometimes one or two may be far more preferable to others. Outcome preferences might reveal fair equal choice is lacking, but not conclusively on their own.

States must ensure such choices are available. There is no fair equality of opportunity for young people to have a career as a doctor or lawyer (for example) if such roles do not exist in a society with a weak economy. Nor is fair equality of opportunity secured if roles exist but beyond the reach of most individuals who might wish to pursue these options had they been available.

Equality does not require exactness to account for the different interests and preferences individuals have. But fair equality of opportunity *choices* is linked to a fairly similar distribution of outcomes *chosen*. In other words, we can evidence that fair options are available equally when there is an equitable distribution of opportunities chosen.

Consider the role that outcomes play for fair equality of opportunity. Imagine there are two applicants for a job. The first has no experience and little training, but the second applicant has worked in the area for many years and fully qualified. How should egalitarians decide which to hire?

It might be argued that fair equality of opportunity allows us to consider applicants on their individual merits (Barry 2001: 55). So long as all had the ability to apply, we should decide outcomes on merit. This puts the emphasis on deservedness instead of other factors, such as wealth or personal networks. The focus on merit is meant to help us focus on equal opportunities.

It is no surprise that meritocratic ideals have popular resonance. They reinforce the widely held ideal that employment decisions (including the decision to hire oneself) were made on the basis of quality and deservedness. After all, an employer might say, we always want whoever is best for the job. Moreover, to hire on merit is to ensure that equal opportunities lead to beneficial outcomes as it ensures those who will produce the most value receive the job.

One criticism of merit-based selection is that *implicit bias* might enter into our decision-making. This is where we make decisions without being aware of our preconceptions that might disadvantage job applicants unfairly. These could be assumptions that only people from a particular background are a better or worse fit – not because of what they have done individually – but informed by background assumptions that may be unfounded and untrue.

But if such bias were acknowledged and controlled, there is perhaps a more challenging criticism. This is the concern that merit-based decision-making makes existing social and political inequalities worse. This is presented powerfully by Daniel Markovits. He argues that to use a merit-based metric for determining outcomes instead of wealth creates an illusion that deservingness, not affluence, is the deciding factor. But the result is, according to Markovits, that relative wealth counts most.

His argument goes like this. A merit-based process would look at things like academic performance or work experience. The applicant with the best profile would be seen to merit the job over rivals. What Markovits explains is that the use of merit masks the wealth possessed that created and fostered the relevant merit indicators. Children from affluent homes have more resources available to study at better schools, receive additional tutoring and get more support for exams. They are better connected tapping into powerful networks to enjoy better work experience opportunities. In these ways, when we judge someone using the metric of merit to assess credentials and experience we are actually scoring them on the basis of the effective use of family resources enabling those results. Merit-based procedures appear friendly to fair equality of opportunity widening access to the deserving, but the affluent are the most likely to benefit. And so meritocracy creates unfair political inequalities (Markovits 2019).

This does not require us to reject the use of any merit-based process. The key problem is the equal opportunities for all to apply for a merit-assessed job does not start from a level playing field. Instead, the affluent are able to use their wealth to protect their relative advantage. If everyone had access to the same starting point, then merit-based outcomes would reflect individual achievement because wealth would not be a decisive factor in what outcomes were achieved by specific individuals. Fair equality of opportunity is only possible where applicants share a similar background of support. Otherwise, a system open for all to enter will lead to the wealthy cementing their privileged position. We must show concern not only for the distribution of goods equally, but the distribution of opportunities for achieving them (Williams 1973: 240). Equal choice is more than having an equal option, but choosing from an equal position.

## 3.5   Economic Equality

When we think about equality, we likely think of it in terms of relative *wealth*. Equality is about reducing the gap between the rich and poor where much of the debate focuses on how resources might be redistributed from the former to the latter.

This view of equality as about economic equality is perhaps due to the deep, and sadly growing, economic inequalities we see in many countries today. Such inequalities are a significant problem. This is because economic inequalities can impact so many other areas. The affluent are usually the most powerful; the poorest are so often the powerless. The distribution of wealth depends on laws governing contracts, ownership, trade, and much more that can be to the advantage of the affluent (Dworkin 2000: 1). After all, property law might only benefit the property owners, not the homeless.

Moreover, economic equality has extra importance as any inequalities over wealth can amplify inequalities in other areas. Hence, the rich are not merely unequally affluent, but often unequally influential legally, socially and politically (and not necessarily *vice versa*). If we can improve *economic* equality, we might improve equality in other areas, too. Now that its significance is clear, let us examine what it is.

Economic equality concerns the division of resources among community members. There are different ways resources might be divided. Consider the view that equality requires everyone to have an equal share. We gather up all the resources held within the community and divide these into equal shares distributing the exact same amounts to each member. This would create an equality of resources from day one.

There are several problems with this approach. The first is it does not consider whether the resources I possessed prior to redistribution are rightfully mine. Such a radical redistribution from everyone assumes no one has a right to their original share before resources were collected. If I cannot retain my rightful possession, then the redistribution might be said to have harmed me.

A second problem is that it only creates economic equality when the redistribution is complete, but not afterward. As soon as we buy, sell or trade with others, the amount of resources we possess changes. It would not take long for community members to start the first day all with the same equal amount, but end the day where all have different amounts. What this shows is that economic equality is implausible and impractical, if not impossible, if it aims at everyone having the exact same amount all the time – even if we could start with the same resources.

A third objection is that in reducing the resources so that all meet a shared equal measure the state has leveled down. Part of the concern is that redistributing resources (or other goods) to satisfy general equality may infringe my individual rights, such as to private property as these resources are legitimately mine. But an additional part of the concern is that equality should not aim to level down but level up. When we level down, we reduce everyone to the lowest common denominator. Suppose there is a country called *Borderlinese*. Most of its citizens live above the poverty line, but there are a number living who fall below this threshold. If we were to level down everyone's income until it was the same, everyone would fall into poverty. Economic equality as leveling down has made all worse off. In contrast, there is the view of economic equality as leveling up. This is the idea that we want to raise up those in poverty so that we close the gap with the more affluent. In this way, we seek to bring everyone out of poverty and seek equality by helping raise them up to an equal level. So, the problem of just dividing up equal shares and redistributing is this risks leveling down instead of leveling up.

Having an equal share may not impact everyone equally (Dworkin 2000: 12). This becomes clear when we compare equality in terms of well-being, or welfare. Suppose we distribute the exact same share of resources to everyone around the world. Individuals living in environments that are overly cold or hot will have different resource needs than others who do not. They will require using more resources than others elsewhere. Or consider those living with disabilities. They may require additional resources than others without disabilities to maintain a similar living standard. Giving all an equal share does not treat everyone equally, as different people may have different resource needs for living under broadly similar conditions. Thus, a problem with per capita shares is they might be equally divided, but do not have equal impact as they do not satisfactorily account for individual differences.[11]

Now imagine we all receive an equal share, but we do different things with it. Prudence looks after her resources carefully as she plans for the future. In contrast, Jack is careless losing the full amount suddenly in a game of chance. Is poverty Jack's bad luck? Richard Arneson says:

> The concern of distributive justice is to compensate individuals for misfortune. Some people are blessed with good luck, some are cursed with bad luck, and it is the responsibility of society – all of us regarded collectively – to alter the distribution of good and evils that arises from the jumble of lotteries that constitutes human life as we know it . . . Distributive justice stipulates that the lucky should transfer some or all of their gains due to luck to the unlucky (Arneson 2010: 80).

His argument is that we are *not* fully responsible for our luck and, thus, should *not* be at its mercy. Suppose Jack had a gambling addiction and felt compelled to bet his money away. For Arneson, this lack of voluntary self-control might justify supporting Jack from the full impact of his actions. As Arneson argues, society has a responsibility to mitigate the gains and losses arising from luck so as to mitigate the impact of chance on our lives. A general system of redistribution collects from the gains of those with good luck and shares these with those worse off from their bad luck.

Suppose Kevin loses his resources when gambling, but this is not due to an uncontrollable addiction. Instead, Kevin is aware of the

---

[11] A similar argument might be made for the problematic use of gross domestic product per capita. This is a measure of national wealth divided by national population. This is a problematic measure for measuring both developmental progress and, most especially, equality because general averages mask individual inequalities. Consider two countries where Affluencia has a per capita gross domestic product of $30,000 and Bestily's is $25,000. If we only consider the overall average, Affluencia is generally better off. But suppose we examined the income data and saw that the average income for 90% of its population was actually half at $15,000 (and so the wealthiest 10% share an average income of $165,000). We then see that the income of everyone in Bestily is $25,000. If interested in measuring the relative wealth of most people in each country, we would find most in Bestily with average earnings much higher. This example is meant to show that general averages mask individual inequalities that are relevant to how we understand equality within a community and should be accounted for in some way. See Sen (1995).

risks and chooses to take them in the hope of earning a small fortune. Instead, he loses everything. How should society treat Kevin? For *luck egalitarians*, Kevin's responsibility is crucial. They would argue that those who know the risks and take them should shoulder the burden of those risks. So, on this view, Jack and Kevin both gamble away their resources, but only Jack might access some support from the state because his case is bad luck stemming from an addictive factor outside his control. Because Kevin could have done differently but chose not to, he does not deserve the same assistance.

This illustration raises a concern. If luck egalitarians allow individuals to take great risks but suffer the full negative impact if they are unlucky with their choices, it may incentivize most to do little that is productive. If Kevin bears the costs of his bad luck and may not claim full ownership of his good luck, he may choose a risk-averse life spent waiting for the gains of the good luck from others to trickle down to him.

Now suppose a different example. Cindy is a naturally fast runner. She makes a living from winning track and field competitions. Cindy's running seems a product of good luck. Because she is not fully responsible for her good luck, part of her earnings should be distributed to others.

But consider a change to the example. Suppose Cindy decides to train to run faster. Her improved speed allows her to win more competitions and earn more. Should this require her to pay more? It could be argued that part of her earnings are from hard work, not mere good luck. If so, this raises a very difficult issue of trying to separate how much benefit was a product of good luck and how much a product of good training.[12] Such a distinction seems implausible to draw and, yet, if our luck matters significantly then this is a decision we should make.

It could be objected that these examples consider people as unfree. The concern is that they treat us as unable to meet our needs except through exploiting some advantage from natural talents we had at birth; it assumes we exercise no choice in how we meet our needs rendering us slaves to our talents unable to pursue alternative goals. It is, of course, true that not every talented singer is in the music business nor every gifted footballer plays professional sports. What we do can be a combination of following our inclinations alongside opportunities; we do what might have some interest in doing depending on

---

[12] The distinction between good luck from natural endowments versus good training and effort is also describes as the distinction between nature and nurture.

available options to us for finding work. So, I might be a talented guitarist and not a natural at economics. But I apply myself to learning the latter as there are more lucrative available opportunities in economics than, sadly, there are playing guitar for me. In such circumstances, it would be rational for me to not pursue my natural talents. Thus, it is mistaken to claim that everyone who succeeds is not fully responsible for it because some share of that success is a product of our given talents, not our industry.

Rather than argue that the better off should support through general taxation a welfare system that protects all from destitution *because they necessarily benefit from natural talents that are not of their choosing nor fully deserved*, we might instead say such support should be made *because they are best placed to do so as affluent*. This corrected view accepts that individuals can deserve their wealth whether gained from talent, hard work or both with the demand for equality based on some other factor – such as promoting solidarity and/or avoiding poverty – but *not* that natural talent has or could play a role in one's affluence. Such a position might appear consistent with Karl Marx's statement: "From each according to his abilities, to each according to his needs!" (Marx 1978: 531).

This scenario raises the question of when, if at all, general taxation should be used to support those in destitution. Suppose Cindy has a choice between running a race to earn money or gambling on a competition where she hopes to make more from winnings. While aware of the risk that she could lose her property and become destitute, Cindy thinks it unlikely and gambles instead on running the race. She loses the race and so becomes destitute. What should egalitarians say about her case?

Defenders of *luck egalitarianism* would claim that Cindy should bear the consequences of her choice. Provided others had equal opportunities to place a bet too and Cindy could foresee the possible risks, she is responsible for her misfortune (Anderson 1999: 295). This is despite the fact she has no control over the *option luck* of the gamble itself, as the gambled outcome could have been won and brought financial reward.[13] For this reason, luck egalitarianism may seem an odd view of equality that can accept deep inequalities between people

---

[13] A related issue is to consider my *choice luck*. Suppose Cindy benefits financially from her natural talent for running, but she has expensive tastes and chooses to spend much of her earnings on designer brand running shoes leaving nothing left over for redistribution. Should it matter for deciding what amount is redistributed whether her expensive tastes matter? These seem added costs that she should bear. See Dworkin (2000: 15, 55–56).

if they knowingly made decisions that went wrong and leaving little or no safety net.

Elizabeth Anderson argues that this kind of egalitarian justice would see redistribution as about addressing the inferiority of the unlucky. Any support is not grounded in a shared equality, but only in virtue of saving from destitution those that found themselves in that position (Anderson 1999: 306). In other words, luck egalitarianism supports acting when unlucky, not necessarily because of inequality. Anderson's concern is that such a view fails to treat others with equal concern and respect.

Instead, Anderson claims equality should be seen as a more substantive relationship between equals who are "not marginalized by others," "not dominated by others" and "not exploited . . . To live in an egalitarian community, then, is to be free from oppression to participate in and enjoy the goods of society and to participate in democratic self-government" (Anderson 1999: 315). Equality is achieved through equal citizenship (Scheffler 2003: 22). This view is consistent with the idea that fair equality of opportunity is not enough; there must be fair equality to make effective use of opportunities which Anderson's view of equal citizenship supports.

There is an interesting point raised by philosophers defending a view called *prioritarianism*. Suppose that creating equality in our community requires providing more support (including, but not necessarily, resources) to a group of individuals. Should the claims of anyone who falls below some threshold or standard of equality be treated equally themselves?

Prioritarians claim that in any redistribution we should give priority to those who are worst-off (Parfit 1997).[14] This position takes the view that some may be unequally unequal. Consider individuals Alan, Betsy and Cindy. Suppose they are very unequal economically to the point that Alan is very affluent while Betsy and Cindy are homeless. Prioritarians might argue we should redistribute resources from Alan to both Betsy and Cindy equally. But suppose there is also Danny, who is poor but not as worse off as Betsy or Cindy. Prioritarians might argue that we should prioritize support for Betsy and Cindy prior to supporting Danny because Betsy and Cindy are worse off than Danny.

A concern with prioritarianism is whether we can make interpersonal comparisons of well-being sufficiently well to make judgments

---

[14] See also O'Neill (2008).

about how to apply priority. We need to be able to judge whether some are worse off than others with a means of assessing their relevant difference such that it can be rectified. The problem is that people can have very different views on their needs and whether they are satisfied. Alice enjoys three large meals each day while Eve likes to eat small dishes or snacks instead. Is Alice better off if her meals add up to more than Eve's small dishes? It is difficult to assess as each might enjoy different-sized meals, but both are equally satisfied by that. To be a prioritarian is to know *who* should be prioritized in relation to *what* measure and *how* much of it – and we may lack more than a vague idea of each.

Alternatively, we might argue for *sufficientarianism*. This is the view that we should not, perhaps cannot, aspire to equality for all. Instead, egalitarians should focus on setting the correct level of sufficiency required for satisfactory well-being. We are equal when all of us equally have enough, even if some may have much more than others. The focus of sufficientarianism is ensuring all meet minimal needs. But similar concerns apply as was seen with prioritarianism, as we need to make interpersonal comparisons of well-being to determine when everyone has enough and this can be challenging.

A final concern focuses on our duties to resource egalitarian redistribution. It might be argued that, if we felt strongly that more support should go to the disadvantaged, nothing prevents us from voluntarily contributing more to the state than owed from taxation. Individuals who can and wish to give are free to do so; as those who can but do not want to are only required to pay their share of tax and no more. Such views consider the resources under our control as fully "ours" – sometimes described as the view of being able to eat whatever we kill – and that any duty to resource the state infringes our liberties. In essence, equality is incompatible with freedom: to have more of one, the other must be cut.

This view of equality and freedom has deep roots. As R. H. Tawney noted, "Freedom for the pike is death for the minnow" (Tawney 1931: 164). Equality means accepting limits on our liberties. In this way, a more egalitarian society is where individuals are less free to do as they please. We cannot maximize equality *and* freedom; our choice is to prioritize equality *or* freedom. Or so some have argued.

But are these concepts necessarily opposed? Consider the viewpoint of the individual's freedom. My ability to choose to do whatever I want may be curtailed by a community's efforts to improve equality among its members. But notice what is happening in this case. The freedom in question is not the freedom of all, but the freedom of an individual. Others might wish to exercise their liberties in different ways. When we talk about freedom, we might have in mind the freedom of individuals *collectively*, but we do not conceive of freedom as unique to each specific individual, such that my freedom to do one thing is different in character from yours to do another. The apparent conflict between freedom and equality begins to melt away when we recognize that the concepts we use, like freedom and equality, are to apply to all at the same time.

In other words, my freedom to do or be is not a freedom to do or be in any way that I wish for myself right now. On the contrary, it is constrained by the freedoms of others. For example, no one would say we are free to murder or steal. And such constraints allow an equality among citizens within the justified bounds of their freedom. This shows us that where we relate concepts we need to compare them in similar ways, such as in the freedom of all and the equality of all, rather than the freedom of one versus the equality of a group if we want to get a clearer sense of how they relate. Individuals do not live in total isolation but in community with others. A community's approach to securing freedom while enabling equality can do both from the viewpoint of the community relevant to both freedom and equality (Cohen 2000: 148–179).

## 3.6   Conclusion

Everyone claims to want equality. But of what? And for who? This chapter has explored a range of ideas about the different kinds of equality, including formal, legal, political, social, and economic. They have in common ways of understanding relationships between two or more individuals or groups about some measure of value. When we consider equality in the relevant sense, we examine normative relationships. To understand equality is to consider equality in relation to something valued.

As we have seen, this can take a number of different forms whether formal, legal, political, social, or economic. The way equality is usually presented is as a desirable and just end – no doubt arising from a need to address socio-economic and other inequalities that can seem endemic. While equality is conceptually distinct from justice, arguments for greater equality are typically justified in reference to some view of justice. As Tawney observes, the equality we might want "is not equality of capacity or attainment, but of circumstances, institutions and manner of life" and the inequality we might deplore "is not inequality of personal gifts, but of the social and economic environment" (Tawney 1931: 48–49). The next chapter will examine theories of justice more closely.

## Further Reading

Anderson, Elizabeth. 1999. "What is the Point of Equality?" *Ethics* 109:287–337.

Dworkin, Ronald. 2000. *Sovereign Virtue: The Theory and Practice of Equality*. Cambridge: Harvard University Press.

Parekh, Bhikhu. 2006. *Rethinking Multiculturalism: Cultural Diversity and Political Theory*, 2nd edition. Basingstoke: Palgrave Macmillan.

White, Stuart. 2007. *Equality*. Cambridge: Polity.

# 4

# Justice

## 4.1 Introduction

Political philosophy might be thought synonymous with justice. To have a political theory is to have a view about what is justice. And yet, what *is* it?

One classic view is that justice aims at doing the right thing primarily for the right reasons. An alternative is that justice aims at bringing about the best consequences. Both views might accept a third approach that claims justice is only legitimated through a social contract that a community agrees together. Political justice is justified when we consent to a constitution and public institutions that govern our activities. This approach is taken by the most influential political philosopher of the last century, John Rawls, who develops what a social contractarian theory of justice might look like. But there are many challenges to his approach, and they argue that social contracts work differently than Rawls claims or that justice should be based on ensuring our well-being and a minimally decent life, as is defended by the capabilities approach. Moreover, there are important contributions made by feminist approaches and stakeholder theorists, too.

In this chapter, we explore these different ways of thinking about justice. Each major approach will be explained drawing on leading figures from both contemporary political philosophy and its history,

*Political Philosophy: The Fundamentals*, First Edition. Thom Brooks.
© 2025 John Wiley & Sons Ltd. Published 2025 by John Wiley & Sons Ltd.

with an emphasis on the influential theory of justice developed by Rawls. The aim is for readers to have an insight into the main ideas and debates within a large and ever-growing field.

It will also become clear that theories of what is just connect with theories about freedom, rights, and equality. Few argue that a just state is a political community where all are slaves answerable to an unaccountable tyrant. Instead, a just state is regularly conceived of as a place where free and equal citizens might flourish although how these different concepts relate may vary depending on which theory of justice we find most compelling. This chapter aims to build on some of the familiar figures and ideas found in earlier chapters, show their relevance to justice and deepen understanding of how they fit within political philosophy more broadly.

## 4.2   Deontology

A theory of justice provides a compelling justification for how our activities should be governed. But this is only what a theory of justice provides, not which theory is found compelling. Of course, which view is best is a matter of debate. In the history of philosophy, two general approaches to defining justice stand out. The first is *deontology*. This approach claims justice is where we do what is right in-itself independently of future outcomes. Justice is a matter of procedure or application where our choices are governed by moral standards. A choice is right where it is consistent with this criteria. Consequences are generally irrelevant for determining whether an act is just (Alexander and Moore 2020). Thus, a deontologist would argue lying is wrong because it is wrongful to do, and whether or not telling a lie might lead to better future outcomes.

The most influential view of deontology is Immanuel Kant's moral law, or "categorical imperative." He argues for a *formula of universal law*, claiming we should "act only in accordance with that maxim through which you can use at the same time will that it become a universal law" (Kant 1997: [4:421]). Kant claims his moral law is universal and timeless governing all human interactions. In order to assess whether we are following the moral law, we examine how closely our actions conform consistently with it (Kant 1997: [4:399–400]). All that we require is showing that our actions do not contradict themselves (Kant 1998: [B xxix]).

Kant's moral law is useful for identifying actions we would want to find unjust. For example, the murderer breaches the moral law because he cannot universally claim a maxim that individuals can be murdered. This cannot be a universal maxim because if everyone was murdered there would be no one left alive, and so clearly not an action we can universalize and perform at the same time. Another illustration is theft. The thief breaches the moral law because she cannot universally claim that the thief can own (stolen) property, but others cannot own it. It is not a universal maxim as it would undermine the possibility of property rights for anyone.

The main appeal of deontological theories is their claim to objectivity and certainty. For instance, Kant's moral law is a universal law governing all actions by everyone. Whether our actions are justified (and so "just") according to the moral law is a matter of examining whether our actions meet the moral law's criteria. Deontological theories focus on the duties we have because they are the right duties for anyone to have.[1] Examples might include that wrongs, like murder or lying, are always wrong independently of whether doing so would lead to beneficial consequences (or not).

There are some general concerns that are made about deontological theories. One historical criticism specifically targeting Kant's moral law is that Kant's theory reduces justice to satisfying an empty formalism (Hegel 1990: §135R, Brooks 2013a: 55–61). The argument is that crimes like murder or theft are wrong because they are evil, not because they cannot be universal maxims. In other words, wrongs are wrongful as a matter of their substance and not merely because they satisfy some formalistic requirement.

A broader second criticism of deontological approaches is that their appeal to doing duty for duty's sake trivializes the importance of consequences. Famously, Kant claims that we should not lie, even if we wanted to deceive a murderer at our door looking for an innocent person hiding in our home (Kant 1996a: [8:427]). This view holds that the means define the end; we do what is right because it is right for us to do, not for what end it might produce. So, wrong actions like lying, as a wrong, is prohibited always, even if we thought there could be beneficial consequences in specified circumstances.

---

[1] A connection rarely highlighted is that most defenders of deontological approaches in domestic justice also defend universal norms of cosmopolitanism in the global justice arena. Similarly, defenders of consequentialism in domestic justice are more commonly associated with liberal nationalism in global justice. This will be explored in Chapter 7.

Or consider a train is moving at speed along its tracks unable to stop, often referred to as *the trolley problem* (Thomson 1976). If the train continues unabated, it will run over two people who have been tied together onto the train tracks and will be killed when the train drives past. In this hypothetical thought experiment, you stand next to a lever that, if you should pull it, the level will change the direction of the track so the train will be diverted from running over the two tied together. However, this second track has a third individual tied onto it by themselves and would be killed instead.

The trolly problem example raises important questions to think about. Does justice require us to act so that the greater number survive at the expense of another? If it is did, then perhaps we would divert the train to avoid killing two instead of one. Would it matter if the two on the track are convicted murders, but the lone individual was a well-respected political leader? If so, then perhaps we might not opt to save the greater number of people but rather aim at what might be more deserved or important. However, such views require further explanation to make this case.

Such scenarios can be difficult for deontological accounts. This is because they challenge the generality and universality of deontological theories, as we reflect on whether it is preferable to do one's moral duty for its sake *in-itself* without regard for which outcome yields the most beneficial outcomes (Brooks 2002b). While many have argued it is generally worse to actively do harm than passively allow it – known by philosophers as the difference between *doing* and *allowing* (Thomson 1976: 217).

While the examples can be complex, the general idea is that there is a moral difference between what we do and what we allow. For instance, suppose there is a building on fire with someone trying to get out. Their only escape is to jump and you have a safety net to catch them. We would all agree that we should rescue them if we can. But imagine that while setting up our net, we see a second building on fire with multiple people trying to escape. For many people, the best course of action is to save the greatest number we can. And yet, if we did so, we would be moving our safety net away from the burning building with one person giving them no means to escape. Few argue that we would be responsible for their death, as it was something that was allowed but not something that we did.

Now consider a third scenario. We set out a safety net to catch the one person from the first burning building. When we notice the second burning building, we did not need to move the safety net because, in this hypothetical scenario, we have a second safety we use to save those in that other building. While our backs are turned, an evil villain moves the safety net away from the first building. In the second and third scenarios, the same outcomes happen: namely, there is a safety net for the individual in the first burning building to jump onto, but it is moved with only those in the second burning building saved. But, it is argued, the two cases might have similar outcomes, but there are not morally similar. This is the difference between our moving the net so we can save more people and the evil villain moving the net out of the way so that it does nothing. In the former, we might be thought to have done nothing wrong and the tragic problem at the first burning building merely allowed. But in the latter third example, the evil villain has done wrong insofar as he has done, not merely allowed, a wrong to happen in moving the safety net away so that the individual in the first burning building does not have a means of escape (McMahan 1993).

The importance of such hypothetical examples is helping us to consider whether doing or allowing should make a moral difference and, if so, where lines should be drawn. There are real practical consequences for how we think about these cases, such as whether we should enable the gravely ill to choose euthanasia or not. Those who claim it is better to allow than do might oppose euthanasia on those grounds, whereas those that believe it can be justifiable to do will not oppose the practice. Moreover, these cases help us reflect more on whether consequences can matter for our moral judgment making (or not) as we will explore next.

## 4.3   Consequentialism

A second classic approach to defining justice is *consequentialism*. It claims what is just is what yields the most beneficial consequences (Scheffler 1988, Sinnott-Armstrong 2023). There are many different forms this can take. One group of consequentialist views is *utilitarianism*, which claims that justice is about maximizing *utility* (Smart and Williams 1973). The original modern version proposed by Jeremy Betham and centered on his Greatest Happiness Principle.[2] He defined

---

[2] See Bentham and Mill (1987: 65–112). This book is a collection of separately written works. My citation is to an essay authored only by Bentham.

utility as "that property in any object, whereby it tends to produce benefit, advantage, pleasure, good, or happiness (all this in the present case comes again to the same thing) to prevent the happening of mischief, pain, evil, or unhappiness to the party whose interest is considered" (Bentham and Mill 1987: 66). An example might be acting in such a way that pleases the most people, or as Bentham says when we seek "to augment the happiness of the community" and not diminish it (Bentham and Mill 1987: 66). An example is justifying punishment as a deterrent. For utilitarians, punishment should be set at an amount that deters would-be criminals. The additional "pain" severity in punishing is thought to be outweighed by the extra "pleasure" in fewer crimes being committed. The Greatest Happiness of the community overall is secured where crimes are less frequent because of punishment's deterring effect (Mill 1986).

Recall the trolley problem discussed above. If an unstoppable train was traveling toward a group of people on one track, a utilitarian could justify pulling a lever so the train switches to a second track that might kill only one person if this would maximize the greatest happiness of the greatest number. Alternatively, consequentialists might not switch tracks if it meant the train would run over convicted murderers but not a well-respected political leader if they thought the greatest happiness would be better secured this way. So, how we calculate the greatest good on a case-by-case basis determines how we might justify what action to take. Bentham's view is sometimes characterized as *hedonism* because of its aim of maximizing pleasure. It is also sometimes referred to as *act utilitarianism*, as we are to choose those *acts* that maximize utility within our community.

A different form of utilitarianism is *rule utilitarianism*. This is where there are moral restraints on how we maximize utility. For example, a concern might be that if killing an innocent person contributed to more beneficial consequences than not doing so – perhaps because the individual is disliked despite being innocent of any wrongdoing – then consequentialism might justify killing the innocent. Rule utilitarians might apply requirements that consequences are maximized subject to protecting individual rights, which would reject killing the innocent to promote consequences no matter what these are. We can protect rights while promoting consequences.

The main appeal of consequentialism is its adaptability. Consequentialists might reject the idea we should not lie to a murderer seeking to kill an innocent person hidden in our home on the grounds that doing so leads to a better outcome (e.g., an innocent person not being murdered outweighs deceiving a murderer looking to kill).

Critics make three key arguments against consequentialism. The first is that those claiming we should maximize utility – understood as pleasure or value – wrongly assume that every individual judgment is comparable. In other words, we aggregate the expected happiness or pain experienced by individuals and choose outcomes where the greatest happiness is realized. But this assumes that utility is comparable across individuals. The utilitarian must claim that we can score our expected pleasure or pain along the same scale. It assumes that my enjoyment of listening to Metallica can have the same utility units for you when enjoying a beer, but for some this will be positive and others it may be the opposite. The problem is that we need to make such judgments with some precision to calculate expected utility and so have a view of just outcomes.

The unitary nature of utility is even challenged by leading utilitarians. As John Stuart Mill argued, pleasures are not of the same kind. He claimed there were two different kinds of pleasure and each should be weighted differently. Mill claims there are higher pleasures that should be the object of utility maximization, including acts that were intellectually complex, imaginative, and made good use of our *moral sentiments*. These had greater value than what he called our lower pleasures, such as our bodily appetites for food, sleep, and sex (Mill 2015). On this view, we should seek to maximize our utility; but, specifically, to focus only on our higher pleasures as these are of far greater value than our lower pleasures.[3]

A second criticism is that consequentialism is justified by achieving desired outcomes, but these come in the future and are unknowable at the time we choose. Suppose I justify punishment because it is expected to have a satisfactory deterrent effect. But after someone is punished, the deterrent effect does not materialize. If punishment is justified by future effects that do not happen, this undermines the justification for the practice. The problem here is that we cannot know if our

---

[3] Whenever I discuss Mill's distinction between higher and lower pleasures with non-academic audiences, the usual criticism is nobody should be surprised to hear that a philosopher thinks a life engaged with ideas is of great value, but more must be said about why non-philosophers ought to share the view. Some might simply call it the "we'll he'd say that, wouldn't he?" counterargument.

consequentialist-based decision is correct until after it was decided and implemented. Whether beneficial outcomes materialize justifying what we have done belongs to the future, and therefore to at least some degree out of our control as we lack certainty about outcome results.

I am surprised the point is rarely made that there is a *problem of consequentialist timeframes*. If I claim a course of action is justified because it will contribute to a desired outcome in the future, it is unclear when that future point is. Should it be clear in a few days, weeks, months, or years? Or longer? Suppose Olivia bases a judgment on consequentialist grounds and the outcome supports doing some action about a month later, such as making an important decision. Suppose Grace does the same, but the outcome does not support hers until a year later. Which is the better consequentialist argument? This seems impossible to judge from the limited information available. Perhaps consequentialists should not only specify the expected outcome that justifies an action but provide a timeframe as well. Yet, it is clear that if the expected outcome does not materialize at some time in future, this is fatal to the justification of the action: consequentialism requires consequences happen. But it is unclear if an expected outcome that took much longer to materialize than planned makes any necessary negative impact on our finding that the consequentialist basis for justifying it was present. And yet I think we would want to resist an argument that said, "well, the expected consequences haven't materialized *yet*, but this does not disprove my consequentialist argument; we can only say the judgment is unproven, not disproven, and allow further time as consequences *might* materialize at some unknowable point *in future*." This is because it would leave consequentialist arguments either evidenced or pending evidence, not justified or unjustified. Perhaps it might be said that, until the fullness of time plays out, we cannot disprove consequentialist claims. Such a view would render consequentialism difficult to falsify and so undermine its claim to offer a compelling alternative theory of justice that we should model political decisions around.

A third criticism made of utilitarianism in particular is that it is overly demanding on individuals to perform it. Utilitarianism claims we should maximize utility. The problem is that whenever we might enjoy leisure activities or get sleep we might better maximize general happiness if only we spent this time having fun or sleeping instead — and perhaps at the expense of our own happiness. Utilitarianism is not only a theory about maximizing the greater good but also an ethical demand on us. The criticism is this demand could require our spending every waking minute maximizing utility and the greatest happiness if we can do so. This criticism does not mean the theory is inconsistent, only likely unappealing, as it would demand too much from individuals to be plausible in the eyes of most people.

However, the primary criticism made of consequentialism is that it could justify wrongs as a means to achieving beneficial ends. The most common criticism is that a consequentialist might justify executing an innocent man if it caused an expected deterrent effect reducing future murders and, thus, save the lives of innocent others. Critics argue that it's always unjust to infringe fundamental individual rights, like our right to life, to achieve some future goal. Consequentialism may justify beneficial outcomes, but it is open to doing so in unjust ways that go too far, or so it could be argued.

In response, consequentialists can claim that such potential flaws can be avoided. For example, the criminal law should be conceived as a system of threats whereby citizens are warned that criminal convictions will receive punishments intended to deter them and others from engaging in future criminality. So, if citizens should fail to heed this warning, then they deserve to be punished as they had been warned and, crucially, no one punished is innocent as all had performed a crime despite receiving warnings. In this way, deterrence can be a goal of punishment that punishes wrongdoers, but not at the expense of punishing anyone who is innocent (Ellis 2003).

## 4.4   Moral Sentiments

Emotions are important for justice. Experiencing or witnessing injustice can bring out our sentiments about what is just and unjust. In Plato's *Phaedrus*, he claims that we should see ourselves like a charioteer driven by two horses as we race across the Earth in the sky (Plato 1997: 246a–b). One of our horses seeks to pull us higher to the heavens, representing our rational selves. The second horse attempts to drag us lower down towards the Earth. If we go too far up, we will lose all sight of the world. But if we go too far down, we will crash into the ground. For Plato, the horses represent our rational and irrational parts that must be held in "moderation" for our safe travels (Plato 1997: 442d). We are like a charioteer managing these two parts to ourselves by maintaining a steady grip on the reigns. In this analogy, our emotions are to be restrained.

A different view of emotions is developed by the Scottish Enlightenment philosopher David Hume. He argues that our *moral sentiments* inform our views about what is right or wrong. He says:

> There is an inconvenience which attends all abstruse reasoning, that it may silence, without convincing an antagonist, and requires the same intense study to make sensible of its force, that was at first requisite for its invention. When we leave our closet, and engage in the common affairs of life, its conclusions seem to vanish, like the phantoms of the night on the appearance of the morning; and 'tis difficult for us to retain even that conviction, which, we had attain'd with difficulty (Hume 2000: 293).

In other words, great efforts are put into concocting rational arguments for or against some view – that may also take great efforts to understand. While we may come to grasp the meaning of such intricate explanations, they "convince" us only superficially. As soon as we leave the lecture room and go into the outside world, such arguments may carry little weight or have a minor presence in our thinking in our everyday lives.

Hume claims that our "morals . . . have an influence on the actions and affections" of all of us because it is felt and, it is assumed, felt similarly by others, too (Hume 2000: 294, 302). Imagine you look outside your window onto the street. You see an unprovoked attack on an unsuspecting innocent person. How would you *feel*? Hume's claim is that we would naturally know this was a serious wrong. This wouldn't be because we had learned it from a book or had spent time reflecting on what actions we'd find wrong hypothetically. Instead, his view is that we'd know this was wrong because it would be *felt*; we can make such moral judgments through the intelligence of our emotions applied to specific circumstances (Nussbaum 2001).

In other words, when we see wrongdoing we can feel our hearts race and become agitated as we are emotionally impacted by the experience. Hume argues that our moral sentiments are of two kinds. Sometimes they are "natural" in that they are present from birth. Examples include the idea that we all innately know, through our natural sentiments that murder is wrong. We do not need to be taught this; it is felt. A second variety of moral sentiments are "artificial" and learned since birth, such as the morality of keeping promises and honoring contracts (Hume 2000: 307–322). We do not have an innate knowledge about contractual agreements, but soon learn them. While moral sentiments may have different sources (e.g., natural or artificial), they weigh on us in the same ways. For example, we may not have the same feeling of deep concern when discovering my car is parked illegally as we might if witnessing a violent assault. Hume's point is that our moral sentiments can inform us of what is right and wrong by the way that we emotionally respond to ethical situations. We reflect on how we would react to a situation as a guide to determining the rightness or wrongness of taking some form of action.

A criticism of Hume's approach is that it assumes we all react broadly the same way. There should be no differences between what our moral sentiments inform us is wrong either because we are all thought to be wired the same way and so react in the same manner in similar situations or because we have all learned how we should react in circumstances relating to our artificial sentiments. This raises the issue of how to deal with disagreements about what our moral sentiments should be. Clearly, this is an issue: if everyone felt broadly the same way about justice, it might be supposed we would argue much less about it – and virtually everyone would naturally obey the law. The fact that not everyone does take such a view might be a sign that some have not reflected sufficiently about what their moral sentiments are telling them or perhaps that we can perceive and relate to the same situations differently.

An alternative method to Hume's is proposed by Adam Smith, who claims we might manage disagreement by using a novel attempt at an impartial standard. Smith accepts that individuals may disagree about what their moral sentiments say about how to act in ethical situations. So, he argues that we should imagine the moral sentiments of a hypothetical "impartial spectator" who observes a situation alongside us (Smith 2002: sects. 1.1.5.4, 3.1.2). We consider whether the impartial spectator would approve or disapprove and not our own personal feelings (Brooks 2012b). In imagining what an impartial spectator might feel, it is supposed to identify a neutral third party that all sides might support, at least as a means of resolving any differences.

One problem with Smith's view is that we adjudicate issues about what is right and wrong with reference to an imaginary figure who does not exist. While it may often be good advice to put yourself in another's shoes and see a situation from another point of view, the issue here is that the impartial spectator is truly a view from nowhere and an unreliable guide to ethical conduct.

These accounts highlight the importance of our emotions for how we think about justice and attempts to better understand their relevance. We regularly assess standards like guilt according to whether it is beyond reasonable doubt or what a reasonable individual would do under specified circumstances (Nussbaum 2004: 33). These are ways in which we might be thought to regularly consider our moral sentiments in matters of justice. For instance, suppose gunshots are reportedly heard coming from an alleyway late at night. The police are promptly contacted and an officer is sent to the area where shots were heard in order to inspect. While searching an alleyway, the police officer finds an individual holding what looks like a rifle in his hands although the street is poorly lit. Thinking he may have found the suspect gunman, the police officer orders the individual to stop, but they attempt to run away. Unsure if this is the suspected gunman and concerned they might shoot, the police officer fires a gun at the individual which kills them. It turns out the individual was not the suspected gunman. Worse, what appeared to be a gun was actually a piano leg carried in a bag. In this case, the officer pleaded self-defense and was acquitted of any charges. The argument made was that any reasonable individual would be justified to act in self-defense out of a reasonable fear to protect their life, even if it turned out the fear was unfounded.[4] It was a reasonable fear that he might be shot at and seriously or fatally injured that justified use of lethal force. Situations like this show that our emotions matter in making reasonable assessments of lawful conduct. As Nussbaum rightly observes, "law without appeal to emotion is virtually unthinkable" (Nussbaum 2004: 5).

When thinking about what is reasonable to want from a theory of justice, it is essential we assess our arguments in light of our having moral sentiments and in context. Otherwise, our view of what is reasonable to do is only partial. Emotions cannot be excised from how we experience and understand the world any more than our reason. Like Plato's charioteer, we hold both in balanced moderation when considering the demands of justice on us. A society that does not share a common *sense* of justice will not have just principles embedded in

---

[4] The example is based on an actual case. See *R. v. HM Coroner for Inner North London* (2005).

its heart and have weak bonds between citizens. If we better appreciate the importance of the emotions for our politics, we can build a more flourishing sense of community that wins over hearts as well as minds (Nussbaum 2013, Brooks 2022a).

## 4.5   The Idea of a Social Contract

A classic view is the idea that we consent to a social contract and so agree to being governed by its terms, a view deontologists and consequentialists can both accept. This raises the obvious question of why we would consent to any such contract in the first place. Social contract theorists have usually appealed to thinking about what life might be like without the state. Such a hypothetical world without laws or public institution is thought to be both chaotic and dangerous. This place is called a state of nature where life is "nasty, brutish and short" and where individuals face each other in a war of one against all without any police or institutions to protect individuals from their possible mistreatment by others (Hobbes 1996: 89). While everyone would be free to do as they like, they would lack safety and security, always having to fend off miscreants without help where such occasions arise. We are, as Rousseau says, "born free, and everywhere . . . in chains" (Rousseau 1997b: 41).

Social contract theorists have claimed such a state of nature would be an unbearable way of life. They argue that it is intuitive that all of us would want to leave a state of nature and create a political state instead. This state is, in essence, a product of choice: it is held that we would all consent to creating a political state in order to escape from a state of nature. Our consent is key to creating the state and to its legitimacy (Rousseau 1997b: 41). Accordingly, Rousseau rejects the view that *might is right* and that forcing others to act however one sees fit is consistent with any legitimate exercise of power. This is because, for Rousseau, to act as we are forced to act denies our agency and, thus, does not create any duties. Therein is an important distinction made between being forced where we react like automatons under threat versus having a duty where we act from our consent to being part of a social contract with others. Consent is required for legitimate political power and essential to its sustainable use over time. Rousseau claims our continuous consent is what maintains political legitimacy, whereas maintaining control through mere force is exhausted more quickly, as it relies on continuous threats (Rousseau 1997b: 44).

The social contract is a product of popular consent. Yet, it may appear that Rousseau faces a significant difficulty. If we can only exit the state of nature by all of us consenting to a social contract, how can such unanimity support political stability? It is clear that we often disagree about what we think justice is and what the state should do. So, if everyone must consent to everything, this seems too high a bar for any realistic view of political justice as we might expect at least some to dissent.

In reply, Rousseau claims:

> There is only one law which by its nature requires unanimous consent. That is the social pact: for the civil association is the most voluntary act in the world; every man being born free and master of himself, no one may pretext whatsoever subject him without his consent (Rousseau 1997b: 123).[5]

Our one act of unanimity is full agreement that we become members of a shared, social contract, creating a political community. We do not require full consent to every decision made by the political state, as the state itself is a creation of our full consent.

But some may find this perplexing. After all, if our full consent is required for creating a social contract, why should it not be required for agreeing to every decision binding on members? It might appear that the problem of – so, what to do if we disagree about law making? – has simply not gone away.

Rousseau offers a novel answer to this concern. If consent to a contract binds us, it is problematic when we do not all agree on its application. Rousseau acknowledges that disagreement happens, perhaps unavoidably. But he calls this a matter of a *common will*, which he defines as a mere statistical majority. For Rousseau, the common will is simply a product of adding up the particular views that individuals might have at a particular time. In his view, a common will cannot justify nor ground political decisions. The problem is not that he is against majority decision-making (or "majoritarianism"), but his concern that simply siding with whatever view has the most support fails to be inclusive of those who disagree. How can we consent to decisions where some disagree with the majority?

---

[5] The quote uses the language of "every man" but this should be interpreted as "every individual."

Rousseau's answer is that – instead of a common will – we should base outcomes on a *general will*. So, what's the difference? A general will is formed by focusing not on our particular individual wish but instead on our shared "mutual" interests (Rousseau 1997b: 61–63). Or, in other words, we make decisions in our community based on what is best for *all* and not our mere *self-interest*. Rousseau says: "The constant will of all the members of the State is the general will; it is through it that they are citizens and free" (Rousseau 1997b: 124). His claim is that a majority based on decisions focused on what is shared is majoritarian decision-making, but not merely because it is a majority (Rousseau 1997b: 124). While a minority will disagree (at least when on the losing side of any vote), a majority based on a view of the general will produces outcomes that connect with all our shared, mutual interests, whether in favor or opposed. In this way, we need not have unanimous decisions about every law we want to pass but yet reach outcomes that are inclusive of everyone's interests, whether or not they are in support.

So, we can see how consent plays an essential role in creating a social contract and the importance of basing future decisions on the general will shared by all. But like other social contract theorists, including Plato and Hobbes, Rousseau claims the social contract's essential constitution is consented to by all members but not produced by them.

Instead, it is typically argued that we appoint an outsider, someone who is not a part of our social contract and so not a member of our political community. The name usually given to the role is "the Lawgiver" (Rousseau 1997b: 68–72, Hobbes 1996: 120–129, Plato 1997: 1325 [630d–631a]). Rousseau claims we need an outsider described as one "who saw all of man's passions and experienced none of them, who had no relation to our nature yet knew it thoroughly" (Rousseau 1997b: 68–69). This individual is imagined to distil from our particular interactions our shared values and shared view of justice, a view thought too difficult for us to discern ourselves within the society as its members.

One concern that could be raised is that such a task is superhuman, overly demanding and fanciful because we might doubt any single person could, or even should, perform the task of a Lawgiver. Rousseau seems to acknowledge their godlike abilities when he says that a Lawgiver is necessary because "it would require gods to give men laws" (Rousseau 1997b: 68–69). This naturally raises the worry that if such a role is impossible to undertake – and yet essential to the launch of a social contract – the whole scheme seems flawed. Rousseau claims the Lawgiver must "persuade without convincing" (Rousseau 1997b: 71). In other words, they should help us, as community members, come to share the view given of what our constitution, as ours, should be and not because he merely says it should be. While we might find this argument is not realistic, it does highlight important questions, such as whether decision-making based on a general, not common, will can be inclusive of all and the importance of strong agreement about the constitutional essentials setting out our political institutions as a necessary precursor to their application to more contested policy areas.

A second concern is with a phrase Rousseau uses to describe our freedom within a state. The social contract is a constraint on what activities we might pursue that is shaped by our shared values. So, we are free to do what is in keeping with the general will that is developed within our state. And, yet, we are not free to do whatever we please, as this would return us to a state of nature. We are thus "forced to be free" (Rousseau 1997b: 53). This is a controversial phrase that looks like an oxymoron: how can anyone be *forced* to become *free*? Rousseau's phrasing might be thought a poetical flourish. If we act freely, our activities are consistent with the general will: there is no force or coercion of any kind. But if we act contrary to the general will, such as by infringing the law, then we would face coercion to prevent our law-breaking and revert us back to law-abidingness. In this way, we might be said to be forced into acting freely.

A third concern, noted in the last chapter, is that basing the justification of political legitimacy on the idea of a social contract is deeply flawed because no such event happened where we – you and I – agreed to exit a state of nature by signing up to a social contract. Thus, the idea of a social contract is a mere thought experiment, a philosophical fiction (Hume 1994: 186–201). Social contract supporters might accept the critique but argue that the hypothetical model highlights the relevance and *essentiality* of consent to justifying political legitimacy. If we cannot all consent to our political institutions, then they are unjust and illegitimate. Critics might counterclaim that, without an actual contract to draw on, individuals may form very different views about what the imagined contract is and how it applies, rendering it unworkable.

Of course, there are various written documents whose historical background may echo the likes of a social contract. Examples that may come to mind include England's 1215 Magna Carta, or "Great Charter," that limited the king's powers through a publicly acknowledged declaration signed by many of those directly affected or the American Constitution of 1787. However, these real-world illustrations are different from the hypothetical social contract in at least two key ways. First, neither document was a unanimous agreement. For example, King John signed the Magna Carta under duress in an arrangement with barons, not commoners like the public. But, of course, even if all such historical documents like this *were* universally consented to, it is unclear why any past unanimous agreement made by individuals now dead for centuries should be as binding on us all today.

A final concern about social contracts is that they are exclusionary and can wrongly leave members out. The reason is because not all individuals in our community may have the capacity to offer informed consent, perhaps due to their having disabilities that prevent them from doing so (Nussbaum 2006: 9–154). If consent is necessary to become part of a social contract (and for creating political equality among members as equally consenting to the contract), then those unable to do so risk being left out and not having the political equality available to others. A possible response to critics is that the social contract is ultimately based on a general will that tracks our essentially shared values and common interests. However, it is supposed to be knowable by every individual in terms of knowing how to discern the general will, and so this response will not satisfy the concern about those who are unable to grasp the general will because of their disabilities.

## 4.6    Rawls's Theory of Justice

John Rawls is the most influential political philosopher of the last century. His importance is in developing a new theory of justice – described as *justice as fairness* – that takes some familiar ideas from past philosophers, such as the social contract, and reimagines them in ground-breaking work that is essential for any political theory student to know. It is a testament to his influence that Rawls not only revolutionized how many do political philosophy today but also he popularized this area, sparking new interest in political thought more widely. The fact that so many continue to study and work within this area is a legacy of his enormous contribution. In the words of one of his Harvard colleagues, Robert Nozick, "political philosophers now must either work within Rawls's theory or explain why not" (Nozick 1974: 183).

Rawls begins from a similar starting point as used by Rousseau. Rawls is interested in understanding justice in terms of what might justify political legitimacy. He accepts several important assumptions before explaining his argument. Rawls says we organize a theory of justice around two fundamental ideas. The first is that justice, whatever else it is, is "the idea of society as a fair system of social cooperation over time from one generation to the next" (Rawls 2001: 5). This is probably uncontroversial, but his point is that a just society is governed by a fair system that is intended to continue into the future. A second assumption is that he conceives citizens as "free and equal" (Rawls 2001: 5). This is equally uncontroversial, but notice that Rawls has said nothing about what makes a system fair or what form of justice is required if citizens are assumed to be free and equal. A third is that Rawls assumes that the just state is a "well-ordered society," by which he means a society that is effectively governed by a public conception of justice (Rawls 2001: 5). Note again that Rawls does not say anything at this point about how it should be ordered.

Finally, Rawls assumes that these free and equal citizens have two moral powers: the first that they can conceive of themselves and others as being able to have some conception of the good and, second, that they are capable of assessing and advancing claims about the good (Rawls 2001: 21–23). This last assumption is vulnerable to the criticism of social contract theories generally that they may exclude individuals, such as those lacking these moral powers perhaps because of a disability. In reply, it might be said that Rawls makes no secret that he conceives of his theory of justice as a *realistic utopia* (Rawls 2001: 13). It is utopian insofar as it is an ideal model, but realistic insofar as he believes it can offer practical guidance for how a theory of justice might be applied.

With these basic assumptions in mind, Rawls invites us to conduct a thought experiment that is intended to help flesh out a new, compelling theory of justice. Based on the tradition of social contract theory inherited from figures like Rousseau, Rawls agrees that unanimous consent to a constitutional arrangement is essential. However, he is aware of criticisms that our choice is not whether to leave an actual state of nature. And he wants to have a way of handling the concern of why we should – you and me in the here and now – agree to such a contractual arrangement. This is where his famous thought experiment comes into view.

Rawls asks us to imagine we are a member of an *original position*. We are in this position as representatives alongside an unspecified number of other people. In the original position, we are to think about justice behind a *veil of ignorance*. Rawls says that when behind this veil we "are not allowed to know the social positions or the particular comprehensive doctrines of the persons they represent. They also do not know persons' race and ethnic group, sex, or various native endowments such as strength and intelligence, all within the normal range" (Rawls 2001: 15). In other words, when behind a veil of ignorance, we do not know what kind of protected characteristics or natural abilities we might find after we remove the veil. This is critically important because it means that we are to consider how we would make decisions without regard to our sex, ethnicity and other factors. Nor are we to argue from a position of defending any specific view of the good (or what Rawls calls a "comprehensive doctrine") either. Rawls claims that we can respect individuals as free and equal where these characteristics about ourselves are hidden from us.

Rawls's original position is used to consider which principle of justice we would want to unanimously endorse to govern what he calls "the basic structure" of our society, including our social and political institutions as well as our family life (Rawls 2001: 10). We examine possibilities without regard to our social or economic position, individual characteristics nor natural abilities. In this way, Rawls claims that members of an original position would not agree on principles of justice that would favor those who had social status, affluence or benefited from personal attributes they gained at birth. They would not be guided by private self-interest; but, instead, by a shared, collective interest – akin to a general will – held in common.

In the original position and behind a veil of ignorance, Rawls claims everyone would unanimously support two principles of justice. The first principle is that "each person has the same indefeasible claim to a fully adequate scheme of equal basic liberties, which scheme is compatible with the same scheme of liberties for all" (Rawls 2001: 42). Rawls defines basic liberties to include political liberties (such as the right to vote or hold public office), freedom of speech and assembly, freedom of thought and liberty of conscience, integrity of our person, freedom from arbitrary arrest or harm, and the right to own property (Rawls 1999: 53).

Rawls argues we would all agree, in the original position, that each of us held the same full set of equal basic liberties. Importantly, he claims we would also share a basic minimum of "primary good" that satisfy our needs and the social bases of self-respect (Rawls 1999: 54).

Rawls claims a theory of justice should allow for social and economic inequality *if* the first principle of justice is satisfied and subject to his second principle of justice. This is defined as:

> social and economic inequalities are to satisfy two conditions: first, they
> are to be attached to offices and positions open to all under conditions
> of fair equality of opportunity; and second, they are to be to the greatest
> benefit of the least-advantaged members of society (Rawls 2001: 42–43).

So, the second principle of justice is in two parts. The first part has priority over the second. This first part of the second principle is that every individual has a *fair equal opportunity* to any social or political office. For example, a President or Prime Minister will enjoy more privileged opportunities than other citizens. Rawls claims this inequality can be justified *if* everyone enjoys the same set of equal basic liberties and primary goods and *if* everyone has the same opportunities to hold that office. Should it be the case that the wealthy or those with social prestige have greater access to these positions, then the inequality of power is unjustified. Everyone must have the same fair opportunity to hold a political office, for example, if that position is to carry greater power than ordinary citizenship. Otherwise, this inequality is unsupported.

The second part of the second principle of justice – which Rawls calls "the difference principle" – is more controversial. If all have basic equal liberties and if all have fair equality of opportunity, then the difference principle allows inequality where the least advantaged receive the greatest benefits (Rawls 2001: 43). Suppose we wanted to give the wealthy a tax break, making them even better off, perhaps in the hope it might incentivize their investing more in the economy. (Of course the wealthy might simply pocket their savings instead.) For Rawls, this can be justified if the least-advantaged were made even better off, such as receiving a bigger tax break or being removed from income taxation altogether.[6] In this way, the position of the most-advantaged to the least-advantaged would not grow apart, and any gap might shrink over time.

---

[6] I have remarked to my British students that we can see the difference principle is in vogue where the big tax announcement from successive UK governments is to raise more lower income earners out of income tax brackets benefitting the least-advantaged.

Rawls's two principles of justice are not equal. He claims the first has lexical priority over the second.[7] We only consider the second principle where the first is satisfied. The idea is that we must all have equal basic liberties as a priority. If this condition is met, then we might consider social and economic inequalities – but, even then, this does not alter the equal basic liberties we should have at all times. I describe the lexical priority of these principles and their parts to students as follows. Suppose we call the first principle of justice "A" (basic liberties), the second principle of justice's first part "B" (fair equality of opportunity), and the second principle of justice's second part "C" (difference principle). The priority of principles and parts runs A, B and C. We must satisfy A before considering B and satisfy A and B before considering C.

Readers might wonder: how do we know that anyone in the original position would actually support these two principles of justice and in this way? (A fair enough question to be sure!) After all, and as we have seen before, the problem with hypothetical models of social contracts is that they usually turn out to be fictional scenarios: no one was there, no agreement was struck and no contract agreed. So, how to know what would happen in such cases?

Rawls claims his social contract theory is different. His evidence that there really are two principles of justice all in an original position would agree to in the way he claims is because any one of us can see for ourselves any time. Rawls's evidence is our own individual intuitions about justice. We can verify it at a moment's notice "here and now" (Rawls 2001: 17).

In essence, we're invited to enter the original position ourselves. Imagine we are behind a veil of ignorance and, with others, considering what principles of justice would apply to the basic structure of our social and political society. Rawls's claim is that, if we accept his assumptions, including the idea that we are all free and equal, we will see for ourselves that all would accept equal basic liberties and would only accept inequalities, provided equal basic liberties remain intact, where there is first fair equality of opportunity and the difference principle.

Rawls accepts his approach is an "ideal theory" and he is aware that no society may be organized as set out by his principles of justice (Rawls 2001: 13). Nonetheless, he rejects the idea that his theory of

---

[7] Rawls describes the priority of the first principle of justice over the second principle as a "lexical priority." See Rawls (1999: 37–38).

justice is merely idealistic. Instead, he argues his justice as fairness is "realistically utopian" because "it probes the limits of the practicable" (Rawls 2001: 13). He claims his theory provides a benchmark for what any just society should aspire toward. Our political community is more consistent with justice the closer it comes to realizing the practicable aspirations of justice as fairness, even if no society is perfectly consistent (and so none is perfectly just).

Before turning to other parts of Rawls's views, we should pause to consider criticisms raised about Rawls's theory thus far. Most of these concerns are focused on Rawls's claims about our intuitions. For example, Rawls claims that those in the original position would not be overly risk adverse. This explains why he argues that intuitively we should agree: given his assumptions, those behind a veil of ignorance would agree that all should be guaranteed a basic minimum of primary goods, but would allow wide disparities in wealth, allowing some to enjoy unequal advantages. It certainly was *not* my intuition either when I was reading Rawls's work for the first time nearly 30 years ago. I imagined that those in an original position might be far more likely to find agreement about all of us enjoying a higher minimal standard of living and permitting much less extreme gaps in wealth and power in a broadly egalitarian state than Rawls allows. Nor was I alone in having different intuitions about what might be most likely to be agreed in this hypothetical scenario (Cohen 2008).

A second concern is that Rawls asks us to do the impossible. In his theory, we are to imagine ourselves behind a veil of ignorance without knowledge of our particular characteristics, natural abilities or background. This requires us to strip away defining aspects of who we are. But can we? It might be argued that my knowledge of the world is mediated. Different languages can use different concepts to convey meanings that are not always exact equivalents. My past experiences can shape my perception of new experiences. While we can heighten our awareness of how knowledge is mediated, it is unclear that we can see the world in some unmediated way and entirely separate from many of the characteristics that help define how we see ourselves and how others see us. As Bernard Williams observes, "our arguments have to be grounded in a human point of view; they cannot be derived from a point of view that is no one's point of view at all" (Williams 1985: 19). Thus, the view from behind the veil of ignorance is a view of no one situated nowhere (Sandel 1998).

A final concern is that Rawls's view of distributive justice is unjust. As Robert Nozick observes, Rawls's difference principle aims at creating a just outcome. Any redistribution should provide most benefit to the least-advantaged. Inequality is only justified where this benefit is enabled. However, Nozick argues that Rawls's argument for a just outcome ignores the issue of whether individuals possess just acquisitions (Nozick 1974: 150–151). If I own my property legitimately, it is rightfully mine and so to redistribute it to others infringes on my property rights. Thus, for Nozick, Rawls fails to account for desert (Nozick 1974: 217). In wanting to do justice by distributing goods to others, it is claimed Rawls does an injustice who rightly possess these goods in the first place.

To illustrate his point, Nozick uses the example of a celebrity from the early 1970s when he was writing.[8] But we can simply imagine any famous entertainer from music or sports. Suppose this entertainer is performing at a venue nearby and that they are performing with others. Suppose further that the entry ticket costs $10 each and we, alongside many other fans, buy tickets to sit in the audience. Nozick argues that we consent to transferring our money to the entertainers and what they receive from us is deservedly theirs. Now suppose further that when we buy the ticket, we are told that half of it will go to the main entertainer performing that evening. This is the primary reason we chose to attend and so we agree to buy tickets. For Nozick, the transfer of money here is legitimate because of our consent to the exchange. The entertainer rightly possesses the money received because the audience consented to this transfer to watch the performance and so it is deserved. In contrast, in Nozick's view, Rawls sees distribution in terms of an "end-state" focused only on redistributing to achieve a preferred outcome; but, in so doing, it interferes unjustly with our freedoms and infringes our property rights (Nozick 1974: 163).

Nozick famously argues that taxation is essentially "the violation of people's rights," akin to "forced labor," whereby we are forced to work for another's purpose (Nozick 1974: 168–169). This does not mean that the state cannot levy taxes, and it might be argued that it can be reasonable to consent to some basic tax to resource essential public services. But the point is that any redistribution from original holdings

---

[8] The original example in his 1974 book is the then famous basketball player Wilt Chamberlain, a figure who may be unknown to many readers today. See Nozick (1974: 161). I always wished he used someone from baseball instead like Reggie Jackson.

requires consent. The problem, for Nozick, with Rawls's theory of justice is that members of the original position distribute resources like it is "manna from heaven" belonging to no one, whereas it matters how we acquire resources in the first place before we consider how any might be justifiably transferred to others (Nozick 1974: 199).

## 4.7   Rawls's Political Liberalism

Later in his career, Rawls became convinced that his theory of justice as fairness needed to be developed further and was missing something important. He believed it had a "serious problem" of ensuring political stability over time (Rawls 1996: xviii). To explain, Rawls claims that individuals have "comprehensive doctrines," which are conceptions of the good. He defines reasonable comprehensive doctrines as any major philosophical view or world religion. These doctrines can exist as libertarianism, utilitarianism, Catholicism, Judaism, Hinduism, or others. In Rawls's view, these doctrines are not essentially politically incompatible with one another. For example, libertarians and Catholics can both accept similar ideas about the value of human dignity, even if understood in very different ways, and so on. The only views that we exclude from consideration are what we might call unreasonable doctrines. These are defined as ideologies like fascism or white supremacy which are exclusionary by nature and reject any place for alternatives. Such exclusionary views are deemed unreasonable because their rejection of any differing view is thought to fly in the face of the pluralistic society that we inescapably live within.

Rawls claims that anyone supporting a reasonable comprehensive doctrine can endorse the two principles of justice. One issue is that, for Rawls, these principles set constitutional boundaries but do not provide satisfactory guidance for determining public policies. For example, respecting citizens as free and equal does not illuminate how to settle policy disagreements, such as whether to allow abortion, capital punishment, euthanasia or other matters. However, our reasonable comprehensive doctrines might provide the guidance we need. So, a utilitarian might argue for a policy based on an assessment of how it maximizes overall happiness. The problem is that different doctrines may take different sides. We may naturally wonder: how to choose?

Rawls argues that all societies are characterized by what he calls "the fact of reasonable pluralism" (Rawls 2001: 4). In other words, there is no society where every member supports a single, shared comprehensive doctrine. Instead, there is pluralism. If we are to respect citizens as free and equal, it is essential that we respect their right to endorse different doctrines. This raises the challenge of how to secure political stability over time when citizens support different conceptions of the good while respecting their equality. Thus, we cannot simply adopt one doctrine instead of others, as this would treat the reasonable pluralism in society unequally by favoring one over rivals.

Rawls calls his approach *political liberalism*. This begins with a distinction between the *rational* and the *reasonable* that complement each other (Rawls 2001: 6–7). The justification of two principles of justice is rationally produced through the thought experiment of an original position. It is meant to be unanimously supported and serves as the boundaries for political legitimacy: in other words, political justice must be consistent with these principles. But, as noted already, this leaves a space within the rational boundaries that provides unsatisfactory guidance for determining policy outcomes – and this is especially problematic where equal citizens hold different conceptions of the good. Within these natural boundaries, we need a way to determine how we might decide these outcomes.

Rawls's answer is that citizens should engage each other through the use of *public reasons* (Rawls 2001: 26–27). These are reasons that we may reasonably offer to others for mutual acceptance. Consider claiming the reason for adopting a policy was because it was the doctrinaire of the Catholic Church, such as the doctrine of papal supremacy. Catholicism is a reasonable comprehensive doctrine and the view of paper supremacy, which is a part of its doctrine, is reasonable to it. However, this reason is not accessible to alternative doctrines because it is exclusive to Catholicism.

Instead, reasons must be made relating to values and interests that connect with one's own doctrine but are also acceptable to others. In this way, public reasons can link doctrines together. Rawls says we create *an overlapping consensus* through the use of public reasons (Rawls 2001: 32). He argues that public reasons provide the right links, as they can be acceptable to any other doctrine. These reasons create a basis – through a consensus – that allows citizens to determine public policies on the basis of the weight of public reasons, not the size of a majority for one reasonable comprehensive doctrine. In this way, the free and equal status of citizens is respected, as doctrines do not have priority over others.

The process of creating an overlapping consensus is determined by weighing the relative merits of different public reasons. We consider their persuasiveness through *reflective equilibrium* (Rawls 2001: 29). As a community, we choose public policies that are consistent with the two principles of justice and which are best supported by public reasons in an overlapping consensus.

Rawls's defense of political liberalism is complex (readers will notice several references to new terminology like comprehensive doctrines, fact of reasonable pluralism, an overlapping consensus and more) and controversial (Brooks and Nussbaum 2015). One criticism is that some may doubt that the fact of reasonable pluralism requires that we need more than Rawls's two principles of justice. These critics claim that his two principles create a communal bond because of their universal support and, it is argued, can guide a useful guide to just policy outcomes on their own (Barry 1995). A second criticism is that an overlapping consensus is too weak of a foundation for political stability over time. The argument is that the main reason why I hold a view might be a reason that is specific to my preferred doctrine, and so I use public reasons to gain acceptance for it from others with different doctrines than mine. But while these public reasons may help create a consensus with people holding differing views, the consensus forged is fragile because the interlinking public reasons may not substantially connect with why I support one view over another (Wenar 1995). For example, my substantive position in favor of a view about human dignity might be based on specific religious convictions that others might not share with me. In order to engage in public reasoning, I trim down and remove parts of my actual position so that it is a more acceptable public reason to others that might be accepted by other citizens with different convictions. Perhaps they ultimate would agree. The criticism is that the public reasons that connect us may be fairly weak if stripped of much of the substance for why we, individually, hold the views we have in the first place.

A third criticism is that Rawls's political liberalism may aspire to impartiality relating to different doctrines, but it is not neutral itself. For example, it is an explicit endorsement of liberalism and the priority it gives to individual equality and rights. We might agree that this view is right and any theory of justice we would support would have the similar priority. But it is neutral to all views of the good, not least its own core values.

In conclusion, Rawls's work is deeply influential in the field. Even where philosophers might reject his conclusions, they may do so using his terminology. Rawls's legacy is not only his theory of justice but also the language he introduced to develop and defend it. Let us now consider important alternatives and they build off from or connect with Rawls's political liberalism.

## 4.8 The Capabilities Approach

A major contribution to how we might think about justice is broadly called the *capabilities approach*, which we considered in Chapter 2. A capability is the ability to do or be. Our capabilities identify our fundamental freedoms that any just government should secure and protect.

Thinking about our capabilities as a foundation for justice is believed to have many benefits. One is that it can respect the separateness of persons. This is understood in contrast to utilitarianism, where we aggregate the views of individuals in pursuit of actions that promote general happiness. The problem is that aggregation can mask inequalities and so fail to ensure all individuals receive equal concern and respect. The capabilities approach demands that we ensure capabilities for every individual so that unequal capability satisfaction is avoided.

The leading philosopher advocating for the capabilities approach is Martha Nussbaum. She claims that we have 10 different capabilities that must all be satisfied at or above a threshold that guarantees at least a minimally decent life. Nussbaum identifies our capabilities as: life; bodily health; bodily integrity; senses, imagination, and thought; emotions; practical reason; affiliation; other species; and play and control over one's environment (Nussbaum 2011: 33–34). We might broadly group these into three sets, including the body (achieving capabilities of life and bodily health), the mind (achieving capabilities of senses, imagination, thought, emotions, and practical reason) and our boundaries with others (achieving capabilities of bodily integrity, affiliation, other species, play, and control over one's environment). While Nussbaum claims there is no priority or ordering within her list, I have argued that securing capabilities of the body is necessary for enjoyment of others capabilities and that securing capabilities of the body and brain, or mind, is essential to enable exercise of the rest on her list suggesting some are more essential than others in relation to each other (Brooks 2020c: 204–205).

Nussbaum argues that justice is possible if every individual has the freedom to do or be in relation to every capability at or above a minimal threshold. The only essential is that every capability is available to us to exercise if we wish to. We need not exercise any or all capabilities, but they must be ever-present. There is no injustice if we choose against exercising any capability.

Capabilities do not require the state to always intervene. In fact, sometimes the state should probably not, such as where we have an affiliation capability to make friends (Nussbaum 2000: 79). In other areas, such as ensuring a capability to have "good health," the state could play a role in creating a national health service or instead running a privatized system (Nussbaum 2000: 78). For Nussbaum, it is unimportant if the state is a provider of capabilities – and so its view of justice can be accepted by libertarians. On the contrary, the only thing that does matter is that every individual can exercise all capabilities, whether secured by the public, private or charitable sector.

One criticism about the capabilities approach concerns the claim that everyone must be able to exercise all capabilities to enjoy a minimally decent life, but that, at the same time, we do not need to exercise them. If I need not enjoy any capabilities, it is unclear why being able to do something that I might refuse to do ensures a minimally decent life.

Compare two hypothetical communities. The citizens in the first community exercise all 10 capabilities all the time; in the second community, no citizen chooses to exercise any capability at any time. For Nussbaum, both communities are equally just if they each allow all citizens to exercise their capabilities. The example is akin to one community where all choose to eat and another where all choose to fast. Each differs in how citizens actually function but not in terms of their available capabilities – and it is having all of their capabilities available above a threshold that makes a difference, not actual functioning.

There seems something, at least to me, intuitively problematic about saying that options must be available that, in fact, nobody in the society decides to choose to do. Indeed, it is doubtful we would say the mere formal option to politically participate for all is sufficiently satisfied if it transpired that the overwhelming majority that actually did stand for office come from only a narrow demographic, such as wealthy white men from privileged backgrounds. If a more inclusive range of members do not participate, it raises questions about how well secured equal rights to participation are embedded. Our having, and also enjoying, capabilities both seem important (Brooks 2014a: 100–106). My view is that this concern might be resolved by proponents of the capabilities approach arguing that it must be *both* possible *and* probable that we can, and that we do, exercise our capabilities most, if not all, of the time. The *problem of probability* for the capabilities approach is that if their exercise is not probable, it raises questions that its availability for all to freely exercise is not satisfactorily possible.

While capabilities is an alternative approach to Rawls's theory, it has been claimed the two views can be made compatible. Nobel Prize winning economist Amartya Sen claims capability should be seen as a continuum (Sen 1999). We can measure development from low to advanced along this continuum, and our aim is to raise ourselves ever higher. For Sen, there's no such thing as having "too much" capability.

Sen argues that a capability approach, such as his formulation, can be compatible with Rawls's theory of justice by replacing Rawls's thinner view of primary goods with the thicker conception of capability (Sen 1999: 306–307). Rawls's view of primary goods is primarily as a *means* of satisfactory human living but not its *end* (Sen 2009: 234). Sen claims replacing these goods with his approach would make it so. However, Rawls rejects this suggestion, claiming that Sen's view of capability is incompatible with primary goods because he seeks to maximize capability – and, for Rawls, endorse a comprehensive doctrine in its own right that might clash with other doctrines (Rawls 1996: 188).

Nussbaum claims her approach of 10 capabilities satisfied up to a minimum threshold is compatible with Rawls's theory, but in a different area. She argues that her understanding of capabilities, which does not aim at maximization, can be endorsed from any other reasonable doctrine. So, the way capabilities might fit with Rawls's theory is as part of an overlapping consensus (Nussbaum 2006: 79). As I have argued elsewhere, Nussbaum's approach would not, in my view, necessarily be the object of a consensus across all reasonable doctrines. The issue is the content that she gives to define her capabilities. For example, Nussbaum claims the capability to bodily health includes reproductive health and choice (Nussbaum 2000: 78). While I agree with her that it should, the problem for Nussbaum's position is that not every reasonable comprehensive doctrine accepts reproductive choice in this way and, therefore, an approach defining capabilities in such a way and incompatible with other doctrines is necessarily incompatible with the object of an overlapping consensus.

Of course, one way to resolve this problem is to redefine capabilities so that the incompatibility is overcome. A second way is to make a case for implanting Nussbaum's approach where Sen had attempted to install his own. Whereas Sen's approach was thought incompatible because it was a comprehensive doctrine in its own right, Nussbaum's capabilities are set at ensuring a basic minimum that is more in keeping with the way that Rawls conceives primary goods but in a more substantial way (Brooks 2015a: 154–164). If we replaced Rawls's primary goods with Nussbaum's more substantive 10 capabilities, this might offer a more compelling view about our primary goods in a way consistent within Rawls's theory of justice, but then not as a part of an overlapping consensus.

## 4.9    Feminist Justice

Feminist approaches to justice are an important and influential alternative to Rawls's views as well. It is a mistake to think there is one "feminist" view and it is a diverse tent, as if half of humanity shared only view about justice. However, a defining thread that speaks to what most, if not all, feminist approaches defend, then it is a concern about power and inequality between men and women. Feminist justice examines political inequalities in order to expose them and point toward their change.

One key approach is *radical feminism*. They are called radicals because they call themselves it. Radical feminists see their self-identity as radical, akin to a badge of honor, and the name is not given as a criticism. Radical feminists *own* their radicalism.

Andrea Dworkin and Catharine MacKinnon are leading figures of this approach (MacKinnon 1991). In their work, they focus on gender inequalities as essentially problematic that may lead to bans. For example, they famously drafted an anti-pornography ordinance. Their claim was that women may lack consent to participate and they can be abused during production that impacted those participating for many years afterwards (MacKinnon and Dworkin 1998). Moreover, Dworkin and MacKinnon argue that pornography is harmful to the equal status of women in society. This is because pornography is a medium that sends the message that women are second-class citizens, where men are the actors and women are, in effect, the acted-upon. Unless pornography is banned, their concern about these problems will persist.

A second key approach is *liberal feminism*. This group focuses on gender inequalities but applies a liberal outlook. Central to liberalism are the importance of consent and the priority of individual rights. Liberal feminists challenge inequalities but may often develop arguments for what conditions must apply to avoid bans. Leading figures in this area, like Nussbaum, accept that the way much of pornography is produced and distributed is deeply flawed (Nussbaum 1995: 286, 290). However, they disagree with radical feminists that this means that pornography is essentially problematic and unredeemable. Instead, liberal feminists have argued that if the pornographic industry was regulated better so that women's individual rights were protected and that participation requires informed consent then, under these more stringent conditions, liberal feminists could justify the right of individuals to make and watch pornography.

Broadly, we can see the differences between radical feminists and liberal feminists over pornography replicated when examining their position on other political issues. One such example is prostitution. In general, radical feminists draw attention to the lack of consent, the risk of serious harms to their health and of violence, and the gendered nature of a practice where, typically, most prostitutes are women and the overwhelming proportion of those paying prostitutes are men. As a structurally unequal practice, most radical feminists oppose the practice, including Dworkin and MacKinnon. On the contrary, liberal feminists like Nussbaum draw on the same background facts to argue the problems could be overcome if there was better regulation of prostitution. This would ensure all taking part had given informed consent and the rights of all parties respected and upheld.

A final example is polygamy. This is a kind of pluralist marriage. It is found in the world in one of two ways: as *polygyny*, where there is one husband and multiple wives, or *polyandry*, where there is one wife with multiple husbands. Polygamy is almost always in the form of polygyny: the question of whether to allow polygamy is essentially a question of whether men might be permitted multiple wives, embedding polygyny far more than polyandry. As practiced, polygamy has been linked with harmful effects, including more likely gender inequality, a higher risk of depression, and higher incidences of domestic violence than in non-polygamous marriages (Brooks 2009: 111–121).

Liberal feminists, such as Nussbaum and Cheshire Calhoun, have argued that polygamy may be problematic how we might find it, but that it is possible for polygamy to be lawful for women (and men) who consent and have individual rights protections in place. So, perhaps polygamous marriages are more likely to involve underage brides than monogamous marriages, and there may be power inequality between men and women. For Nussbaum and Calhoun, we must ensure proper standards are in place so polygamous partners are adults who fully and freely consent to joining this pluralist form of marriage (Calhoun 2005, Nussbaum 2008).

As I have pointed out, liberal feminists have overlooked a problem with their solution. This is the fact that polygamy is a structurally inegalitarian institution – and so this is objectionable to a liberal view based on equal rights between men and women. The concern is that polygamy's structure is like a hub and spoke where, typically, a man is at the hub in the middle and his wives connect to him like spokes. This model is structurally unequal because the man at the center is the only one who can consent to marrying everyone in the relationship. He is a direct part of who joins or leaves. In contrast, his wives only consent to join or leave a marriage with their husband; they need not consent to other wives joining the marriage. So, polygamy is structurally unequal between the center and its spokes. Moreover, the overwhelming share of polygamous marriages are polygynous. This raises a concern that if polygamy became easier to create, then virtually all might be polygynous and, therefore, allowing everyone to form a polygamous marriage will likely lead to more women in an unequal position in comparison to men.[9] For liberals prioritizing individual rights and equality, this is a serious problem.

These examples are aimed at demonstrating that feminisms are not the same and different feminist approaches can take radically different sides on debates. Feminists might all focus on gender inequality, but their various forms can argue for very different conclusions.

However, one important point that feminists have made clear is challenging the traditional division between *the public* and *the private*. In traditional liberal theory, political justice was found within the public. It can be seen in the rules that regulate our behavior in our employment, owning property, resolving conflicts, and political participation. In this traditional view, the private was one's home where justice did not apply. Every individual was the king (or queen) of their

---

[9] See Brooks (2009: 114–117). It is worth noting that those seeking pluralist relationships that are not structurally inegalitarian might consider *polyamory*, where an individual can have multiple partners, and these can also have partners, but all are not necessarily partners of everyone connected.

own metaphorical castle. The state ought not intrude, or so it was commonly claimed.

Feminists helped challenge this position. They rightly argued that justice is not only applicable once I walk out my front door. There are significant issues pertaining to justice within our private spaces, not least relating to violence within the home, especially concerning violence against women and girls. But it also extended to whether boys and girls, as well as men and women, receive fair equality of opportunity within the home and outside it. When Rawls originally claimed justice applied to a basic structure, he did not believe it included application to the family. But in his later work, he changed his mind – and so has virtually everyone else working in the field since.

## 4.10    The Stakeholder Society

Finally, we turn to a new alternative view that I have developed: the idea of *justice as stakeholding* (Brooks 2016c: 115–132). Stakeholding is a principled approach that says that *those who have a stake in outcomes should have a say in decision-making*. Those with a stake have an interest in how decisions might impact them. If we ignore the interests of stakeholders when deciding public policy, we deny their equal concern and respect.

The origins of stakeholder theory are found in work about business ethics, especially regarding corporate governance, where the aim is showing a compelling way of guaranteeing corporate accountability and transparency (Freeman 1984, Hutton 1995). Traditional stakeholder theory says that a business should not only focus on outcomes like profit-making but also the way it manages decisions for achieving these outcomes. If corporate members were understood to be stakeholders in the success of the business, they should be seen as partners engaged in some shared conception of the good that business seeks to achieve. A stakeholder model is seen as a way of creating a more inclusive form of decision-making that delivers a more sustainable business model, harnessing members more effectively toward a successful business (Freeman et al. 2007, Hutton 2010).

A stakeholder model for good governance and sustainable productivity can inform how government is organized, not only the structure of successful businesses (Gould 2011: 249–250). At the same time, there are some important differences. The first concerns failure. If a business fails, it can have a devastating impact on those losing their livelihoods and the communities that had benefited from its operations. However, new positions can be found and communities rebuilt. In contrast, if a government fails, its impact can be more consequential impacting everything from the everyday economy to law and order. It's far more arduous to launch a new government than start a new business. So, as Rawls highlights, we need to think carefully about how we promote political stability and "for the right reasons" where citizens receive equal concern and respect (Rawls 1996: xxxix, xli–xliii). The promise of stakeholder theory is that it delivers a more inclusive and sustainable form of governance that improves long-term success (Brooks 2015b).

A second difference is the way in which we might seek to identify who are the relevant stakeholders. Businesses will have a chief executive, maybe a senior management team, shareholders, and employees. But it will also have customers, the local community of which the business is a part, and the wider economy (Hutton 2010: 151). Yet, this view casts the net too wide. Decision-making would be unworkable if everyone had the same impact over decision-making. Moreover, it is intuitively obvious that some will have greater stakes than others: the success or failure of a business will impact its employees generally much more significantly than non-employees. And within the organization, employees fulfill different roles, and these are reflected in some having greater stakes than others (Fassin 2009).

The main *political* problem that stakeholding can address is the problem of *political alienation*. The alienated are not "at home" in the world but feel disconnected from their society. Alienation may be fueled by personal circumstances. It may become more likely to view oneself as alienated from society when living in economic insecurity, where opportunities are few or none and where their society is seen as a body that has a separate existence. But what defines alienation principally is a conviction of the self and others. Alienation is the view that, no matter how much I try, my voice will not be heard and that my interests are ignored now and into the future.[10]

For many of our most well-known theories of justice, alienation is not considered a significant problem nor threat to political justice if

---

[10] This *future condition* for alienation is important. Someone who felt their interests were ignored or disregarded on a single matter may be disappointed or frustrated, even rightfully so. But alienation is not a one-off feeling, but a conviction of my identity as separate in a longer-term timeframe.

rights, liberties, and opportunities are maintained. For example, Rawls's theory claims that so long as a society is governed by two principles of justice, guaranteeing basic liberties and fair equality of opportunity, and we have the possibility of offering public reasons to others, then it is not a problem if we choose to never take part. Likewise, the capabilities approach only requires that we have the opportunity for affiliating with others and politically participating. So long as this is guaranteed above some minimum threshold, we are free to choose to do or be as we like – including the choice to avoid participating. Similarly, defenders of republican theories of freedom claim that we must have opportunities for deliberating policies with others, but we need not take part (Brooks 2025b).

This state of the discipline seems to me intuitively worrying. How can we claim to achieve justice for our state when many of our fellow citizens identify themselves as separate from, or even hostile to, it? Standard justice theories are correct that citizens should not be coerced into public reasoning, enjoying capabilities relating to lifelong social affiliations, or taking part in deliberative politics. At the same time, it is mistaken to claim that it is not essential to justice that citizens choose, without coercion, to be engaged in the social and political life of their state to some significant degree overall. To claim that justice is achieved because everyone could vote or deliberate, but only a privileged few do so, ignores the importance of citizens having a conviction that they are a part of their community, that their community values them as members and that citizens have, and see themselves as having, equal concern and respect.

Justice as stakeholding addresses this important gap. We must ensure that citizens conceive of themselves as stakeholders. This requires that greater protections – and support – is in place so that those with a stake identify themselves as stakeholders and have a conviction their voices are valued.

Stakeholding is not conceived as a separate, freestanding theory of justice. It is a principled approach that is compatible with other leading theories: political liberalism, the capabilities approach, republicanism and other views can all integrate stakeholding into their models (Brooks 2016c: 121–129). If citizens shared convictions of themselves as stakeholders with a stake and a say, this will foster greater interaction in a collective enterprise with others – whether in engaging in public reasoning, capability enjoyment or exercising republican deliberation.

Admittedly, changing convictions is difficult. But the risk of not doing so leaves us with models of participatory politics that many do not participate in, whether available opportunities are seen as closed to them. When conceiving what a just society should look like, a community that takes seriously the inclusion and integration of its citizens seems essential and, if so, some form of stakeholding is required.

## 4.11   Conclusion

Justice can seem synonymous with political philosophy. This chapter has examined various approaches to how we might understand the topic – with special attention given to the hugely influential work of John Rawls. It is hoped that students are more familiar with the main approaches and leading thinkers. Whether you are more convinced by deontology or consequentialism or by Rawls or his critics, the principle that those with a stake should have a say in a society of stakeholders who identify themselves this way can cohere with your view. But it raises questions about the just workings of our society, in particular, the place and application of democratic participation. We shall turn now to this.

## Further Reading

Nussbaum, Martha C. 2000. *Women and Human Development: The Capabilities Approach*. Cambridge: Cambridge University Press.

Parekh, Bhikhu. 2006. *Rethinking Multiculturalism: Cultural Diversity and Political Theory*, 2nd edition. Basingstoke: Palgrave Macmillan.

Rawls, John. 2001. *Justice as Fairness: A Restatement*. Cambridge: Harvard University Press.

Sandel, Michael. 2009. *Justice*. Harmondsworth: Penguin.

# 5
# Democracy

## 5.1 Introduction

The word "democracy" comes from the Greek word *dēmokratia* formed from *dēmos* meaning "the people" and *kratos* meaning "power" or "rule." Thus, democracy is defined as *rule by the people*. Central to the idea of democracy is that the people should decide through an election process who should hold political power. But there is a deep disagreement about what form this should take. Almost every country holds elections, even countries that are not actually democracies, including North Korea (whose official name is the *Democratic* People's Republic of Korea, after all). As Robert Dahl observed, "there is no democratic theory – there are only democratic theories" (Dahl 1956: 1).

In this chapter, we will examine these different theories about how the people rule. We will begin with democracy's origins in ancient Athens to highlight the ways in which our understanding of democracy has changed over time since then. We will explore different conceptions of democracy, including popular democracy, representative democracy and deliberative democracy. Through this discussion, we will consider whether democracies are best because they have the most just process (akin to a deontological approach) or because they lead to the best outcomes (in line with a consequentialist approach).

*Political Philosophy: The Fundamentals*, First Edition. Thom Brooks.
© 2025 John Wiley & Sons Ltd. Published 2025 by John Wiley & Sons Ltd.

The chapter concludes considering the place of unelected experts in a modern democracy.

When I ask students the question *why democracy*, this can strike some of them as an odd thing to ask given how many take for granted that any just government must be democratic. So, when I ask them for *which kind of democracy is best* this further takes them by surprise as there is rarely much engagement among different democratic models and relatively little knowledge about democratic options. This chapter aims to speak to these issues and provide a clearer understanding of *why* democracy is so ever-present and *what* it is.

## 5.2   Why Democracy?

Before examining the different ways we can understand democracy, we should first consider the fundamental question of why have a democracy at all?

It is easy for today's generation to overlook the fact that democracy has not always been the main political system over the last 2,000 years. The defining feature of all democracies is that political leaders are chosen through popular elections held at regular intervals. Each democracy may have different ways of how they choose leaders and which kinds of positions are chosen. Elections are conclusive in this process: the winning candidate has the position they sought.[1] No democracy elects its political leaders for life. Regular elections are held to re-select political office holders.

Democracy is characterized by *participation*. In a traditional hereditary monarchy, future leaders are born within families. An aristocracy of nobles or authoritarian oligarchy are different political systems, but both are where a small group hold power with few opportunities for others among the citizenry to take part. These political systems may be led by those who seek to bring prosperity to their communities – or, if taking Machiavelli's advice, seek to rule by being feared rather than loved (Machiavelli 1995: 93–95). Whatever their intended goal, political decision-making is made by the few, not the many.

Democracies are different because they allow more opportunities to participate first hand as candidates for political office and for

---

[1] An exception is where election law is breached. This can lead to candidates being disqualified.

public participation in selecting candidates to take office. As Alexis de Tocqueville observed in his study of early America, "democratic peoples have a natural taste for liberty; left to themselves, they will seek it, and be sad if it is taken from them" (de Tocqueville 1969: 506). Moreover, democracies *require* participation. A hereditary monarchy is a system that creates its next leader from birth. But, in democracies, participatory effort is essential. Citizens must stand for election or no one can serve in the position. And the public must vote or no one can take office. Democratic politics is essentially participatory and this distinguishes democracies from alternative political systems.[2]

Participation plays a justificatory role for democracies, too. Following social contract theory, democracies are believed to be governments chosen by the people from their free consent. Democratic systems, including the legitimacy of their elected officials and the decisions they make in their official capacity, are believed to be justified because of the free and equal consent of the political community. Over time, successive groups campaigning for expanding suffrage so more could participate highlighted the lack of legitimacy for excluding many in society from full involvement.

Greater equality in democratic participation has played a key role in democracy's historical development. Citizens with rights to participate do so on a formally equal basis with each able to cast a vote.[3] Most democracies have expanded participation to allow more people to take part as candidates and voters. Where this may have been limited only to men with large property holdings, contemporary democracies commonly exercise universal suffrage, the right of all adults to vote in elections.[4]

Robert Dahl offers a definition of an "ideal" democracy intended to help us model how actual democracies should be constituted using five criteria. The first is *effective participation*. This requires that all citizens have equal and effective opportunities for contributing to democratic decision-making. The second is *voting equality* mandating

---

[2] On democracies as promoters of equality and freedom, see Aristotle (1984: 2091 [1136.40–1317.17]).

[3] I use the word "citizen" (instead of "member") because every democracy allows opportunities for its citizens to vote, subject to conditions like age, but not every democracy allows non-citizens who are lawfully resident to vote. The reference to "citizens" (not "members") is intended to avoid confusion. But it should be noted that some democracies allow limited political participation for lawfully resident members who are not among its citizens.

[4] This right can be subject to exemptions, such as prohibiting adult felons from voting.

that each of us has an equal vote and equal opportunity to vote. The third criterion is *enlightened understanding*. This is the view that voters should have equal and effective opportunities to learn about and reflect on relevant policy outcomes, including their expected consequences. The fourth is curiously called *control of the agenda*. This means that citizens can decide for themselves the matters to be considered as a community and that policies agreed are always subject to change in future. Finally, the fifth criterion for democracy is *inclusion of adults* providing universal suffrage (Dahl 1998: 37–38).

Many of these criteria are value laden. For example, we must not simply be able to participate, but participate *effectively*. What is required to meet this test? Must we set aside time every day away from our work or families to engage politically? We might be *able* to participate effectively, but choose not to, for example. Yet, it seems odd to have an ideal conception where we could take part, but nonetheless most choose to ignore it. Or take the criterion of having an enlightened understanding. How much learning and effort is required? Clearly it would not mandate all citizens to pass a knowledge test in order to be allowed to participate. However, it might include an expectation that all of us acquire at least some understanding about broad policy choices so that everyone can contribute in an informed and meaningfully way.

It would be an understatement to say that those who study politics for a living are passionate about their subject. I know many brilliant political scientists who argue that a healthy democracy requires informed debate and regular political engagement. (Or, in other words, a healthy democracy would be a political community made up of people with their same interests and passion for political affairs.) Yet, these models of our "ideal" selves can seem one sided and perhaps out of touch with most citizens, as if the only meaningful activity in our lives is to talk about politics and policy making. Such ideals of we-the-citizen characterize us as only part of some kind of full-time assembly while wrongly ignoring to our other meaningful roles in work, family life and recreation. This point is crucial to keep in mind (and as my family regularly reminds me!).

But one element that we should include in any ideal – and actual – view of how democratic politics should work is the need for *integrity* in our politics. As I've argued before, "trust is also essential for our democracy. It's its life's blood . . . Democracies hold elections with winners and losers. But their future health depends on all sides accepting and respecting results with trust in the process being fair"

(Brooks 2022d: 1, 4). Dahl's criterion should include a requirement that political engagement is done with integrity. Otherwise, individuals may have an ability to participate and the enlightened understanding to do so, but yet fail to engage others honestly and sincerely.

Citizens will not agree about everything all the time. Differences about what is best are unavoidable. But what is avoidable is conducting debates in ways that undermine our trust in each other and our governance. This requires not only understanding about issues, but a politics that is accountable, transparent and fair.

As parties to a debate, it can be easy to focus on your own side "winning" by getting approval for a policy change. But as citizens, we must focus more on how *we* all "win" in the ways that we conduct our decision-making. Deception, false promises, personal attacks and untruths may be useful in the partisan pursuit of gaining individual political influence or power in the short term. However, to let these factors take root is to undermine the value of understanding in decision-making and introduce a rot into our collective political lives that should never be allowed to take root.

This is especially important when we consider that government functions include its ability to resolve disputes among its members, including provision for remedies and sanctions. As Raz notes, "a government's power can and normally does quite properly extend to people who do not accept its authority" (Raz 1986: 102). So, it is vital that democracies command public confidence of all community members. This major challenge is made more difficult where integrity in public life is lacking. The best protection that the public may have is by insisting on standards of integrity in political debate and public life with consequences for breaches, including at the ballot box, to ensure that such problematic conduct is discouraged and avoided (Brooks 2016e). If Aristotle is right that "man is by nature a political animal," then it must become domesticated toward promoting a common good, not its impulsive pursuits for personal political gain at the expense of the community's well-being (Aristotle 1984: 2029 [1278.19]).

Modern politics is discussed in the context of a 24-hour news cycle. This has been positive in allowing citizens more time to gain information about current affairs. A negative development is continuous news coverages require a steady stream of news to broadcast. An effect is this can highlight short-term problems as they happen over longer-term matters on the political horizon. The consequence is that short-term decision-making can lead to less optimal outcomes over time. For example, if a government were to simply react to the news of the day, whatever it was, its handling of relevant policy areas would be haphazard. In contrast, a longer-term approach could provide a plan for achieving targets and measuring progress that would provide a better structure for managing policy successes.

Bernard Williams put the issue like this: "Why should I hinder my future projects from the perspective of my present values rather than inhibit my preset projects from the perspectives of my future values?" (Williams 1981: 10). He argues that it is only through our present projects that we conceive ourselves and our future. In other words, we must see our short-term projects as part of a larger, longer-term strategy; it is this strategy that provides justification for those shorter-term steps that lead up to it.

A final point about *why* democracy is because it works: we are happier and better off in a democracy. As Aristotle observed, "a multitude is a better judge of many things than any individual" (Aristotle 1984: 2041 [1285.31]). This wisdom of the crowd harnessing the contributions of its members is a significant advantage over political systems reliant on only a few with most cut off from participation (Estlund 2008). Internationally, some have claimed the *democratic peace theory* that holds that historically, democracies avoid war with one another; and so global peace might be achieved if more countries became democracies (Russett 1993). In these ways, democracies are thought to make better choices leaving people better off at home and abroad.

This does not mean we are at an end of history where democracy is guaranteed forever after it is established. As R. H. Tawney observes: "democracy and extreme economic inequality form, when combined, an unstable compound" (Tawney 1931: 193). Should democracies fail to deliver for their communities, the concern is much graver than a risk that a particular government might end but, that the democracy itself might be cast aside in favor of some alternative. The problem is that any viable alternative is likely to reduce, if not end, popular participation. Those with a stake would no longer have a say and citizens would not be treated like stakeholders in a shared community, but rather like a group to be dominated and managed by others.

As we have seen, the value of democracy is in the legitimacy of its decision-making and of its outcomes as a participatory system that is more inclusive than alternatives. We shall turn now to the forms that democracy has taken from its origins to the present day to deliver this value.

## 5.3   Democratic Models

The word "democracy" has Greek origins and perhaps the first democracy was born in the ancient Greek city of Athens around 507 BCE.[5] At this time, city-states were commonplace, but usually monarchical. Athens created a form of popular government with elected citizens governing through an assembly. All citizens were entitled to vote and participate. A few positions were reserved for electing public officials like generals in the military, but most individuals were chosen by lottery where every citizen had an equal chance of being elected (Dahl 1998: 12).[6] The idea was that, in a democracy, anybody could be called on to be part of the decision-making group. In effect, everybody that could vote might be picked for a position.

With the rise of what became the Roman Empire, Athenian democracy came to an end. There were some democratic elements in the Roman Republic, but participation was poor. This was likely because Romans with a right to take part could only do so from within the Forum building in Rome which could be hundreds of miles away (Dahl 1998: 13–14). For centuries afterwards, monarchies became the most popular model of government. These were seen as a providing necessary unity for the state, as suggested by Hobbes, whereas democracy was viewed as impulsive, uncontrolled, and enabling a disunited polity that made it weak and susceptible to attack (Hobbes 1996: 130). This position no doubt traded on the view of leading philosophers like Aristotle that democracies were governments by the poor, uneducated and generally incapable (Aristotle 1984: 2031 [1279–1280]). This contrasted with monarchies, aristocracies and oligarchies where the poor were not decision-makers and the ruling class were well educated. Fast forward to today and democracies are seemingly everywhere, although it would be misleading to say there was any single model used.

### 5.3.1   Separation of Powers

The first kind of model concerns its structure. These can be broadly divided into a presidential or parliamentary model, with variations of

---

[5] I use the abbreviation for Before Common Era, or BCE.
[6] If this seems odd, remember that the US President is also the Commander-in-Chief overseeing a military whose might is unimaginable to anyone living 2,500 years ago – or even a century ago.

how each operate. The *presidential* model, such as found in the United States, has an elected president serving as both head of state and the head of the executive branch of the government. This creates a unified executive headed by one person.

The US President leads the executive branch and appoints members of their administration's cabinet. The Cabinet's members need not be picked from among elected members in Congress, but, if they are elected to Congress, they must resign their seats. No one can be both a serving Senator while Secretary of State at the same time, for instance. Cabinet members are directly answerable to the President and their role is primarily advisory with power mostly concentrated in the presidency.

The elections for President and members of Congress are held at fixed times. A President cannot dissolve the government and call a general election. This can entail prolonged gridlock and paralyzed decision-making where officials remain in office even if they have lost the confidence of other members and the wider public.

The *parliamentary* model, as the Westminster model found in the United Kingdom, has a hereditary monarch as head of state and a Prime Minister as head of the government.[7] They are not equal with actual power resting with Parliament. The UK's Prime Minister selects members of the Cabinet who must hold active positions in Parliament. This means either they must be an elected Member of Parliament in the House of Commons or serve as a life Peer in the House of Lords. While the Prime Minister can effectively hire or fire ministers at will, those ministers are the decision-makers within their departments and so not merely advisory roles. Their ministerial position is held alongside their position in the House of Commons or the House of Lords where they might debate and vote on measures their government seeks to defend.

While elections must be held within a five-year period, they may be held earlier if the government fails to maintain the confidence of the House of Commons or if the Prime Minister wants to call an early election for any reason. In the UK, it is Parliament that is supremely sovereign. This means that Parliament, not the government, can decide whether or not to hold elections earlier. Often it is the government that chooses when elections are held, but this is generally when it has

---

[7] For simplicity's sake, I will refer to the parliamentary model in its Westminster (UK) version. There are many different ways of having a parliamentary (or a presidential) system, but the focus on the US and UK covers the main points of difference.

a majority in the House of Commons. If the government should not command the confidence of a majority, then it may be forced by Parliament into holding an election earlier than it wants. Ultimately, in a parliamentary system, control rests with the majority within Parliament and it is for Parliament to decide.

The presidential and parliamentary models thus give different powers to the head of government and head of state; senior cabinet members hold different roles in each and the timing of elections can vary. However, a crucial difference between these two models is how the traditional three branches of government work together. These are the *legislature* that creates the law, the *executive* that enforces the law and *judiciary* that administers the laws by interpreting the law when its meaning is disputed (de Montesquieu 1989).

In the United Kingdom's parliamentary system, these branches are not entirely separated. Members of the executive branch hold seats in Parliament and so can both introduce and pass laws they seek to deliver. However, active judges do not have seats in Parliament. A curious position is that of the Lord Chancellor (who also holds the position of Justice Secretary): they currently have a seat in Parliament and so a member of the legislature, they hold a senior position in government so part of the executive and has a duty to uphold the independence of the judiciary and the rule of law across government although no longer the head of judiciary as well (Horne 2015). In this way, perhaps uniquely, the Lord Chancellor has some role to play across all three branches of government.

The parliamentary system has sometimes been called an "elective dictatorship." This is because – even with a slim majority – the government can deliver substantial reforms if it can maintain party discipline. It is common for opposition parties to lose virtually every vote in a Parliament. For example, over the last five years, the government lost only one vote on an amendment.[8]

In the United States' presidential system, the three branches of government are entirely separated.[9] James Madison played a central role in the writing of America's Constitution and widely credited for advocating separate branches of government. He argued that "the

---

[8] This happened with Clause 27 of the Victims and Prisoners Act on 4 December 2023 where the government was defeated by four votes.

[9] America's founders held deep concerns about tyranny and took various steps to create institutions that would avoid it. Originally, there were no political parties. But factional divisions over early constitutional debates soon coalesced into a party system.

accumulation of all powers, legislative, executive and judiciary, in the same hands, whether of one, a few, or many, may justly be pronounced the very definition of tyranny."[10] Separate branches of government were intended to create a system of checks and balances where each branch can impose a check on others. This would restrict the powers of each avoiding any one branch having dominance as a means to ensure political equality among citizens and the branches of their government.

An example of how this system works is how laws are made. Congress legislates, but it requires the approval of the President for a Bill to become law. If the President vetoes it, both Houses in Congress must vote by two-thirds majority to overturn the veto and pass the law. Plus, the constitutionality of laws can be challenged in the judiciary, which has the power to render laws unconstitutional and, thus, invalid. The system is like a complex web where all three branches are designed to serve as checks and balances on the power of each other. No one branch can do whatever it wants nor when it wants within its domain. The result is a political system that can move much slowly than a parliamentary system given there are more obstacles that can slow, if not stop, change – and, as a result, intended to produce a more stable, consistent model. A less charitable view is it produces gridlock.

No discussion of American's separation of powers in a book about political philosophy can ignore the recently decided case *Trump v. United States* involving US President Donald Trump prior to his winning a second term. In this case, the US Supreme Court held that "under our constitutional structure of separated powers, the nature of Presidential power entitles a former President to absolute immunity from criminal persecution" although "no immunity for unofficial acts" (*Trump v. United States* 2024).

Without making any comment about the dispute leading up to this case, the Supreme Court's majority judgment seems wrong in principle and as an in correct interpretation of the law. First a point of principle: if a sitting President has "absolute immunity from criminal persecution," it might allow them to commit crimes harming political opponents for the purposes of remaining in office and without fearing repercussions. The Court makes a caveat that there is no immunity for "unofficial acts," understood to be where the President might act in a capacity unrelated to official duties. But it is unclear this caveat would always

---

[10] Madison writing in *The Federalist* (number 47) and cited in Dahl (1956: 6).

ensure no immunity for a President committing treason or other such acts in order to continue in office in extreme hypothetical cases.

A second reason is the Constitution does not appear to grant such immunity to the President. The Court cites an earlier case claiming only that the judiciary had "'no power to control (the President's) discretion' when pursuant to the powers invested exclusively to him by the Constitution."[11] But as argued by Justice Sonia Sotomayor in a dissenting opinion, she notes that the "Constitution does not shield a former President from answering for criminal and treasonous acts."[12] Indeed, the President takes an oath to "faithfully execute the Office of the President" which explicitly states they will "preserve, protect and defend the Constitution."[13] An "absolute immunity" to any charges is incompatible with acting in breach of the Constitution and the rule of law. Thus, finding that one, and only one, individual is not bound by the rule of law while in office would further appear to undermine the system of checks and balances that has held the American democratic model together. It is a safe bet the debate over this issue is far from over.

## 5.3.2    Voting Systems

Democracies are run by those chosen by the people. This can follow very different procedures. Many countries, like the United States and United Kingdom, follow a *first past the post* system. Voters choose a candidate and the candidate with the most votes wins. The system is favored for producing stable government majorities, but criticized for mismatching popular support overall. For example, a candidate could win their seat with a small share of the vote so long as others fared worse. Furthermore, one party could receive more votes nationally than another, but have fewer seats if these votes are too concentrated in some areas and thinner in others. Suppose the Alpha Party received 100,000 votes in district 1 but only 10,000 votes in districts 2 and 3. The Beta Party scores 10,001 votes in all three districts. The Alpha Party would win district 1 and the Beta Party would win districts 2 and 3. This is despite the fact the former received 120,000 votes in total while the Beta Party received only 30,003 across all three districts.

---

[11] Trump v. United States 2024 [Roberts, CJ].
[12] Trump v. United States 2024 [Sotomayor, J].
[13] See Article II, Section 1 of the US Constitution (1789).

The counterclaim in favor of the first past the post system is that voting areas are not the same. Each can represent very different areas and face different issues. It could be that the Beta Party was much better aligned with relevant local issues which is won more seats. Moreover, if it does not matter where votes are coming from, it might be that a political party could simple focus on voter turnout in an urban area without once seeking votes from across the country. Whether we are concerned by that will turn on what we mean by a "majority" (as in a "majority *of what*"). If we think that it important for politicians to win a *bare majority* of wherever it comes from, then whoever has the most votes overall should win. There is no problem if every vote came from only place and nowhere else. Or if we think that our elected leaders should represent a majority of the country, not only a majority of its votes, then we will support a constituency-by-constituency or electoral college system found in the first past the post model, which we might call a *qualified majority*.

An illustration that helps show the distinction is the difference in the US between the popular vote and the electoral college. The popular vote is the bare majority of votes cast overall, such as in a national election for a new President. While this is counted, it does not determine the victor. There is also the electoral college system whereby states have a number of electors equal to the number of representatives it sends to Congress in both the House and Senate. As more populous states have more congresspeople, these states are worth more electoral college delegates than less populous states. The candidate who wins the most electoral college delegates is elected President.

It is regularly asked by my students why such a system is used when it can seem more intuitive to decide the outcome from a bare majority of the popular vote. The counterargument is that if a bare majority is all that mattered, a candidate from a populous state like California or Texas might canvass only within their area, speaking only to citizens there and not engage – nor visit – states further afield, as this might be unnecessary if one only needed to win the most votes overall. The electoral college system of a *qualified majority* requires candidates to canvass in multiple states and campaign across the country. While the electoral college winner has not always won the most votes overall, it will be the candidate who has won over the most delegates from individual states that secures a wider geographical spread than might otherwise be necessary.

A similar argument applies to the UK's parliamentary elections. The party that wins the most votes nationally might not win the most seats. Instead, parties contest constituency-by-constituency. It is possible for a party to win far more seats than another with fewer votes if these votes are spread out more evenly enough to win constituency elections by only the margin necessary.[14]

The main alternative to the first past the post is *proportional representation*. This system aims to distribute seats in proportion to voter support overall. One form is as a *party list*. Citizens vote for one political party. Parties win seats proportionately. So, if the Alpha Party won half of all votes, it would win half the seats. Some systems require a minimal vote share like at least 5%, which would keep small fringe parties from gaining a nominal seat.

The party list system has its pros and cons. The primary benefit is that it is believed to better capture the proportional preferences of all voters. If a large minority supports a political party, they might lose every seat under the first past the post system because they are not a majority but they could win a minority share of seats under the party list system. The main criticism is that the system creates weak governments, as most require some form of a governing coalition because parties rarely win more than half of all votes and so must form a government that are comprised of two or more different political parties.

A second form of proportional representation is the *single transferable vote* system. Voters rank their preference for candidates. The election counters set a quota. This is calculated by dividing the number of votes cast by the number of available seats and adding one. So, if 100,000 people voted to elect 10 candidates, the quota for each candidate would be 10,001. The election counters then count the number of first preferences. If any candidates reach the quota or higher, they are duly elected. But that is not all. If not all positions are filled, the candidate with the fewest first-preference votes is eliminated. The votes for the eliminated candidate are redistributed to the remaining candidates based on the voters' next preferences. This process is repeated until all positions are filled.

---

[14] For example, in the 2024 parliamentary elections in the UK, the Liberal Democrats won 72 seats while the Reform Party won 5. While the former outperformed in winning more constituencies seat-by-seat, it received about 3.5 million votes while the latter won over 4 million votes. In another contrast, the Green Party received nearly 2 million votes and won 4 MPs while the Welsh nationalist party Plaid Cymru also won 4 MPs, but on less than 200,000 votes (BBC 2024).

The main benefit is this system allows for more tactical voting which has seen an increase in independent candidates winning elections. It is also thought to better track preferences as voters can rank various parties very differently. The final result represents a broader support base than alternatives. The main criticisms are it is a more complex system to work out. Other critics claim it counts votes twice, although they certainly do not count twice since voters of candidates coming last and redistributed are, in essence, counted anew (not again) for their next preference.

Each system has its merits and demerits. Without trying to convince readers one way or the other, I have tried to provide an overview of the main options so you can formulate your own opinion. Should we seek stronger government led by a single party or govern collaboratively across coalitions? Should parties win seats based on popularity across the most individual constituencies or instead the overall vote share? How should a voting system best track voter preferences? These questions have no obvious right answer – and I would not rule out, as artificial intelligence (AI) continues to change the ways we live and work, that new electoral models will be proposed in future. Whereas AI is often feared a threat to democracy insofar as it has the potential to create false and misleading images and videos, it may also identify new ways of managing processes more effectively and efficiently.

After typing this sentence, I asked Chat GPT if it could identify new ways of voting. One of these suggested I will call a *points-based voting system*. This might work in the following way. Voters each get points (for example, five points). They can then distribute these points to candidates at an election however they like. Suppose I have five points and there are five candidates. One option is that I could choose to give all five points to a single candidate. Or maybe a second option is that I am split between two candidates so I give one and three points and the other two points. Or maybe a third option is that I am equally lukewarm about candidates so I give each one point. Or, a fourth option is that maybe I am not keen on any of them so award only one point to my preferred candidate, but do not spent the other four points. Or, finally, a fifth option is that I give each of the five candidates one point. After all voters have distributed their share of points, we add up the points awarded by voters for each candidate. The winner is the candidate with the most points.

Such a points-based voting system model could better track the intensity of support for multiple candidates than alternatives. This intensity of support in relation to other candidates is an important aspect that other electoral systems can miss. However, this system would be complex and difficult for many voters to understand as well as a break from the principle of "one person, one vote." AI has the potential to help us see processes in new ways that could revolutionize how we do politics in a manner still unimaginable at this time. (I would not have thought to include this alternative if not for it.)

### 5.3.3    Rethinking Representation

Democracy is rule by the people, but how should the elected relate to their electorate? In other words, whatever way we choose to conduct elections and whatever model – presidential or parliamentary – we support, what is the relationship between the voters and the officials they empower through winning elections?

The first variety are forms of *indirect democracy*. This is where the public vote to elect officials, perhaps on account of supporting the policy preferences of officials, and these officials are thereby enabled to make political decisions on behalf of the public. The public indirectly contributes to public policy-making by choosing the decision-makers who will determine what these policies will be.

One variety of indirect democracy is the idea of *popular representation*. This view sees the role of elected officials as representing the majority in their constituency. As Aristotle says, the "people are supreme" (Aristotle 1984: 2029 [1278.10–1278.11]). Popular representatives give supreme control, in a sense, to the public. These representatives make decisions that they believe matches the popular views of their voters. It is a model where the views of the representative are relatively trivial. For example, it is unimportant whether a popular representative prefers option one if their voters mostly support option two. Elected officials might seek to change the minds of their voters if they thought their support for a future decision was the wrong one but, ultimately, would continue to track popular preferences and vote accordingly.

One criticism of this view is that while, of course, democratic officials must please their voters – otherwise, they might not be re-elected – sometimes the voters might get things wrong: while elected officials should act in the best interests of all, their decisions do not necessarily reflect whatever happens to be the public mood at that moment. This critique views the public's support as a tight constraint on the discretion of their elected officials to make political decisions. A response is to say that there is wisdom in groups and the collective views of voters can be a useful compass to sound decision-making. It echoes a famous speech by the ancient Greek statesman Pericles, who said: "Our ordinary citizens, though occupied with the pursuits of industry, are still fair judges of public matters . . . and instead of looking on discussion as a stumbling block in the way of action, we think it an indispensable preliminary to any wise action at all" (Dahl 1998: 39). The public view is an aggregate of collective knowledge and experience. Instead of a hindrance, it could serve as a helpful barometer not only of voter support but of the best course of action. Indeed, for most citizens, the biggest political activity they may be involved in is voting. This commands respect whatever one's assessment of the final outcome.

But a related second criticism is that the public mood can be fickle. Issues rise and fall in importance from day to day. To be guided on what the state should do on an aggregate of not fully informed guesswork makes for short-term, haphazard decision-making. It undermines following a strategy should the public mood at some point differ. And there is a risk that misinformation among the public might warrant ignoring voters' views in extreme cases.

Popular representation is not necessarily *populist* (Dahl 1956: 45–50). Populism is the view that politics has become disconnected from ordinary people, disregarded by a privileged and empowered elite. In essence, that governments are making unpopular decisions that are opposed to the public interest. Populists claim they stand for a collective "the people" in opposition to a perceived elite-run establishment. Populism is neither necessarily right wing or left wing with varieties of both kinds (Norris and Inglehart 2018). Often the term "populist" is used pejoratively for the ways in which many populists mythologize notions of people versus the elite and oversimplified or unworkable means of addressing complex issues.

Examples include enacting so-called three strikes and you're out laws whereby someone convicted of a third imprisonable felony was automatically sentenced for life. Populist supporters claimed the criminal justice had been run for too long by out-of-touch experts, become increasingly less punitive and so contributed to growing crime rates. It was claimed this was out of line with where the people are and that a much harsher punishment would act as an effective deterrent. But that is not what happened. The prison population grew quickly as more were imprisoned and for much longer with spiraling costs – the California state auditor estimated the policy added a whopping $19 billion to the state's prison budget with a negligible effect on crime rates. Less than a decade after it was passed, California voters passed a new proposition that began to significantly reduce the numbers of offenders caught up in this plan. An assessment of the state's legislative analyst's office found that as the policy broadly continues it expected to see the prison population continue to grow with "significant implications" for increased capital and operating costs for the future.[15]

There are other examples of populism where a focus has been on seeking to tear up rights protections in order to pursue a policy end. An illustration from the United Kingdom is threats to leave the European Convention on Human Rights, as this has been seen by some as a block on delivering anti-immigration policies. In this case, the government called a snap election and had a historic loss so these threats have come to nothing.

Nevertheless, this is the kind of worry – namely, rolling back rights protections, especially where they may support an unpopular minority – that many fear from some forms of populism. While populists claim the will of the people should not be thwarted by unwanted legal barriers, critics highlight that populist notions of "the people" do not include the full population, including minority groups that might be made much worse off by rolling back individual rights protections. Populists are right to claim it is legitimate to seek making policies that the majority support, but they are wrong if they mistake a majoritarian system with a tyranny of the majority. The majority may choose the officials. However, the everyday exercise of democratic decision-making is imposed by constitutional rights (Brettschneider 2007). The rule of law means no one is above the law and fair terms for all – even political opponents. A healthy democracy must have some means of ensuring a majoritarian democracy does not rule as a mobocracy (or ochlocracy, meaning mob rule) that infringes the rule of law and fails to treat all citizens with equal concern and respect.

It is a striking fact of much populism that it is often not especially *popular*(!). Most elected officials – the ones who have won elections – neither self-identify nor are seen by others to be populists. So, in reflecting on what populism is about, it should be seen as an antiestablishment

---

[15] See url: https://lao.ca.gov/2005/3_strikes/3_strikes_102005.htm.

ideology which can struggle managing its positioning against the establishment when it becomes the established government.

There is much to dislike about populism as indicated above. However, it often feeds off of real concerns within many democracies that large parts of the public feel left out to the point of becoming alienated. Where citizens do not see themselves as having a stake in how society manages itself, this can fuel their interest in supporting political parties that claim they will not forget them, their interests should be valued and given hope for a better future. An oft-recommended remedy for populism is to have an inclusive democracy that enables improvements in well-being.

A second form of indirect democracy is *representative government* and it is the most common. This model holds that the public elects officials who represent the public in a democratic body, but the elected are chosen to exercise their own judgment and not required to decide however the public might wish they did on the day. As Joseph Schumpeter says:

> The voters outside Parliament must respect the division of labor between themselves and the politicians they elect. They must not withdraw confidence too easily between elections and they must understand that, one they have elected an individual, political action is his business and not theirs (Schumpeter 1962: 295).

The role of voters is to decide who should make decisions on their own behalf. An apt slogan might be something like: voters elect officials and officials govern the voters.[16] This model sees a more passive role for the public which are like patients in a democracy juxtaposed against officials who are active agents tasked with the responsibility of making the correct decisions based on their own expertise or experience rather than drawing on the collective wisdom of the crowd.

The benefit of this system is it provides a division of labor. The public may not have sufficient expertise to guide every decision and be thought more productively focused on non-political matters like family, work, and recreation. Meanwhile, representatives are free to make decisions they see as best. This could allow decision-making to

---

[16] Schumpeter refers to democracy not as rule by the people, but "rule by the politicians" as it is the politicians who make policy decisions. See Schumpeter (1962: 295) and I have always found it an apt description.

be guided more by reason and evidence than the fickle views of the public and make for higher quality decisions that will benefit everyone more than alternatives.

The criticisms are that this model can fuel public apathy and political misconduct. The reason is that, if representatives need not be concerned much about voters think except at election time, the public may feel ignored because they are ignored. Furthermore, if voters are only relevant for deciding election outcomes, it can lead to a lack of sufficient scrutiny by citizens during their representatives' time in office, such as challenging them on pledges made and ensuring representatives act with integrity. The guard who protects the people are the people.

### 5.3.4   Deliberative Democracy

*Deliberative democracy* is a form of democracy whereby citizens engage with one another to determine policies. It is a mode of *direct democracy* because the citizens directly shape decision outcomes, instead of it being necessarily mediated by others. Deliberative democracy is a reaction against representative democracy: while the latter sees citizens as playing a generally passive role, the former conceives an active position. In this sense, it has echoes of democracy's ancient Athenian origins of everyone involved in collective decision for the community.

Deliberative democracy has two key drivers. The first is a concern that our politics should be more substantive. At present, politics involves few opportunities for most people to play any role in shaping political decisions beyond voting periodically. Most engagement is generally passively, such as observing superficial media campaigns or partisan political advertising. This could change if the power to decide was put back in the hands of citizens. This could foster improved civic engagement and raise the quality of our political debates (Gutmann and Thompson 1998). Otherwise, the primary, and usually only, way citizens actively engage with politics is in the act of voting. Those who become involved in political campaigns whether in developing strategies or delivering leaflets are usually a small minority.

A second driver is a concern that communities experience political polarization, even deep disagreement. It is believed that if citizens came together to discuss issues and decide outcomes collaboratively that we can reduce disagreement and better converge on mutually acceptable policies (Shapiro 2003: 23–25). Deliberative democracy is not just about making better decisions, but making communities more inclusive and cooperative.

The idea of deliberative democracy is consistent with many variants of republican theories. Republicans define freedom as non-domination. The idea is that we are free where others do not dominate us and infringe our autonomy. If someone were to coerce us, then this would restrict our ability to act autonomously and so we would risk being unfree. This raises questions about how we might agree to being bound by laws, as they are coercive by their nature.

Republicans, such as Philip Pettit, argue that we must engage others through what he calls "discursive interaction," which he defines as "to discourse is to reason and, in particular, to reason together with others" (Pettit 2001: 67). Pettit claims that we can engage each other discursively on an equal level. Neither is like a second-class citizen and we approach one another with equality (Pettit 2001: 72). Discursive interaction requires the absence of coercion. This is because coercion is contrary to "co-reasoning" with others (Pettit 2001: 75).

Republican deliberative democracy is a means of creating laws and policies that may have coercive effects. However, our republican freedom is intact because these are justified under our collective *discursive control* and not an arbitrary imposition on us. Republicanism focuses on the process, not the outcome. In other words, it matters *how* we decide collectively more than *what* we decide. As other scholars have noted, like Robert Talisse, real discursive freedom is at work in our deliberative engagement when they are conducted without predetermined answers to deep and substantive moral disagreements (Talisse 2007, 2009).

There are different forms of deliberative democracy. One example is James Fishkin's argument for the use of deliberation opinion polling (Fishkin 1991). The idea is that a time would be set for debates on key issues with representatives of each side to make the argument for a potential decision with interlocutors. The general public would watch these debates at home. When they conclude, every household would have a box with buttons to register which decision was preferred. The outcome with the most public votes would be enacted. The attractiveness of this view is it shows a way in which all citizens could be included no matter a country's size and hand decision-making directly to the people. However, the criticisms are that such a plan would be enormously time intensive for seemingly little pay-off, as there is no compelling evidence the decision-making would be better or that such a scheme would be popular with citizens forced to regularly drop other plans so they can continually register their votes. Moreover, there is no clear interactive deliberation as the overwhelming majority of those participating do so passively at home.

A second example is the use of *citizen juries*. These are mini-publics of jury-like group of randomly selected citizens in a deliberative body which is used to help define laws and policies in connection with the wider public. This aims to harness the collective wisdom of the public that is more inclusive of a country's diversity (Landemore 2020). Citizen juries have been used increasingly, usually as a forum for generating recommendations for local or state governments. Their benefits are fostering civic engagement and providing useful feedback to policy makers about impending decisions to be made. However, there can be high participation costs. Not everyone can satisfy the time commitments even if these are short and not everyone may wish to participate if they did. Of course, deliberation "cannot be mandated" (Shapiro 2003: 49). This does not mean we should discourage further use but, rather that we are sensitive to ensuring these bodies are diverse and can play meaningful roles.

The main criticism of deliberative democracy is not whether more civic engagement is a good thing (it surely is) nor whether it could help address the problems of apathy and polarization (it surely would), but how strong the public appetite is for it. In their study of popular perceptions of public participation, John R. Hibbing and Elizabeth Theiss-Morse confirmed:

> The last thing people want is to be more involved in political decision-making. They do not want to make political decisions themselves; they do not want to provide much input to those who are assigned to make these decisions; and they would rather not know all the details of the decision-making process. Most people have strong feelings on few if any of the issues the government needs to address and would much prefer to spend their time in nonpolitical pursuits (Hibbing and Theiss-Morse 2002: 1–2).

This chimes with Niccolo Machiavelli's saying that "the majority of men live happily so long as they are not deprived of either their property or their honor" (Machiavelli 1995: 99). In other words, most people want to live normal lives and this does not include much room for substantive political debate.

Moreover, Hibbing and Theiss-Morse found:

> Participation in politics is low because people do not like politics even in the best of circumstances; in other words, they simply do not like the process of openly arriving at a decision in the face of diverse opinions (Hibbing and Theiss-Morse 2002: 3).

If correct, the problem is not that people choose not to participate in politics because they lack the time; it is because they lack the interest and find negotiating agreement with others holding different political views uncomfortable. It must be said that this is anecdotally my experience, too. Most people I know who are not political philosophers or politicians are usually far more keen to talk about different subjects like the final results of a big sporting event or the antics of contestants on reality television shows than the latest policy announcement or the key pledges in an election manifesto.[17]

Suppose these findings – anecdotal or otherwise – are correct. Most people do not want to deliberate. They would find the experience awkward and stressful. This only points out how most people are; it does not speak to how we should strive to be. A key lesson, as I see it, is that deliberative democracy could be used more widely and could bring many benefits. Part of its mission must be to continually developing a compelling model for how this can be operationalized institutionally. But a second, no less important, part is that it must be made more compelling for the wider public so more want to engage with it.

## 5.4   A Role for Experts?

A longstanding criticism of democracy is it lacks expertise. Many of its most famous critics, including Plato, argue that political leadership requires "the expert knowledge of kingship" that democracies lack (Plato 1997: 426d, 477d–477e; Brooks 2006). He claims they are "like people groping the dark" and merely "feed, fatten and fornicate"

---

[17] Sometimes statements like this are said in a perjorative sense, namely, that people ought not be as interested in such matters and should be more concerned, and interested, in political and public affairs. I disagree with those who make such claims. Anyone dismissive about why others care so little about political matters should reflect on why they care so little about non-political matters. Both can have value. If politics is about people, this factor should not be ignored or dismissed as unimportant.

(Plato 1997: 99b, 586b). Plato argued the common citizenry were simply incapable of self-government on their own.

Plato argues that there should be a mixed form of government bringing together expertise in governing with popular consent (Plato 1997: 693d–693e). He says:

> I suppose that, when a democratic city, athirst for freedom, happens to get bad cupbearers for its leaders, so that it gets drunk by drinking more than it should of *the unmixed wine of freedom*, then, unless the rulers are very pliable and provide plenty of that freedom, they are punished by the city and accused of being accursed oligarchs (Plato 1997: 562c–562d).

Noting the ancient Greek practice of always mixing wine with water, Plato rejects drinking the "unmixed wine of freedom" – a freedom to do as one likes that he associated with democracies of his time – perhaps because to do so may be intoxicating, but yet also lead to ill judgment and errors. Instead, our wine – and our freedom – should become moderated and allow us to exercise "good judgement" (Plato 1997: 693d–693e).

This idea that an elite group of experts should play some role in political decision-making is commonly referred to as *guardianship*. These experts are seen as essential to good government because of their impartial expertise. For example, Cicero claims: "The management of the republic is like a guardianship, and must be conducted in the light of what is beneficial not to the guardian, but to those who are put in their charge" (Cicero 1991: 33–34). So, experts possess both the requisite knowledge to govern which the public lacks and also use their knowledge for the common good, whereas members of the public are assumed more likely to be led more by self-interest. Of course, possessing political knowledge does not mean it would never be used to pursue individual partisan ends – expert political strategists use their insights to assist political parties contest elections all the time.

The challenge to democracy from guardianship is best summarized by Robert Dahl, who says:

> almost all of us do rely on experts to make crucial decisions that bear strongly and directly on our well-being, happiness, health, future, even our survival, not just physicians, surgeons, and pilots but in our increasingly complex society a myriad others. So if we let experts make decisions on important matters like these, why shouldn't we turn government over to experts? (Dahl 1998: 70).

There are two key reasons why he thinks this challenge fails. The first is that this challenge assumes that political experts can govern effectively because they have knowledge about governance. As Machiavelli argues:

> No state should ever think it can always make secure decisions. On the contrary, it should consider all decisions it takes as risks, because it is in the nature of things that in seeking to avoid one difficulty you run into another (Machiavelli 1995: 115).

Every decision is a risk. As former British Prime Minister Tony Blair has argued, "the moment you decide, you divide" as taking a side in decision-making will rarely receive unanimous approval (Blair 2010: 28). Political experts are far from perfect at predicting the future: Philip Tetlock's studies claim these experts are often little better than chimpanzees and so he tries to develop new methods for performing much better (Tetlock 2005: xix).

The second reason why Dahl claims the guardianship challenge fails is because "to govern a state well requires much more than strictly scientific knowledge" (Dahl 1998: 71). Governments are elected by the people, they are run by people and their success or failure is assessed by people; governments are people-driven collective projects. Technical mastery of policy strategy is important, but not sufficient. Governing is as much about people – their hopes, dreams, fragilities, and fears – as it is about the policy detail. Expertise alone is not enough.

These arguments against the use of experts are only reservations against putting experts in sole control. Of course, experts can play many important roles within a democracy that help it function better. To cede subordinate decisions to experts is not to give final control over major decisions (Dahl 1998: 71). Indeed, some deliberative democrats like Pettit, argue that some public policy decisions – such as setting interest rates – can and should be done by relevant experts, so long as the people have the power to take back this control should they want it in future (Pettit 2004, 2012). Such decisions are technical, even technocratic, in nature and where specialist expertise is relevant and necessary so long as overall control is retained by a deliberative public.

Moreover, it can be said that the proper functioning of contemporary democracy requires a team of unelected experts serving the delivering of the government's plans, including the civil service.[18] This is a necessity given the complexities of managing the affairs of the state in an interconnected global environment. It is impossible to imagine modern governments functioning without a highly skilled civil service today.

Self-government requires the self-control that an expert team supporting successive elected governments can enable far more effectively than without them. The rule of law requires legal experts in a well-functioning judiciary to ensure a democracy is governed properly by its own rules (Breyer 2010). The argument is not that these experts have the same view, but that their views – even if contested – contribute significantly to the success of government's governing. No modern polity could operate effectively without it. As Schumpeter argues: "the management of some of these affairs requires special aptitudes and techniques and will therefore have to be entrusted to specialists who have them. This does not affect the principle, however, because these specialists simply act in order to carry out the will of the people exactly as a doctor acts in order to carry out the will of the patient to get well" (Schumpeter 1962: 250).

Of course, a government could add expertise into its decision-making process by supporting experts as political candidates who win elections. An alternative way that expertise could be incorporated is following a model like the UK's House of Lords (Russell 2013). This is an independent body from the elected House of Commons. Peers are appointed for life to the House of Lords broadly for their expertise and relevant experience. Their main focus is as a revising chamber that challenges proposed legislation and recommends improvements. It can only delay, rather than veto, most Bills. The work of the Lords is of a consistently high standard, and where its members are widely recognized leaders in their field with many also drawn from having served in senior positions while elected members of the House of Commons. While the selection process has attracted attention that has not always been positive, the House of Lords is an example of a functioning unelected body in the heart of the world's first parliamentary democracy complementing the work of the more powerful elected House of Commons. There are continuing calls for its abolition and replacement by an elected body. One can only expect this is on the

---

[18] Karl Marx and Friedrich Engels called the civil service "a committee for managing the common affairs of the whole bourgeoise." See Marx and Engels (1967: 82).

near horizon. In the meantime, it stands as an important contribution to how democracy may function with an added layer of expertise.

Such examples highlight for us the idea that democracy is rule by the people is true insofar as their choice in free and regular elections determines who governs. But this speaks only to the procedure for choosing a government. Democratic governance is legitimated by the will of the people, but delivered, in significant part, by unelected experts.

## 5.5   Conclusion

Democracy is everywhere, but it operates differently from place to place. In this chapter, we have considered democracy's early roots in ancient Athens leading to models of parliamentary and presidential models today. We have considered the different methods of voting and contrasting approaches to how we might conceive democracy whether as essentially popular, representative, or deliberative, as well as the possible role of unelected experts within a democratic system.

Everyone might claim to support democracy. But what does this mean? Democracy is more than elections: it is the method we conduct them, the roles elected politicians play, the model for governing and the ways in which the public may inform the decision-making between casting votes. In other words, democracy is about much more than elections alone. It is hoped this chapter has helped to explain how and why.

## Further Reading

Dahl, Robert A. 1998. *On Democracy*. New Haven: Yale University Press.
Estlund, David, ed. 2002. *Democracy*. Oxford: Blackwell.
Gutmann, Amy and Dennis Thompson. 1998. *Democracy and Disagreement*. Cambridge: Harvard University Press.
Shapiro, Ian. 2003. *The State of Democratic Theory*. Princeton: Princeton University Press.

# 6

# Punishment

## 6.1 Introduction

Crimes happen. Every community justifies the punishment of offenders who commit crimes. Yet, there are a wide variety of approaches taken. One view is that punishment should be deserved and proportionate, but it begs the question of in proportion *to what*? A second view is that we should aim to deter others from committing the crime. So, how severe should a deterrent punishment be? Another view is that offenders ought to be rehabilitated so that they do not re-offend in the future. But what if they would engage in crime again anyway? Or we might want to punish in all three ways – a deserved, proportionate punishment that deterred and reformed. However, these different penal goals can go in different directions: the punishment deserved could be different than the amount that would deter and *vice versa*.

This chapter examines the justification of punishment. After discussing its definition, we will consider five models: retribution, deterrence, rehabilitation, restorative justice and a unified theory of punishment that aims to bring these different penal aims together. We will find that each model of punishment can be understood in different ways. So, to claim to be a "retributivist" could refer to numerous approaches with consequences for how it might work in practice. More importantly, these theories do not exist in a vacuum – they exist

*Political Philosophy: The Fundamentals*, First Edition. Thom Brooks.
© 2025 John Wiley & Sons Ltd. Published 2025 by John Wiley & Sons Ltd.

as responses to crime and so it is crucial we can view the two together. Any theory of punishment must be applicable to acts or omissions that we would want to criminalize. It should meet a high justificatory bar, too. Individuals have rights. If we are to justify the state interfering with our rights, then this is a serious matter that demands we exercise caution and ensure any use of punishment meets this test. This chapter will examine different ways of approaching these issues.

## 6.2   Defining Punishment

Before considering *theories* about justifying punishment, we must first consider the issue of what it *is*. We can define through several conditions. The *first condition* is that the kind of punishment we are interested in is where someone has broken the law. We talk of "punishment" in many different contexts. For example, suppose our child does not complete their homework. We might say that they were "punished" by not being allowed to watch television or play games. Or consider a case where your employer became upset that a colleague came into the office late so they "punished" them with extra work. In these hypothetical examples, someone is punished in a colloquial sense, but in a very different way from how legal punishment works. For instance, when a parent punishes their child, they act for whatever reason they find most appropriate: the matter is mostly private between parent and child. Different parents may enforce different rules on their children and in various ways. Likewise, employers may treat employee lateness in multiple ways largely at the company's discretion.

What these examples have in common is that rules may be arbitrary and so too the consequences for breaking them. Parents may raise their children and employers discipline their employees however they like within strict legal limits. State punishment is very different. The rule of law requires that we apply the same rules to everyone. We cannot apply different standards from one person to the next to decide if someone has broken the law or how they might be punished for it. Moreover, the rules we apply are part of a criminal justice system within our democratic state. This entails that the laws binding on us have legitimacy that can warrant our obedience. So, while we may often speak of "punishment" in various contexts, this is probably best described as disciplining in non-legal circumstances. *Punishment* is inextricably connected to the breaking of state-sanctioned laws and administered by public institutions. Or, in the words of Cesare Beccaria, "only the law determines the cases in which a man deserves punishment" (Beccaria 1986: 53).

The *second condition* is that punishment is a response to crime. One famous distinction, made by Joel Feinberg, claims "penalties" are different from "punishments" (Feinberg 1970: 95–98). He defines penalties as fines and warnings, while punishment is understood as hard treatment such as prison. The difference is that punishments are not only more severe, but, critically, he claims that only punishments are justified as an expression of the public's censure of the offender's conduct.

Feinberg's distinction is problematic. First, fines and warnings can express public censure for wrongful conduct, too. Indeed, *any* state sanction might do this. For instance, a monetary fine might be a far less severe sanction than a year in prison. But this difference is proportional in terms of the amount of censure that might be expressed – where a more severe sanction would convey greater censure. They are not different categories. Second, Feinburg sets up the distinction as if our only options are to impose *either* a fine *or* imprisonment when we punish, but not both together. However, the fact is that most convicted offenders do not receive only a custodial sentence and, if they do, it is common for sentencing to include financial penalties, including reparations, in combination. So, it is a mistake to see the choice of penal options as an either-or of one or two alternatives with different justificatory sources: both might be imposed on an offender for the same crime and at the same time. Instead, it is more accurate to define punishment *as a response* to crime which might take multiple forms, including in combination. This is consistent with the first condition that we only punish lawbreaking and punishment is a response to it.

The *third condition* is that punishment must be of a person for breaking the law. This is an important requirement. Suppose a murder took place on your street. If punishment need only be a response to lawbreaking *in general*, then we might be justified in punishing *anybody* we liked as a crime had happened – whether or not they did it. This would be deeply objectionable, as innocent people should not be punished for crimes they did not commit. When we punish in response to a crime, we must only punish the person(s) who broke the law(s). An implication of this view is that we cannot justify the punishment of the innocent. If the state were to jail an innocent person, this would be unjustified. Strictly speaking, an innocent individual sentenced is *wronged* rather than *punished* (Brooks 2021a: 4).

The *fourth condition* is that punishment must be administered and imposed intentionally by an authority within a legal system. This requires that punishment is dispensed in a specific way. Imagine we come across a thief carrying recently stolen smartphones. The thief has committed a crime and punishment is a legitimate response. However, we could not take matters into our hands and simply "punish" him however we thought justified on the spot. We convict offenders through a the relevant legal system and it is this process that determines which crimes are committed and how, if at all, offenders are punished. Punishment is not imposed arbitrarily, but an intentional sanction imposed by the state on an individual for committing crime.

The *fifth condition* is that punishment must involve a loss. This can be understood in a myriad of ways, such as a loss of liberty, a loss of money because of a fine or some degree of suffering. That punishment must involve loss does not reduce punishment to a form of sadism. Not all losses are justifiable and any that are imposed must be supported in relation to some justificatory penal purpose. It is required that punishment imposes some burden, otherwise it would reward, subject to legal safeguards.

Finally, punishment must have a *general justifying aim* and a *distribution* (Hart 2008: 4). The general justifying aim is the general justificatory purpose for punishing. Any punishment must meet the five conditions spelled out above. This does not tell us which purpose is intended for punishing nor which is most compelling. This general aim justifies the imposition of punishment. But this begs the question of its amount. The distribution of punishment refers to how we achieve punishment's aims. For example, if we claim punishment's justifying aim is to deter future offenders, we must also have some means of understanding how this amount of punishment is to be determined. We will now consider several possible justifying aims.

## 6.3   Retribution

Perhaps the most familiar – and most misunderstood – theory of punishment is *retribution*. Its definition is deceptively simple, but can be understood in complex ways. Generally speaking, retributivists claim that punishment is justified when offenders *deserve* it and in *proportion* to their deserts. Retributivism is a broadly deontological theory where punishment is merited when deserved and without regard for its consequences as a result. The basic idea is that offenders must have offended to be punished. Desert is necessary and sufficient for justifying punishment. Their punishment is set in proportion to their offense. But this is where the simplicity ends.

Retributivism is sometimes thought to be synonymous with vengeance, but this is a mistake. Retribution is punishment administered by the state. However, vengeance is where private individuals take matters into their own hands "punishing" individuals they believe deserving as much as they think deserved. On the contrary, retribution is not a private judgment about desert and proportionality outside the rule of law. Instead, retribution is where punishment is deserved in proportion to crimes as determined by public institutions within the criminal justice system. Vengeance is arbitrary as individuals doing the same kinds of crimes might be punished radically differently depending on who was doing vengeance. In contrast, retribution aims to treat like cases alike where the deserving receive the same kinds of punishment in proportion to their wrongs.

The *lex talionis* (or "eye for an eye") found in the Code of Hammurabi is a retributivist principle that helps makes clear how retribution differs from vengeance. First, punishment is public justice. The *lex talionis* makes explicit that the law and punishment for any breaches is to be imposed by the state. This is opposite to vengeance which is not public justice, but private violence. Second, the *lex talionis* stipulates clear limits. While a system enforcing "eye for an eye" or "tooth for a tooth" will look extreme, even macabre, to contemporary readers and for good reason, the key element to focus on is that justified punishments is strictly proportionate. In other words, an offender who takes an eye loses an eye, but not their life.

But this leads us to the thorny issue of what serves as desert and sets these limits. Classic retributivists defined having desert as possessing moral responsibility for wrongful conduct. For example, Kant says:

> whatever undeserved evil you inflict upon another within the people, you inflict upon yourself. If you insult him, you insult yourself; if you steal from him, you steal from yourself; if you strike him, you strike yourself; if you kill him, you kill yourself (Kant 1996b: 106 [6:333]).

Crimes are defined as varieties of "undeserved evil." However, not all evils are equally immoral. We cannot strike someone who had only insulted, nor may we kill someone that had stolen property. Retributivists punish crimes like murder and theft because they are deemed to be forms of "undeserved evil." However, they would not punish them the same way. Instead, retributivists would punish crimes like murder more severely than theft because they would argue murder is the greater evil and, therefore, should be punished more severely than theft. For retributivists, we generally punish proportion to where a crime is thought to sit on along a scale of its evilness.

This broad view that we punish the deserving for their moral responsibility for evil conduct is widely popular, too. If I ask students to name the first kinds of crime that come to their minds, the usual reply is to name crimes such as murder, theft and assault. These crimes are identified as wrongful in every major religion and philosophical theory. It is easy to see all crimes as evil with examples like these. Moreover, most people would say that crimes like murder and theft are wrongs that should be prohibited even if they were not illegal already. Such crimes can be classified sometimes as *mala in se* which means that they are wrongs-in-themselves independently of any state declaring them as crimes.

The first problem with seeing desert linked to immorality is that, simply put, we disagree about which moral theory is best and, therefore, can disagree about what desert is. This is because different moral theories may justify different views about desert. For example, someone who is a deontologist applying Kant's moral law may claim that some conduct is immoral that somebody else who is a consequentialist might not accept. In other words, on the one hand, a Kantian following the moral law might argue that we avoid certain actions because they are wrongful regardless of their potentially positive effects. On the other hand, a consequentialist might claim we ought to do those actions due to their potentially positive effects. Thus, the Kantian might punish all forms of lying as a moral law breach, while the utilitarian punishes only some lies depending on whether utility is maximized. Different views about morality can mean differences about what is deserved and why. This disagreement does not require us to reject retributivism. The point is that what counts for desert and how we proportionately distribute punishment in relation to it can differ from one moral theory to the next.

A second problem is more significant: namely, that not all crimes are immoral. Possible examples include drug offenses and most traffic violations. Some might add prostitution and sex work although this is controversial. The argument is that these kinds of activities are not necessarily immoral. We might think it is discourteous, even selfish, to discover someone has parked their car illegally especially if it blocked street traffic. But if our double parking blocked no one's movement, this would not appear to be a wrong for any other reason than it is simply illegal, even if not obviously wrongful. Likewise, possessing cannabis in New York City was illegal when I was growing up in the vicinity about 20 years ago. But now it is widely available from smoke shops. Has cannabis possession become morally justified by the waving of time's magic wand? Perhaps views about its wrongness have changed during my lifetime, but the key relevant factor is that it is no longer unlawful. The view that cannabis use is wrongful is still held by many people despite this change. This example highlights the idea of crimes as *mala prohibita* which means that they are wrongful primarily because they are prohibited, and their wrongfulness may change over time.

A third problem is that retributivism claims punishment is deserved when someone is morally responsible for evil conduct. This is problematic if the unlawful conduct is not itself immoral, but we can go further. Most criminal offenses are crimes of *strict liability*. This means that, in law, one's responsibility – moral, causal, or otherwise – is irrelevant for receiving a conviction. To take a few common examples found in most jurisdictions: drug possession is usually proven by the fact that drugs were found on one's person and mistaking it for something else is no defense, driving above speed limits is unlawful regardless of how excellent the driver nor how clear the driving conditions are and statutory rape occurs whenever there is sexual intercourse with anyone under the age of consent regardless of circumstances. This range shows that strict liability crimes can be across the spectrum of seriousness. If retributivists want to insist moral responsibility always matters, they would need to rewrite most of our criminal laws creating various defenses for where our responsibility was impaired or absent.

Perhaps one of the bigger challenges for retributivists is the need to know that we are morally responsible for immorality and how much we are. Kant says:

> The real morality of actions, their merit or guilt, even that of our own conduct, thus remains entirely hidden from us. Our imputation can refer only to the empirical character. How much of this character is ascribable to the pure effect of freedom, how much to mere nature, that is, to faults of temperament for which there is no responsibility, or to its happy constitution, can never be determined, and upon it therefore no perfectly just judgments can be passed (Kant 1998: [A552/B580]).

Kant's point is that we can determine retributivist punishments imperfectly at best when making a link to other's "real morality" behind an action. We cannot read the minds, nor hearts, of others with any certainty. We can render no perfect judgment that others did, in fact, possess desert and determine its proportional value. Such human error is inevitable. Yet, this does not mean no judgment can be made or that retributivism is theoretically impossible. In practice, we apply standards like *beyond a reasonable doubt* in making our best efforts to discern others' desert and set punishment in proportion to their deservedness as best we can.[1] After all, what more can we do?

There are a variety of other ways that retributivists have attempted to understand desert and proportionality. Many have noted the difficulties of applying strict proportionality. For example, suppose that we have a system of punishing offenders in like cases alike. If someone murders another, then they are punished by death. But what if they steal property, such as my bicycle?[2] It seems absurd to say that we should simply steal it back, or perhaps take a second bike from the

---

[1] When this is applied to capital punishment, the problem of ascertaining desert is far more serious. If we know that no such judgment about another's desert can be made perfectly, then we know that mistakes will be made. This is perhaps inevitable for any human-run institution. But if the errors we anticipate might lead to our knowingly, foreseeably and avoidably executing individuals who will later be found innocent, we lack a means to remedy our mistakes (assuming life imprisonment is an available option). Of course, someone might not be condemned but sentenced for many years and, despite pleading their innocence, may die in prison before exonerating evidence comes to light. In these cases, we were mistaken but not acting in a way that would make a remedy impossible as exoneration remained an option. This is a different situation from executing someone on the mistaken belief that they were deserving, only to discover later on that they were not. It is on this basis that I have argued that retributivists should reject the use of capital punishment on grounds of desert. The finality of execution is incompatible with a making of judgments where we know remedies should remain available when any errors are made. This is all the more important given that we cannot know in advance which cases, nor kinds of cases, of individuals sentenced to death will later lead to exoneration no matter how unanimous a jury, a compelling narrative and all appeals exhausted. We know this because it has happened that future scientific evidence may come to light that confirms mistakes are made even in cases like these. This argument for why retributivists should oppose the death penalty is cited in the case *Santiago II* where, in my native US state, the Connecticut Supreme Court ruled the death penalty unconstitutional in Connecticut. I very much hope other states follow this Court's lead. See Brooks (2011b: 232–245) and *State v. Santiago (Santiago II)* (2015).

[2] I note for any interested readers that, this example is not entirely hypothetical. When I was younger, my father made me a bespoke BMX bike at his bicycle store which was subsequently stolen from our home and never recovered afterwards. It is the same store, Ed's Enterprises, where I once fixed a flat tire for a bike used by former US President George W. Bush's daughters when visiting the area, as his uncle (and brother of his father, when George Bush the elder was the US President at that time), was a regular customer.

thief for our own. Or what if someone did criminal damage like scratching my car door with a key? It would similarly sound nonsensical to argue that we should do criminal damage to the offender's car or other belongings in a form of retaliation. While the idea of strict proportionality may sound attractive *in the abstract*, punishing crimes in a like for like manner *in practice* leads to mostly absurd and objectionable results.

As an alternative option to strict proportionality is *proportional retribution*. This is defined by Jeffrey Reiman:

> Proportional retributivism, then, in requiring hat the worst crime be punished by the society's worst punishment and so on, could be understood as translating the offender's just desert into its nearest equivalent in the society's table of morally acceptable punishments (Reiman 1985: 129).

This model works by creating two separate lists. The first ranks the crimes to be punished from the worst to the least worst. The second list ranks the available range of justified punishments from the most to the least severe. We then start at the top linking the most severe punishment to the worst crime and then scale down from there (e.g., link the second most severe punishment with the second worst crime and so on until all are paired). The benefit of this view is that we can set punishments in proportion to crimes, but without our endorsing any punishments that we find objectionable and overly harsh. For example, we might simply rule out the death penalty and set a different punishment as part of our list of what would be acceptable punishments to apply to the convicted.

The main problem with proportional retributivism is that it does not link crimes and punishments in a way that is proportionate to the specific desert of a crime. For example, the worst crime is connected to the most severe available punishment, but this link is made only because they both so happen to be at the same place within separate lists. Suppose we changed our minds and put a different form of punishment at the top of our list of the most severe punishments that we would support. This would change the rank pairings of crimes and punishments. While crimes and punishments might be proportionate to each other *in relation to where they stand within a separate list*, there is *no internal connection based on shared desert* that links them. This is problematic as retributivism demands such a link and it is absent in this form of proportional retribution.

A further problem is it seems impractical to simply link pairs of crimes with a corresponding punishment. This is because perhaps we want to punish two different crimes the same way, such as by life imprisonment. It is far from clear that the badness of crimes has such a strict ranking whereby every variety of punishment can be linked to only one crime. If this were so, then only one crime could be punished by life imprisonment or only one crime could be punished by 12 months in prison. Of course, in practice, most crimes do not have mandatory sentences, such as a compulsory life sentence for specified violent crimes. Instead, most crimes have an upper limit whereby we punish *no more than* a year or some other amount. Thus, to link any crime with a particular amount of punishment is impractical and unrealistic. It is more plausible to argue that we link *categories* of crime based on deserved seriousness to similarly serious *categories* of punishments. In other words, we might claim the most violent or dangerous crimes are of a similar category of wrongfulness for which they share a link to the same kind of penal severity, such as all being punishable by life imprisonment. This kind of approach to proportionality can account for the similarities in wrongfulness with shared proportionality in outcomes that is more defensible.

A further issue is the relevance of harmfulness. This view applies Mill's harm principle, which states that the only justification for interfering with the liberty of others is "to prevent harm to others" (Mill 1989: 13). This view speaks to a wide range of cases, such as violent crimes, which we would want to punish. Problem can arise here with how we define harm and whether we think it is overinclusive or underinclusive. For example, Mill's definition explicitly claims that it is the "harm to others" that justifies intervention and not harm to self. This makes sense our criminalizing behavior like murder, assault and theft as harms to other people. Mill's harm principle excludes cases where a harm is only done to oneself or perhaps no one at all. Examples might include drug possession, traffic offenses or, more controversially, prostitution.[3]

It is not always clear whether an unlawful activity should be seen as a harm to self versus a harm to others. For instance, consider an

---

[3] Prostitution is a contested example. Those who argue that individuals can consent to engage in sex work will claim this activity should be criminal. Any attempt to make it unlawful would be seen as rendering a victimless crime, such as making it unlawful because it is deemed immoral even if no one "harmed" in some other sense. Those who claim that it is an activity that we cannot or should not consent to, including on grounds of wider structural inequality that render it unjust, will argue prostitution should be unlawful and because those who engage it are harmed, directly or indirectly.

addict's use of banned substances. Illegal drug use might be normally thought a harm to self. After all, it is the addict who is using the banned substance and putting himself directly at risk of any related negative impacts on their health. Yet, surely, addicts' behavior can impact their loved ones in a variety of ways. Addicts may harm themselves in feeding their addiction, but they may also harm those around them by the impact of their doing so. So, then does this mean illegal drug use is a harm to others, too? Or does it matter whether they have family, friends or some support network or not? I raise the question to highlight the ways in which fine lines can be difficult to draw.

Furthermore, not all harm to others is obviously warranting punishment either. Players in contact sports can become injured during the normal course of play. Imagine Alice swings her foot to kick a soccer ball in order to score a winning goal; but, instead, she hits Becky in the leg – perhaps as Becky tries to steal the ball away. There is no recognized crime in such cases as the law makes an exception for them, but is the harm principle consistent with it? After all, there is harm done to others. Or think about prize fighters in a boxing match. While this is legal, it is clearly a case where there is harm to others. Would the harm principle allow boxing or would it be inconsistent?

A key distinction is made by Alan Brudner. He argues that we should think about harm in a particular way: namely, not as a harm to morality nor a physical harm injury arising out of consensual activities; but, instead, where there is *harm to our autonomy* (which he calls *legal retributivism*) (Brudner 2009). In these cases, there is harm and it is nonconsensual. Brudner's legal retributivist approach can distinguish between soccer players who get injured and boxers from a thug who assaults a victim. Relevant harm is best understood as a harm to our autonomy.

A final option is *expressivism*. This is defined by Feinberg as:

> At its best, in civilized and democratic countries, punishment surely expresses the community's strong disapproval of what the criminal did. Indeed, it can be said that punishment expresses the judgement (as distinct from any emotions) of the community that what the criminal did was wrong (Feinberg 1970: 100).

In other words, we punish offenders because we condemn their conduct. Their punishment is proportionate to our condemnation. Feinberg is clear that this is not mob justice or punishing others because they are disliked. He is surely right that when the state punishes, it officially certifies public censure. Being sent to imprison sends a message that one has done wrong to some serious degree.

But how distinct is expressivism? It is unclear why it might be practically speaking indistinguishable from retribution. For Feinberg, we do not punish individuals because they are unpopular, but because they did a wrong that is criminalized. So, what is doing the justificatory work is that offenders deserve their punishment. It then seems clear that someone would be punished if it was deserved, and even if the public were not overly condemnatory of the relevant act. (And it is unclear how their censure would be measured without continual opinion surveys that would regularly update sentencing guidelines.) Moreover, it is also clear that if the public strongly disliked conduct that was not criminal, then no punishment would happen. These illustrations highlight the ways that expressivists would punish the deserving to the degree deserved without strictly following public displeasure if it did not closely track desert. Put simply, public condemnation only seems relevant when it supports punishing the deserving, but because it is deserved and not necessarily because the public condemn the behavior to the same deserved degree. Expressivism and retributivism seem the same in practical terms.

An important revision of Feinberg's expressivism is developed by Antony Duff. He argues that punishment is not merely the expression of public censure, but a "communication" whereby offenders are thought to express their remorse back to the community while in prison. Duff claims we must treat offenders "as if he had apologized . . . He might not have paid the apologetic debt owed . . . But something like that debt has been extracted from him" (Duff 2001: 123–124). The difference with Feinberg's expressivism is that Duff's communicative theory is as follows. In Feinberg's expressivism, he claims we punish criminals in proportion to the public's condemnation although in practice we only punish to the degree deserved. The expressivism works one way from the community to the offender. In Duff's communicative theory, the public expresses condemnation and punishment is distributed in proportion to this, but also the offender is assumed to "commute" an apology back even if they never do. The communication works both ways from the community to the offender and then back to the community. However, in practice, offenders need not do anything but serve the prison sentence they are thought to deserve. So, once again, the communicative theory is essentially retributivist whereby we punish the deserving in proportion to the degree deserved even if this amount were different from what a community might want to communicate and irrespective of whatever an offender does (or does not) communicate back. In practice, there is little difference between how expressivism and communicative theory would actually work – and both are consistent with retributivism.

## 6.4   Deterrence

The main alternative penal theories to retributivism are consequentialist. Perhaps the best known of these is *deterrence*. This general theory holds that the main justifying aim of punishment is to deter would-be offenders from committing crimes. The idea is that if punishments deter crime then its beneficial consequences justify the distribution of punishment. Rather than retributivists who justify punishment because it is deserved, deterrent theorists look to punishment's effects.

Deterrent theorists argue that individuals will avoid choosing to engage in crime if the costs of doing so outweigh its benefits. As Hume argues:

> 'Tis indeed certain, that as all human laws are founded on rewards and punishments, 'tis suppos'd as a fundamental principle, that these motives have an influence on the mind, and both produce the good and prevent the evil actions (Hume 2000: 410).

Deterrence presupposes that we each calculate the expected gains and losses that might be a consequence of some conduct. We seek to motivate compliance through fear of punishment. Suppose someone wanted to steal my bicycle. Deterrent theorists claim that we must set the severity of punishment sufficiently high so that it would deter the would-be thief from committing crime.

Deterrence can take two forms. The first is what I call *macrodeterrence* (or general deterrence). This is where we punish an offender to deter the wider public. When we punish an individual offender for a crime, we use them as a means to sending a warning to others to avoid committing that crime themselves by demonstrating what punishment they would receive in order to dissuade others from criminal activities The second form is called *microdeterrence* (or special deterrence). This is where we punish the offender to specifically deter that individual offender from reoffending in the future. It is captured by Mill, who says: "You do not punish one person in order that another may be deterred. The other is deterred, not by the punishment of the first, but the expectation of being punished himself" (Mill 1984: 78). When considering deterrent punishments, we must therefore consider who do we want to influence and dissuade from crime: the general public or the specific offender?

Deterrence should be considered separately from theories of *incapacitation*. These claim the aim of punishment is to incapacitate offenders by taking them out of society and holding them in prisons to reduce crime (O'Flaherty 2018: 216–243). The main flaw with this view is that it could justify imprisoning everyone whether or not they were guilty. This is because if everyone was in prison then no one would be in society to commit crimes. But such a conclusion is absurd.[4]

The primary criticism of deterrence theories is that they could justify the punishment of the innocent. If the punishment is justified by its consequences and the punishment of an innocent person would cause less crime, then innocent people might be punished and justified because of its beneficial consequences. Indeed, some deterrent proponents, like Beccaria, make this point claiming it would be necessary to execute an innocent person if his death was "the only real way of restraining others from committing crimes" (Beccaria 1986: 46). The ends can justify the means.

However, it is not obvious that deterrent punishments should punish the underserving. Suppose the legal system incorporates a range of deterrent threats. Citizens are warned that, if they commit a crime, there will be a deterrent consequence. It could be argued that a system of threats would not punish the innocent. This is because citizens are only punished if, and only if, they fail to heed warnings and do break the law. If they did not, they had respected the threat and avoided criminality. Punishment is only distributed to those who perform crimes and, thus, who did not need the threat of punishment if they engaged in crime. Deterrent punishment would not be justified for anyone innocent (Ellis 2003).

---

[4] This conclusion is absurd for the further reason that it assumes that offenders in prison cannot commit crimes. But, of course, crimes can occur virtually everywhere – and they too often do, including when imprisoned.

A second criticism concerns the *problem of the undeterrable*. If deterrent punishments are justified by their effect on reducing reoffending, what of offenders who is not dissuaded and whose behavior does not change? Since achieving future consequences is crucial, this seems a challenge. If certain individuals were undeterrable, then their punishment might not be justified on grounds of microdeterrence. Instead, punishment might only be warranted on grounds of macrodeterrence, if there was some effect on others among the general public who were deterrable unlike the undeterrable offender.

A third criticism concerns defining success. No one argues the aim of every deterrent punishment is to deter every crime in future; nor do they argue merely for some deterrent effect.[5] The first is too strong; the latter is too weak. Instead, deterrent theories aim at some substantial effect in between these two extremes. In essence, deterrence is reductivist insofar as it aims to reduce crime.

"How much punishment is enough for deterrence, if not all individuals will be deterred?" is a difficult question to answer. This is further complicated by our *not* knowing the full deterrent effects. Think about it. How many people *almost* had their bicycle stolen today, but this was avoided because the potential thief *feared* being punished? We can only measure changes in recorded crime and use this as a yardstick for evidencing if, or when, a policy has any discernible effect on crime reduction. But such measures do not tell us the total number that might have committed a crime if not for their fear of being punished. Furthermore, all this assumes that most of us have an idea of our likely punishment if we did commit a crime – which we don't have. Everybody knows arson is a crime. But do you know the likely sentence if you were convicted? Few do and yet we don't do it. This may strongly suggest that the primary reason why we most often avoid criminality is because we simply think it is wrong for us to do it. We are not motivated by the threat of punishment, but avoid crime because we accept the law and choose to follow it (Beccaria 1986: 51, Green 1986: 113–136).

Deterrence theories also have a unique *problem of time and changing effects*. Suppose you could know the right punishment for a crime that will deter. You change the sentencing rules so that there are all

---

[5] One possible exception is Johann Gottlieb Fichte who said that "the threat of punishment aims to. . . never be necessary." However, this seems more a utopian wish than realistic aim. See Fichte (2000: 228).

set at the right level. The problem with deterrence theories is that the deterrent potential of any crime is constantly changing as social conditions change. So, what might have an effect *today* might be counterproductive *tomorrow*. Moreover, our data will always be measuring actions from the past. In other wordsm by the time we implement changes informed by our studies about what deters, the conditions may have changed again and leaving our evidence-based model out of date. Perhaps such skepticism is misplaced and potential deterrent effects do not shift so quickly over time. But we must remain on guard for their constant shifting regardless. There is no such thing as one, and only one, justified deterrent punishment for every crime and for all time. Deterrent effects can change as our perceptions of crime changes.

Perhaps the biggest issue is whether it matters for most people whether deterrence works, if we could even discern that it does so. In a famous study, it examined support for and opposition against capital punishment (Kahan 1999). Those who favored capital punishment said they did so because it deterred. When asked if they would change their mind if conclusively shown it did not have the effect any longer, they said no because murderers deserved execution. Those who opposed the practice claimed they objected because the death penalty did not deter. But when they, too, were asked if they would change their mind if an effect were proven, they said no because they did not think the state should execute citizens.

The lesson that was drawn from this is that many people presented their public view as evidenced by facts, not their personal values, so to appear objective to others. But it was a mistake to think that any policy maker would win opponents to their side if a deterrent effect could be proven or rejected because the real reason why people took a side was because of their views about relevant values relating to desert and state conduct. Think about your own views. Would you change your mind if the data changed about deterrent effects? Kahan's study makes the case that our values shape our position irrespectively.

## 6.5    Rehabilitation and Restoration

Rehabilitative theories of punishment claim that we should reform offenders in prisoners so that they do not reoffend on release. Like deterrence, rehabilitation theories are also justified in reference to their success in achieving consequences like crime reduction. While deterrence theories aim to reduce crime through the fear of punishment, rehabilitative theories aim to reduce crime through reformative punishment that rehabilitates offenders to avoid future criminality.

Most offenders are released. Their likelihood of reoffending increases each time they are imprisoned, as it gets increasingly more difficult to find economic security and build positive support networks. Some might claim that it should get harder – after all, they have done wrongs and there should be consequences. Nevertheless, this leaves a problem that our criminal justice system may be *criminogenic* insofar as it can turn a one-off convict into a repeat offender over time and with little hope of breaking out of the reoffending cycle. So, we might choose to mete out just deserts or send a deterrent message, but if we want less crime then offenders need to be supported through reform to change behaviors away from criminal activities, or so rehabilitative theorists argue.

One rehabilitative approach is to view punishment like a "medicalization" of crime (Johnstone 1988). Bertrand Russell argues:

> I merely wish to suggest that we should treat the criminal as we treat a man suffering from plague. Each is a public danger, each must have his liberty curtailed until he has ceased to be a danger. But the man suffering from plague is an object of sympathy and commiseration whereas the criminal is an object of execration. This is quite irrational. And it is because of this difference of attitude that our prisons are so much less successful in curing criminal tendencies than our hospitals are in curing disease (Russell 1925: 62).

For Russell, crime is not a moral failure, but a kind of social sickness. Crime is like a pathology to be diagnosed and cured. No doubt many criminals have medical conditions that could benefit from a more healing-driven approach. It is common to find mental health problems, drug and alcohol addictions, and behavioral management challenges. Offenders lack skills and training to find decent work after prison to reintegrate into society and rebuild their lives as law-abiding citizens.

The issue with viewing criminals like ill patients needing treatment is it removes the agency from all criminals. They are the sick; we are the healers. They are the patients; we are the doctors. Reform in prison becomes a one-way street where the state acts and the offender receives, but without any responsibility for their rehabilitation back to law-abidingness.

A second approach is the *moral education theory* of punishment championed by Jean Hampton. She claims rehabilitation should be understood as involving "the inculcation of moral principles" (Honderich 1969: 90). Crimes are moral wrongs. To avoid future criminality, offenders need a greater understanding of why they are moral wrongs. A moral education will ensure offenders are reformed so that they refrain from future offending. Hampton says:

> Thus, according to moral education theory, punishment is not intended as a way of conditioning a human being to do what society wants her to do (in the way that an animal is conditioned by an electrified fence to stay within a pasture); rather, the theory maintains that punishment is intended as a way of teaching the wrongdoer that the action she did (or wants to do) is forbidden because it is morally wrong and should not be done for that reason (Hampton 1984: 212).

This approach claims punishment's aim is to morally educate. If offenders had a better understanding of morally wrongs, they would avoid committing crimes. A problem with this approach is its assumption that all crimes are immoral and not wrongs only because prohibited. As we saw above with retribution, there is reason to question whether all crimes are wrongs according to a single moral view – and, even if many were, not all crimes account for moral responsibility, such as strict liability offenses, so whether one has a more enlightened moral sensibility is no guarantee that criminality will be avoided.

All rehabilitative theories face criticisms around individualization. Suppose Eric and Frank are both convicted of assault. Their crimes are the same kind and equally wrong. The difference is that Frank was immediately apologetic and deeply remorseful about his crime. If we are to rehabilitate according to how long it takes to morally educate, we might punish Frank much less than Eric. In this case, we would punish offenders committing the same crimes for very different lengths. Some readers might think this could be warranted especially if Eric simply takes a bit longer to understand his errors. But let us now suppose that Eric is unapologetic about assaulting a victim and Frank is a deeply remorseful murderer eager to make amends. If our aim is simply to morally educate, Frank seems a less serious case than Eric as the former takes responsibility for his wrongs while Eric does not. But this may sit uncomfortably with some readers. We may instinctively, and retributively, believe Frank deserves greater punishment regardless of who is the most remorseful. Moreover, imprisoning someone until they accept their wrongdoing could lead to punishments that go on far longer than otherwise deserved for no positive consequence.

A newer alternative to the reform and rehabilitation of offenders is *restorative justice*. Most theories of punishment are conceived as theories to be applied from the judge's bench. Restorative justice is different. Its aim is to restore the standing of an offender within a community through an informal process involving dialogue and collaborative engagement. This can take a wide range of forms from resolving conflict between students in schools to South Africa's Truth and Reconciliation Commission. We shall reflect here only on the use of restorative justice as an alternative to sentencing offenders in court drawing on its use in England and Wales (Brooks 2021a: 76–79).

In the UK context, individuals charged with usually minor offenses (and often minors themselves) can have a choice. They can go to court where some short time in prison could be possible or they could engage in restorative justice. If they opt for restorative justice, one big advantage is that prison is not an option provided agreements are honored.

Restorative justice usually takes the form of victim and offender mediation.[6] This is an informal meeting chaired by a trained facilitator who administers the meeting akin to a magistrate holding court in a space like a normal office building. Restorative meetings do not happen at the courthouse: there are no wigs or gowns (as might be found in the UK), no gavels (as might be found in a United States courtroom) and no other formalities. The focus is on dialogue and healing conflict, not the vagaries of the traditional trial process. While both parties may bring a lawyer, this is rare and victims and offenders play an active role speaking for themselves.

Typically, restorative meetings begin with the offender accepting their guilt and make an apology to the victim. The victim has an opportunity to explain the impact of the crime on them. This can be useful in instilling in offenders that their actions have consequences

---

[6] A second format is the restorative conference. This has the same membership as victim and offender mediation, but in conferences the victim and offender may bring a partner or someone to support them. Additionally, there are usually also some representatives from the community present, too. Several of my students have sat on these panels. Typically, these are involve youth justice rather than adult offenders.

on real people that can help them better understand their wrongs to desist in future. The offender has an opportunity to explain why they did what they did. This can provide closure for victims who can see the offender as a fellow citizen.

The facilitator then engages both in a discussion over what terms should be made in a restorative contract. These can be expected to include several hours of community sentencing, a requirement to attend any relevant drug or alcohol treatment meetings, cognitive behavioral treatment if necessary, and some token of reparation to the victim. If the offender does not agree to the restorative contract, he then heads to court and the usual formal process begins. Should the offender agree to the contract, but not fulfill its terms, he may go to court and face the formal process in the same way as if he had never agreed a restorative contract in the first place. But if the contract is agreed and the offender fulfills its terms, he is "restored" and the matter resolved. This means that not only might the offender avoid the possibility of prison, but successful completion of the contract means he will not have a criminal record either. The offender's status resumes to full citizen.

Restorative justice has grown in popularity over the last two decades as studies have found significant benefits in its use. Studies have found about 85% of victims are satisfied with the process which is dramatically higher than their satisfaction with the formal court process. This is likely due to the fact that more than nine in every 10 cases do not go to trial, and victims can rarely participate in trials concerning crimes that happened to them. The same findings show that restorative justice can lead to up to 25% less reoffending than alternatives as well – and all at a cost savings of £9 for every £1 spent (Sherman et al. 2015).

There are various criticisms raised against restorative justice. The first is that if restorative contracts are not honored in full, then the offender can proceed to trial and plead not guilty with the court unable to acknowledge the earlier acceptance of guilt and apology to victims made in the restorative framework. In my view, this deeply undermines the importance of restoration itself. An offender's apology to a victim and agreement to take constructive efforts to make amends is a serious matter and should be taken more seriously within the criminal justice system. Some have argued that admissions of guilt should be legally binding and that failure to fulfill an agreed contract should entail the possibility of prison, an option that might have otherwise been used at first anyway (Brooks 2017b).

The second criticism is that restorative justice is not a real theory of punishment because it is not applicable to all crimes, especially more violent offenses. This is because restorative justice rules out the use of hard treatment, including imprisonment. For its supporters, this is a good thing because, they claim, prisons often make the problem of preventing reoffending much worse. But for opponents of restorative justice, the worry is that some crimes demand possible hard treatment and, since restorative justice would not consider it, restorative justice is only used in much less serious cases, often involving youths.

## 6.6 Unified Theory of Punishment

What is the aim of punishment? We have considered several models. Each claims a single general justifying aim. Retributivists argue that we must punish the deserving proportionately. Deterrence proponents argue that punishment should lead to crime reduction. Rehabilitation and restorative justice advocates claim we must ensure offenders are less likely to re-offend after conviction.

Most philosophers have seen this as a choice: we pick one theory and then defend against the others. This is because each theory has a different justifying aim and these can pull in different directions. Suppose we wanted to punish the deserving *and* deter others. The amount of punishment someone might be said to deserve could be different from the amount needed to deter. We could easily find ourselves having to choose one or the other. If we only distribute punishment to what is deserved, this could be more than needed to deter. But, if we punish sufficient to deter, it might be less than is deserved. Doing two or more at the same time seems impossible.

Our inability to punish according to multiple penal purposes — what I call *penal pluralism* — might be a matter of regret. After all, punishments that were deserved, proportionate, deterrent, and rehabilitative – unifying the main purposes of punishment – might seem the *ideal* penal theory, if only it were realizable. Interestingly, there is an American Model Penal Code that sets out "the general purposes" for sentencing in a pluralistic way. These purposes are:

a. to prevent the commission of offenses;
b. to promote the correction and rehabilitation of offenders;
c. to safeguard offenders against excessive, disproportionate or arbitrary punishment;

d.   to give fair warning of the nature of the sentences that may be imposed on conviction of an offense;
e.   to differentiate offenders with a view to a just individualization in their treatment (American Law Institute 1962: Section 1.02).

The Code makes clear that punishment has multiple aims, including prevention, rehabilitation, proportionality, desert, and publicity. One of the most notable aspects is that the Code's intended purposes – namely, to create a model for use by the individual American states – had an influence that was profound. Since its launch, every US state that has created sentencing guidelines since the Code's launch has done so by enacting in law that punishment has multiple penal purposes similar to what is found in the Code.

Its influence made it across the Atlantic, too. The UK's Sentencing Act 2020 in force in England and Wales states that a court "must have regard to the following purposes of sentencing" including:

(a)  the punishment of offenders,
(b)  the reduction of crime (including its reduction by deterrence),
(c)  the reform and rehabilitation of offenders,
(d)  the protection of the public, and
(e)  the making of reparation by the offenders to persons affected by their offences (Sentencing Act 2020).

The legal guidance states that the court must have regard to one or more sentencing purposes. Punishment is *only* justified in reference to these purposes. The court may appeal to whichever purpose or purposes it chooses to. This cannot be challenged: in other words, justifying punishment on grounds of deterrence that did not, in fact, lead to crime reduction would not undermine the legitimacy of the sentence imposed by a judge. However, there is no guidance for how these different penal purposes should be chosen nor how two or more purposes can work together.

This background makes clear a division. While many philosophers adopt an approach defending only a single purpose to avoid incompatibility between purposes, judges adopt an approach relying on multiple penal purposes but without a framework for providing some coherent way of distributing punishment. Nor is there a rationale for why these five penal purposes and not others, which might give the impression that judges simply pick-and-mix principles from this list. If the philosophers are right, our sentencing practices are incoherent and should change. So, is a *unified theory* of punishment possible?

The answer is *no* if we see existing penal purposes occupying the same weight. We cannot ensure every measure of desert can work coherently with every effort to deter when seeking to do both at the same time. This has led some, like Rawls and Hart, to argue for a two-stage solution (Rawls 1955, Hart 2008). Their idea is that legislatures create laws with a deterrent effect looking to the future, but judiciaries determine actual punishments retributively looking to the past.

This attempted solution does not work. Its problem is the disconnection between how punishments are set versus how they are imposed. If crimes are only punished retributively based on what an offender deserves without consideration of consequences, it is difficult to see how desert and deterrence are combined when the practical effect is a retributivist system with no one punished with regard to its anticipated future effects. Perhaps we might argue that to punish proportionately will have some deterrent effect, but punishment's aim would still be retributively linked to the desert and not an integration of different purposes.

A compelling answer can only be found by identifying some new overarching purpose for punishment that might structure an organize our existing purposes like desert, deterrence, and rehabilitation in a coherent way. If so, different peal purposes might work together in support of some higher goal. An insight into how this might work is made by Hegel, who says:

> Punishment, for example, has various determinations: it is retributive, a deterrent example as well, a threat used by the law as a deterrent, and also it brings the criminal to his senses and reforms him. Each of these different determinations has been considered *the ground* of punishment, because each is an essential determination, and therefore the others as distinct from it, are determined as merely contingent relatively to it. *But the one which is taken as ground is still not the whole punishment itself* (Hegel 1969: 465).

This cryptic passage can be interpreted as making two important claims. The first is that punishment should not be considered retribution, deterrence, *or* rehabilitation. Instead, we should see it as retribution, deterrence, *and* rehabilitation. They are three parts of the same thing. The second claim is that they do not have equal weight. The ground of punishment is not "the whole punishment itself." This is echoed by Green, who was an early exponent of Hegel's philosophy in the late 19th Century, who argued "it is commonly asked whether punishment according to its proper nature is retributive or preventative or reformatory. The true answer is that it is and should be *all three*" (Green 1986: 178).

In my work, I have developed a model built off these historical insights to show how a unified theory of punishment is possible and compelling (Brooks 2016a, Brooks 2017c). It starts from the premise that the criminal law aims at the protection of our legal rights. Crimes are violations of our rights and punishment is a response to their infringement. Thus, the aim of punishment is to protect and maintain our rights as a form of self-defense. For example, if someone steals from me, they breach my right to possess property. Their punishment aims to restore my rights in a way that is deserved, proportionate and secures rights we all share.

This raises the question of how this amount should be determined and punishment applied. Of course, not all rights have equal weight. Some will have greater value than others. For example, my right to life is weightier than my right to possess property. Indeed, my right to property takes for granted that my life is secured. The unified theory of punishment punishes crimes in proportion to the importance of the rights infringed. As Green argues:

> a violation of a right, requires a punishment, of which the kind and amount must depend on the relative importance of the right and of the extent to which its general exercise is threatened. Thus every theory of rights in detail must be followed by, or indeed implies, a corresponding theory of punishment in detail (Green 1986: 177, see Brooks 2012a).

This position is developed still further by James Seth, who says:

> The view of the object of punishment gives the true measure of its amount. This is found not in the amount of moral depravity which the crime reveals, but in the importance of the right violated, relatively to the system of rights of which it forms a part . . . The measure of the punishment is, in short, the measure of social necessity; and this necessity is a changing one (Seth 1898: 305).

Punishment is only deserved if a crime is committed. Crimes are punished differently according to the right infringed in order to protect and maintain the right. This ordering is intuitive. Our rights in protection from violent infringements seem weightier than minor, victimless crimes. Getting this correct requires engaged debate and discussion within a community about its system of rights and the values they embody.

An implication of this view is that crime is a necessary, but not sufficient, condition for punishment. If punishment was not required to protect a right under certain circumstances, then this theory of punishment could warrant pardons or mercy. A further implication is that the importance of rights will change over time, in light of changing social contexts. As circumstances change so too might how we choose to punish crimes. What we criminalize and how we punish will change over time in light of how we, as a community, understand the rights we wish to protect and maintain within our legal system.

A unified theory of punishment aims to protect and maintain rights infringed by crime. It provides a coherent framework for applying penal pluralism without different purposes clashing with each other when we punish (Brooks 2021a: 158–161). Any such punishment must be deserved insofar as an individual must have infringed another's right. The specific combination and amount of crime reduction measures (either preventative or rehabilitative), restorative options and expressivism will all depend on an assessment of what best set of options most effectively protect our rights overall with a view to the future. Crime reduction or rehabilitative measures can play important roles in so far as they facilitate the maintenance and protection of rights. Moreover, and perhaps controversially, the unified theory would choose less costly options where they are roughly similar as part of our rights is ensuring public resources are spent responsibly with regard to value for money. It is a curiosity that most other theories ignore costs: that there is no price too high to pay to deliver retributivism, deterrence, or rehabilitation if the theory calls for it. The unified theory sees cost as the least weighty factor, but no less important.

If penal pluralism is to succeed, it requires some organizing principle that can structure how underlying principles can work coherently. Otherwise, these principles can pull in different directions and render their use unworkable together. The unified theory of punishment is possible if we base it on the purpose of protecting and maintaining rights. We determine punishments in relation to their supporting this overriding, unifying aim. The severity of the punishment distributed is proportionate to the importance of the corresponding infringed right. This can provide a framework used by judges for organizing their use of two or more penal purposes in sentencing decisions.

## 6.7   Conclusion

Every society punishes crimes, but here are very different views about which way of punishing is best. This chapter has considered the definition of punishment and its key distinctions. We have examined the main theories of punishment, such as retribution, deterrence and rehabilitation, and the question of whether it is possible to combine all three into a unified theory.

The power to punish its citizens is one of the most coercive that is exercised by the state against its members. Understandably, it requires a high justificatory threshold. It is hoped that readers will understand more clearly how views of freedom, rights and justice relate to theories of punishment. There remain many other issues to consider, such as how we might justify punishment under different theories. But readers should now have some understanding of how these theories might be applied and consider the merits of rights-based approaches.

## Further Reading

Brooks, Thom. 2021. *Punishment: A Critical Introduction*, 2nd edition. London: Routledge.

Easton, Susan and Christine Piper. 2005. *Sentencing and Punishment: The Quest for Justice*. Oxford: Oxford University Press.

Hart, H. L. A. 1968. *Punishment and Responsibility: Essays in the Philosophy of Law*. Oxford: Oxford University Press.

von Hirsch, Andrew, Andrew Ashworth and Julian Roberts, eds. 2009. *Principled Sentencing: Readings on Theory and Policy*, 3rd edition. Oxford: Hart.

# 7

# Global Justice

## 7.1 Introduction

When I first studied political philosophy, its focus in every lecture was about the freedom, rights and justice that we might enjoy within a shared political community like a state. I do not recall ever being asked to study any texts either classic or contemporary that dealt with global affairs. In his famous *A Theory of Justice*, John Rawls claims to offer a theory of justice for a state that we enter at birth and exit at death; it was a realistic utopia, not a view about justice across borders (Rawls 1999). Rawls's work defined debates in political theory for decades and these focused on justice *within* the state. Political philosophy was about domestic justice. Discussion relatively rarely addressed global issues and global justice.

Everything seems to have changed ever since. Global justice has become one of the biggest and most vibrant fields in political thought today. For many students, the pendulum has swung the other way from my undergraduate days: most of the political thought that they might learn about now is not domestic justice, but global justice. It is easy to see why. We live in a climate emergency and a world where large populations live in severe poverty. These issues represent major challenges for all of us and political philosophy has much to offer in support for how we might understand and grapple with them.

*Political Philosophy: The Fundamentals*, First Edition. Thom Brooks.
© 2025 John Wiley & Sons Ltd. Published 2025 by John Wiley & Sons Ltd.

This chapter focuses on broadly two debates. The first is a fundamental question of our relation to each other and wider humanity. One view is that our primary political identity is located within the state in what is called liberal nationalism. Cosmopolitanism is the second, which claims we are citizens of the world. Each side will be examined. The second debate is about which approach is best to understand our duties, as citizens of affluent countries, to distant individuals living in severe poverty. We will consider the views of positive duties, negative duties and a connection theory of remedial responsibility that aims to bring positive and negative duties together. In examining these ideas, we will engage with issues like self-determination and migration. Climate change is discussed in the final chapter.

## 7.2   Liberal Nationalism

Nationalism can have different meanings. *Classical nationalism* originally conceives of individuals as members of a nation (Miscevic 2020). Their identity is defined through the sharing of common origins, ethnicity, language and perhaps other cultural ties. National membership was generally an identity that individuals were given at birth rather than an identity that was chosen. Historically, many countries were organized as nation-states and where traditionally the community members all shared the same form of national connection. Of course, there can be many longstanding myths about our homogeneity in a collective past. For as long as there have been people, there has been migration. People from different cultures and tradition have engaged, interacted and created families together since the dawn of human history. So, we should remain clear that there is always difference within our communal lives.

The classical view of nationalism is often criticized for basing its view of community on an arbitrary basis, such as one's given ethno-cultural identity. As arbitrary and not a product of choice at birth, political philosophers argue such bonds are threadbare, lack normative justification and are essentially problematic.

This classical view has been superseded by what is called *liberal nationalism* (Brock 2009: 248–273). Liberal nationals see nations as "ethical communities" and not defined through morally arbitrary characteristics like our ethnicity (Miller 1999: 49). Instead, these communities share a connection that has ethical significance. Miller argues:

> Because I identify with my family, my college, or my local community,
> I properly acknowledge obligations to members of these groups that
> are distinct from the obligations I owe to people generally. Seeing
> myself as a member, I feel a loyalty to the group, and this expresses
> itself, among other things, in my giving special weight to the interests
> of fellow-members (Miller 1999: 65).

Identities that are formed through a common character and culture
can carry normative significance. These connections are products of
choice and effort. Contrast this with a group of randomly assembled
individuals we might call a *random nation*. This kind of nation might
be said to have members, but they share only the connection of their
being arbitrarily located to it. Random nation might exist as an aggregate of individuals within a shred territory, but it is *not* an ethical kind
of community. On the contrary, a national community is more than a
collection; it is a *collectivity* sharing an active collective life that is
lived together (Brooks 2023b: 46). This might find expression through
a shared language, group memory, common expressions or cultural
traditions. Liberal nationalism is where individuals are connected to
each other and identify as such.

Liberal nationalism exists within boundaries, but the lines are
drawn around the individual members rather than a piece of land.
This is because the boundary is essentially *ethical*, and *not territorial*,
in its nature (Goodin 1988). The shared communal bonds are the ethical glue that keep members together, not merely their living in close
proximity to each other. This holds them together and defines their
ethical landscape. It is different from what we would find in the random nation example, defined mostly by individuals merely inhabiting
a shared piece of land and lacking any ethical or cultural link.

The bonds of collectivity that create a liberal nationalist community can give rise to *special duties* (or also called "associative duties")
to its members relating to each other (Seglow 2010). In other words,
I can have special obligations to other members based on our shared
communal connection. These are duties that I have only to those with
whom I have a special, not general, connection that is ethical and
duty-generating between us. For example, we might seek to organize
ourselves politically, including conducting elections, creating
community-specific forms of governance and managing public institutions operating from within our community. An ethical community
is more than a place where its members live their lives together; it is

where they create ethical bonds of connection that create duties between members, too.

The way we construct our communal bonds can distinguish our communities from other communities. This is an important insight from Bhikhu Parekh, who argues:

> The identity of a political community consists of those constitutive features that define and distinguish it from others and make it *this* community rather than some other . . . Members of a political community seek to make sense of it and its history, from a general conception of the kind of community it is, and arrive at some form of self-understanding (Parekh 2008: 59–60).

In constructing our community through the shared and specific ethical bonds joining individuals together into a collective project, we shape how we collectively identify ourselves in concert with others in our community and distinguish ourselves from other communities collectively identifying in their own ways. In so doing, we shape and define ourselves in ways that can differentiate our community from others. While the process of community building and the character of associated ethical bonds may be broadly similar everywhere, the direction that is taken and the content that is developed of a community's shared understanding of who they are as a collectivity can differ in significant ways from one community to the next. Thus, a community's sense of itself as "American," "British" or "Chinese" can share similar features relating to each possessing a sense of collective belong, cultural identities and more, but while each having very different histories and ethical content.

Perhaps paradoxically, we may view liberal nationalism as communities other than nations (Brooks 2014b). This is, in part, because other forms of connection can also give rise to intrinsically valuable shared identities that may have normative significance. One example is religious organizations. These may co-create many of the kinds of features we might find with liberal nationalism more generally, such as a shared language, a common historical narrative about the community of belief, cultural traditions, and a strong sense of collective identity (Margalit and Raz 1990). Moreover, it is a collective, whether a church, mosque, synagogue or temple, that can act in matters of global justice, such as helping deliver aid, provide resources, or general support. Thus, it might be argued that we can have a liberal nationalism beyond nations, as these ethical bonds creating duties can exist in these non-national communities, too.

## 7.3   Cosmopolitanism

The main alternative to liberal nationalism is called *cosmopolitanism*. This is the view that all human beings share moral equality. Each individual is "the ultimate unit of moral concern and to be entitled to equal consideration regardless of nationality or citizenship" (Tan 2004: 1, see Held 2010). Nobody chooses the country of their birth. It is arbitrary from a normative point of view that I am born *here* instead of *there*, wherever this might be. It is likewise normatively arbitrary that I begin life as a part of *this* family or raised within the care of *this* community. Likewise, our citizenship is given to us. It is not chosen by us although it might have been chosen for us by others, such as our parents or guardians. Either way, we are of where we began.

Cosmopolitans claim this normative context matters enormously. While we do not choose where we are born nor who raises us, these factors can have a profound, even decisive, impact on our future life chances. For instance, someone born into abject poverty struggling to meet basic needs is more likely to remain in poverty and die much younger than somebody else that spends their lifetime within an affluent society and the many advantages that brings. Those living in severe poverty may lack education and employment prospects, as well as opportunities more generally to enjoy a flourishing future that furthers their individual interests in whatever ways they might value. In contrast, those in affluent societies will have options to choose with greater control over the direction they desire for their lives with the means, the knowledge and the considerably longer lifespan to enjoy it all. A normatively arbitrary start in life can make all the difference to the kind of life we end up with. Cosmopolitans see such inequalities of wealth and well-being as deeply problematic.

The ancient Greek philosopher Diogenes the Cynic famously said "I am a citizen of the world" in perhaps the best known (and repeated) statement of classic cosmopolitanism (Nussbaum 2002: 2). In fact, this view actually expresses the root of the original Greek word for "cosmopolitan," which is *kosmopolitēs*, which literally means "citizen of the world."

There are different ways of understanding cosmopolitanism. One distinction is between the moral and institutional. A *moral cosmopolitanism* claims that all human beings are members of a collective moral community. The moral rights individuals possess are the same across state borders everywhere.[1] This is contrasted with the view of *institutional cosmopolitanism*. This view claims that we are universally bound by global institutions that bring us together and support common standards internationally (Beitz 1999).[2] Of course, these two cosmopolitanisms may overlap. For example, we might argue that our membership in a global moral community might justify the creation of global institutions that foster and protect their flourishing across our world. An illustration might be international human rights regimes. These are born from claims of universal rights requiring protection, such as through international institutional agreements with enforcement bodies to support them.

A second distinction is between weak and strong. A *weak cosmopolitanism* is the view that everyone's claim to justice should be satisfied at least up to some global minimal threshold. This position can be found virtually everywhere, including in the work of non-cosmopolitans. As David Miller, a liberal nationalist, observes, if ensuring that every individual enjoys the same kind of basic liberties and rights protections to at least a common benchmark is what cosmopolitanism, then "we could safely say that we are all cosmopolitans now" (Miller 2007: 28). The differences between liberal nationalists and weak cosmopolitans is not found in whether they think all individuals are entitled to a shared global standard of justice across borders, but rather where this global standard is set. Liberal nationalists tend to focus on securing a more minimal view of "basic needs" up to a minimal common threshold where all must meet this

---

[1] It is sometimes said that moral cosmopolitanism is a moral view that applies the same way to all human beings on our planet. However, strictly speaking, while this is correct, it is also the case that moral cosmopolitanism would apply to all human beings on Earth and in outer space, if people should populate other planets, as the ethical bond is our shared humanity which knows no borders on this planet or extended across other planets. I would be interested and pleased to know if readers consider further how cosmopolitanism might apply to human beings across multiple worlds.

[2] Institutional cosmopolitanism can be further distinguished between a cosmopolitanism where institutional connections are limited to this planet and an institutional cosmopolitanism where institutions were interplanetary.

level while other countries may well do much better[3] In contrast, cosmopolitans claim that we should instead endorse a more substantive level of well-being setting the bar higher than mere basic needs. An example is Nussbaum's capabilities approach, where all 10 capabilities must be available at least up to a common threshold for everyone focused on securing human flourishing for everyone.[4]

An alternative view is *strong cosmopolitanism*. This is the view that everyone shares the same claim to justice to the same degree. The rights for the individual are the rights that should be shared by everyone. Thus, there should be no substantive variations between the basic liberties and well-being someone enjoys in one country versus those of another person in a different country. While it might be morally arbitrary where we are born and which society are brought up in, human beings have equal moral worth and so we should receive equal moral treatment. On this view, where I live should make no moral difference to my moral worth nor equality of welfare. To allow unequal treatment based on state or national membership is to permit morally arbitrary features make a substantive moral difference to individual life chances. Strong cosmopolitans find this incoherent, inconsistent and unjustified.

There are many examples of political philosophers defending strong cosmopolitan claims to universal rights, often inspired by Kant's universal moral law (Kant 1957). For example, Simon Caney argues that everyone "should have the same opportunities to achieve a position, independently of what nation or state or class or religion or ethnic group they belong to" (Caney 2001: 114). Our individual claims are universal, and so we should all be able to pursue them equally, irrespective of where we are.

However, these claims for equal universal treatment often fall far short of calls for a world-state, although there are notable exceptions (Cabrera 2020: 53–70). The most commonly expressed concern is with practicality; namely, that we may all have the same claims, but creating and maintaining a functioning global system that administers the same practical protections for billions of people from all corners of the globe is impractical. It can difficult for any existing state to get

---

[3] See Miller (2007: 163–200). For a notable cosmopolitan exception, see Brock (2009: 65–75).

[4] See Nussbaum (2011: 17–45). On her cosmopolitanism more broadly, see Nussbaum (2019).

it right all the time for its own citizens. To demand that a world-state composed of every human being manage this is impractical and perhaps impossible.

These different views of liberal nationalists and cosmopolitans are relevant in how we might approach major global issues, such as immigration. For example, we live in a world with borders; these are factually given, even if not always normatively justified. For liberal nationalists, these boundaries matter and have special significance. This is because they conceive these borders as essentially encircling a community of individuals that share some substantive ethical connection, ideally as an ethical community. People have the right to self-determination and to forge their conception of justice for its members. These associations can, in their view, create special duties among community members that relate to each other but not to other non-members. We see this in the rights of citizenship. Individuals with citizenship have full rights of community membership, including permanent residency, unrestricted opportunities to pursue employment, stand for political office if desired and vote in elections. Non-members may have only rights to enjoy temporary residency on a fixed-term basis, be restricted in which employers or sectors they might find work in, lack options for direct political participation and be denied a voice in elections. Community membership matters, as self-determined by a community, in practical ways that we find in our own individual communities today.

When non-members seek to cross this border, they are not merely stepping over a line into some new *geographical* space, but crossing into a different *ethical* space that those community members occupy. If immigrants are to become a part of the shared ethical bonds of membership within a foreign community, they must not merely be present within its physical territory but integrate themselves more deeply in becoming a part of its ethical life. It is only when they too become a part of the normative fabric connecting members to each other within a community that they properly take on the special duties and obligations that come with community membership (Miller 2007: 376). Our ethical membership is both a process of identifying ourselves with the community — and of others in the community identifying with us (Parekh 2019: 65). In that way, the shared identity of a community is not fixed in stone and responsive to changes in its composition over time and this is inevitable. Nor is the process of becoming a member a one-way street of new members assimilating to however their new community might conceive of itself; but, rather, members old and new shape each other with the continually evolving identities found in any community. Nevertheless, liberal nationalists argue that the community may set its own terms for admitting immigrants and has a right to exclude them from membership.[5]

In contrast, cosmopolitans defend less stringent border controls. Some strong cosmopolitans may claim there should be none at all arguing that we ought to live in a borderless world. Cosmopolitans argue for our having primarily *general duties* that are owed to everyone everywhere. We may have duties to show equal concern and respect, for example, to all individuals regardless of their nationality. Our borders are normatively arbitrary and so they should not significantly impact life chances so substantially differently from one community to another. This view does not require that I must immigrate from countries that have substantial severe poverty to those with affluence. But it does mean that no one should be condemned to enjoying worse well-being than others simply because of where they happened to be born and not because of the exercise of their freely made choices about where to live.

It is notable that where liberal nationals speak about the need for integration, they talk about citizenship in broadly principled terms. For example, immigrants seeking to naturalize ought to know, respect, and uphold key values that are part of the ethical bonds that make a collection of individuals into a coherent, co-created community. Yet, when we inquire into what these values should be, we find that the values of good citizenship for one community are broadly the same as those for good citizenship everywhere else. For example, the government-approved list of fundamental British values includes democracy, the rule of law, individual liberty, and mutual respect and tolerance for those of different faiths and beliefs. Of course, how these values might become realized can differ from one community to the next. For example, supporting the value of democracy might mean a presidential system for one state and a parliamentary system in another. The forms these take may variate, but their essential substance remains the same. So, while the principle values of citizenship may be universal, the specific demands of being a citizen may vary

---

[5] These exclusions are usually justified where non-arbitrary. For example, a community might deny membership to individuals deemed a public danger or where otherwise not in the public interest, but not because of arbitrary factors like being too tall or short.

and be specific to each community (Brooks 2016b, Brooks 2022b, Brooks 2022c, Parekh 2000). Therefore, the ways in which Americans and British citizens enjoy their shared values in each community might be very different, but the general values themselves – to democracy, to rule of law, individual liberty and mutual respect for others – are broadly similar. The ways in which we achieve good citizenship for one community is similar to how we achieve good citizenship in others.

## 7.4   Tackling Severe Poverty

Global justice covers many issues. The most prominent of these is surely international distributive justice. This concerns the complex human tragedies around severe poverty in our world. No discussion about global justice can ignore it.

Severe poverty is where individuals live a minimal existence suffering from deprivation. Of the eight billion people alive today, nearly half live on less than $6.85 a day. Hundreds of millions live on much less than this. While so many experience real hardship in their daily lives, many others enjoy great wealth and privilege. These deep inequalities between affluent states and the global poor raise pressing questions about what, if any, duties those with wealth have toward those in need. Political philosophers have defended three broad views: positive duties, negative duties, and a connection theory of remedial responsibilities. We shall consider each in turn.

### 7.4.1   Positive Duties

One way to begin thinking about what, if any, duties those with affluence have to the global poor is to consider a thought experiment and perhaps one of the best known in philosophy. Peter Singer says:

> if I am walking past a shallow pond and see a child drowning in it, I ought to wade in and pull the child out. This will mean getting my clothes muddy but this is insignificant, while the death of the child would presumably be a very bad thing (Singer 1972: 231).

Let's call this the *drowning child* case. Imagine the scene. You are out for a walk. You come across a shallow pond. While walking past, you notice that there is a child drowning in the pond. The child cannot save themselves and requires rescue. An important assumption is that the example presupposes the situation involves only two people: namely, you and the child. There is no one else who might jump into the pond and rescue them. Only you might provide rescue. A second assumption is that we do not know how the child entered the pond in the first place. Perhaps they were safely walking along the pond's edge, but fell in deeper water. Maybe, unbeknownst to us, there is a third party who threw the child into the pond, intending to drown them. Any such background circumstances are bracketed out and put to the side. All that we do know is that there is a child drowning, and that only we alone are in a position to provide rescue to the child.

There may be costs involved in rescuing the child. For example, I might be wearing expensive clothes that could be ruined if I were to enter the pond to save the child. Singer says that the possibility of my clothes becoming muddy or otherwise damaged if I rescue the child is "insignificant." The insignificance he references is specifically to the relevant *moral cost* of damaging my clothes in saving the child. Singer argues: "if it is in our power to prevent something from happening without thereby sacrificing anything of comparable *moral* importance, we ought, *morally*, to do it" (Singer 1972: 231). What this means is that we should weigh the moral cost of our acting or doing *to us* against the moral cost of inaction *for others*. Singer's argument is that we morally ought to act if the moral cost to us in acting *is less* than the moral cost to others if we do not.

In the drowning child case, we must decide whether or not to act. The moral cost to us if we act is none. Our clothes might be expensive, but there is no moral cost in getting them muddy, only a financial cost which is morally irrelevant for Singer. We next consider the moral cost *to others* of our inaction. If we do not act, then the moral cost to the drowning child is that they will die. Singer's moral calculus has us weigh up the moral cost to us in acting against the moral cost to the drowning child if we do not act. Since the cost to us is only a muddy suit we might easily replace, but the cost to the child is their death, the moral cost of our not acting to save the child is greatest to the child. Singer's conclusion, therefore, is that we morally ought to save the child. And, of course, who would argue contrariwise that one should not rescue a drowning child in a shallow pond regardless?

Consider a different example. Suppose that we are going past the pond because we are being pursued by an assassin attempting to kill us. Call this *the drowning child and assassin* case. We are faced with a different choice in this scenario. If we are diverted to try to save the child, then the assassin will catch up and kill us. But if we do not save the child and so continue running, we will outpace the assassin and our lives will be saved although the child will drown. The moral cost to us saving the child is higher than our running away because we would be killed doing the former, but not the latter. So, in these different circumstances, we morally do not need save the child where our own life is put at risk.

Singer's example may seem only hypothetical, but its aim is to examine our moral intuitions. He argues that we have *positive duties* to assist and provide rescue to others. We are under a positive duty to help where we can help at no greater moral cost to ourselves than if we did not act. The example is meant to show that those in affluent countries should provide support to those in severe poverty because they can do so. We save those we can – and we have this duty even if we have nothing to do with why others need rescue in the first place. Our distance to others is immaterial. If we can provide support, we should do so where it is needed on balance of the moral costs involved.

While Singer's example and defense of positive duties is much cited and highly popular, it is worth noting a common concern about it. In the example, we are the adult in an active position to save others while those to be saved are children unable to help themselves. While the example is helpful at illuminating what positive duties are and their value, the concern is that as an analogy for addressing severe poverty the example is imperfect. For example, it may be argued that while affluent states may be like the adult able to provide rescue in many ways, they may also bear some responsibility for circumstances in which others are drowning. Moreover, it might be further said that states in severe poverty are not without agency; their sustainable future and flourishing is not simply assistance that others might offer to them, but a right that have for which others are under a duty to ensure, sustain and protect.

## 7.4.2   Negative Duties

An alternative view to positive duties is the idea that we are under an even stronger, and more stringent, *negative duty* if we had contributed in some way to the harm experienced by others. Consider the following example:

> You are walking alongside a pond. You watch an assassin throw someone in a pond. This someone will drown if not saved. Both the assassin and you could save them from drowning (Brooks 2023b: 84).

Both the assassin and you can save the child at no moral cost to yourselves in acting. You both have a positive duty to save the child. The weight of this positive duty is the same, as you both can equally save the child and just as easily as each other.

However, the assassin is under a more weighty *negative* duty to act in this case. This is not because the assassin can save the child more quickly, but because the assassin caused the problem in the first place. Those who are responsible for contributing to another's harm are under a negative duty to negate this harm and provide rescue to remedy it. But notice that where two might both have a positive duty to act, our intuitions likely find a negative duty a stronger reason to do so. If you and an assassin could each save this child, would we not think it was the assassin who had a stronger obligation to act because he had created the problem? If so, then negative duties appear to weigh more heavily than positive duties.

Now consider a different example:

> You are walking alongside a pond. You find two children drowning. You can only save one child.

Call these *two children in need*. Which do you choose? If we follow Singer's positive duties, then the moral cost of acting is less to you than the cost to the children if you do not. Does it matter which is saved? Strictly speaking, no. Neither has more claim to rescue than the other. No injustice to either would be done if we flipped a coin to help decide which we saved.

But suppose that one child was our child. Or not our child, but that the child is someone we know to be a fellow citizen sharing the same nationality as we have. If we can only save one child where two children are drowning, we would still have a positive duty to save one of them because the weight of moral costs has not changed: the moral cost to us in acting is less than the moral cost to the child we save in not acting. However, it can be argued that we would have special duties toward co-nationals and even more so toward our own child. When we weigh up a consideration of our positive duties plus our special duties, we would have an obligation to save our own child or a co-national. Thus, if we have equal duties to save both drowning children but can only save one, then our special duties toward a family or community member might tip the balance in our choosing them over a non-family or non-community member. Intuitively, it may seem wrong to randomly choose which child to save if one was our child. We might even find it cruel for our special connection to be disregarded. Furthermore, it might also seem wrong if our child was safely wading in the pond without difficulty and another's child was drowning that we might not act because our child was ok. Positive duties to act may apply generally whether or not we have an additional special duty to someone in need. However, our special duties can have relevance in determining how we exercise these duties.

A more intricate and controversial theory of negative duties is defended by Thomas Pogge. He builds an argument in several steps intended to show that citizens in affluent countries have a negative duty to provide support to those in global poverty. His argument could be summarized like this:

1. Citizens in affluent countries are predominantly in democracies.
2. Citizens elect their political leaders.
3. These leaders decide directly, or indirectly through those representing them, matters relating to an international global order.
4. The international global order includes institutions like the IMF and World Bank.
5. Through such institutions, the global order knowingly, foreseeably, and avoidably perpetuates a system that maintains severe poverty because its monetary agreements favor affluent states at the expense of developing countries and there are protectionist exemptions favoring affluent states as well (Pogge 2002: 18–19).

Pogge's conclusion is that citizens in affluent countries have a negative duty to those in global poverty. Their duty arises from their essential role in choosing those who make decisions about the international global order in an extended causal link. We have a negative duty to help others because, through our choices of leaders and the consequences of the decisions these leaders make that are detrimental to the global poor, we ultimately bear responsibility for it.

A corollary is that we also have a duty to vote for leaders who do *not* support continuing an international global order that perpetuates severe poverty. Pogge says: "World poverty is actively perpetuated by our governments and officials, and knowingly so. We citizens, too, have enough information to know what is going on, or at least to find out easily, if we care" (Pogge 2010: 2). Thus, we are all implicated and share collective responsibility for global poverty elsewhere – even if we did not vote or, if we did vote, did not foresee the possible consequences of doing so. A common criticism is there are a lot of "ifs" – if in an affluent state, if it is a democracy, if political leaders elected, if leaders decide matters relating to an international global order, if there is such an order and so on – that make any attribution of citizen responsibility for the decision-making of a global order seem weak and somewhat contrived. It might also be questioned how culpable citizens may be for decisions they may not know about, do not support nor can exercise any significant influence in changing in all, or even any, such circumstances.

### 7.4.3   Connection Theory

After considering the use of positive and negative duties, some may think they are insufficient for addressing the real-world challenges of severe poverty. One reason might be that we lack sufficient resources to help others in need as much as might be required. A second reason could be that there can be disputes over whether one state may have a negative duty to act, but they might claim that another state has more of a negative duty – and so, in the end, no one acts. A third reason could be that a community's poverty was caused by a natural disaster that had nothing to do with other states.

Such considerations lead to a new third option for thinking about what, if any, duties affluent states have to those in severe poverty beyond the debate between positive and negative duty proponents. This view is developed by David Miller. He argues:

> Nearly all of us believe that this is a situation that demands a remedy: someone should provide the resources to end the suffering and deprivation. The problem does not end here, but in deciding which particular agent or agents should put the bad situation right. Very often there are many agents who could act in this way. The issue is how to identify one particular agent, or group of agents, as having a particular responsibility to remedy the situation. For unless we do this, there is a danger that the suffering or deprivation will continue unabated, even though everyone agrees that it is morally intolerable, because no-one is willing to accept the responsibility to step in and relieve it (Miller 2001: 453).

Miller calls this a problem of *remedial responsibility*. In other words, we need to work out the responsibilities that states have to deliver remedies.

Miller's solution is to offer a *connection theory*. He claims that "the basic idea here is that A should be considered remedially responsible for P's condition when he is linked to P in one or more ways" (Miller 2007: 99). We examine the weight of connections between our state and those in need compared with other states' connections. The greater the weight of our connections, the stronger the duty on us to provide remedial relief.

Miller identifies six connections we must evaluate:

1. *Causal responsibility*: was a nation causally responsible for bringing about deprivation elsewhere? (Miller 2007: 101–102)
2. *Moral responsibility*: was a nation morally responsible for bringing about deprivation elsewhere? (Miller 2007: 100)
3. *Capacity*: does a nation have the capacity to provide a remedy? (Miller 2007: 103–104)
4. *Community*: is a nation part of a wider shared community with the nation suffering deprivation, such as through "ties of family or friendship, collegiality, religion, nationality, and so forth?" (Miller 2007: 104)
5. *Outcome responsibility*: is the deprivation faced elsewhere a side effect of any nation's conduct? (Miller 2007: 100–101)
6. *Benefit*: did a nation benefit from the deprivation elsewhere, even if it played no part in causing it? (Miller 2007: 102–103)

Miller's argument is that we weigh the relevance of each for our state's possible remedial responsibilities and then compare with that of others. There is no moral calculator at hand; we are simply to "rely on our intuitions about the relative importance of different sources of connection" (Miller 2007: 107). In his view, there is no connection that is intrinsically more valuable than any other. Miller explains:

> We might think, therefore, that some forms of connection should always be given priority over others; I shall argue, however, against this. The point to bear in mind is that the weight of justification is borne by the pressing need to relieve P and the necessity of identifying a particular agent as having the obligation to provide the relief. The fact that some of the links appear morally flimsy when taken by themselves matter less when this point is grasped (Miller 2007: 99–100).

This may make the task seem even more challenging and for good reason. If there is no rank order for how we might weigh these connections against each other and it is left to us to intuitively weigh up the relative connections in our minds, then it may seem obvious that different people may weigh them up the same circumstances and relevant connections very differently, perhaps profoundly so. As a result, this approach has the potential to make agreement on difficult matters about who should provide remedy to those who need it even more challenging.

A significant benefit of Miller's approach is it helps us reflect on how we might assign remedial responsibilities where a country is in need because of human-caused problems, but also where it lacks such a cause. Natural disasters may be more frequent and more devastating generally because of climate change – and this is not doubted. At the same time, natural disasters have existed before there were humans and human-caused climate change – and such disasters continue. While a view of negative duties is helpful for thinking about who has the weightiest responsibilities to remedy harms they contributed to, the connection theory seems better suited for reflecting on different countries with varying connections to others might organize remedial responses to situations where no one country is at fault. Whether caused by a state or by nature, we weight up our connections and use these to determine the relative duties that different countries have to provide remedies to others in need.

*How* this is to be applied is contestable. An example may make this concern clearer. Suppose country A has a moral responsibility for suffering in country B, perhaps due to an unprovoked military attack on country B to annex its lands. Otherwise, country A has no other connection with B. Country C is connected with B only insofar as they both share a common language that no other country uses. Country D has no connection to B other than their financially benefitting from B's misfortune. For instance, suppose an industry in B was devastated because of A's unprovoked military attack. While B's industry became ruined, a similar industry in D profited by having less competition when trading. So, let us weigh up the connections of A, C and D. What might Miller's connection theory say about which should do what to B?

I think most would say that A's moral responsibility connection carries the most weight. In fact, I think most would always say that A's moral responsibility for attacking B would trump other forms of responsibility or connection. Miller might claim connections are not formally equal, but it appears we would not, perhaps never, weigh them equally. He seems to acknowledge this fact when noting that "I assume . . . that negative duties weigh more heavily than positive ones" (Miller 2007: 107). This would give greater weight to our responsibility for contributing to deprivation above other factors.

But there is one connection more important than even moral responsibility. Consider the following connections for comparison where we create a new list of nations that each have a different relation to nation X which is in need:

1. Nation A is causally responsible for deprivation in Nation X.
2. Nation B is morally responsible for deprivation in Nation X.
3. Nation C has the capacity to provide a remedy to Nation X.
4. Nation D shares a national religion with Nation X.
5. Nation E is outcome responsible for deprivation in Nation X.
6. Nation F benefited from the deprivation in Nation X.

Suppose each nation listed (A, B, C, D, E, and F) has only that one connection to Nation X. The only decision we can make is to choose C. Whatever we think about the relative intuitive weight of the other factors, their relevance is to assign remedial responsibility. However, only C can provide any remedy. So, even if nation C has no other connection to nation X and has no responsibility for its deprivation, only nation C can remedy, and so only C can be remedially responsible.

This example shows that it is incoherent to claim that all connections can or should be weighed equally. If a nation lacks the capacity to remedy, then it cannot provide remedy under any circumstances. It does not make sense to claim a nation has a duty to provide remedy where it cannot do it. There is a difference between what a nation *ought* to do and what it *can* do. But if it cannot, then we are unable to insist it fulfills duties beyond its ability. Perhaps every parent ought to save their drowning child, but if the parent cannot swim and would drown in attempting to rescue it is unclear how we might enforce any such duty – and even if we still think the parent ought to risk their lives anyway.

The example above shows that, in fact, Miller's connection theory operates in a two-stage process (Brooks 2002a, Brooks 2011a). The first stage is to consider whether any nation can provide a remedy. If not, then they are not considered further. Weighing up the relative weight of other connections is practically pointless where this makes no difference to whether they can provide remedy, as they cannot do so.

At the second stage, we weigh the connections of only those who can provide remedy and assign remedial responsibilities in relation to which have the greater connections – and so who among those that can remedy possess the strongest connections to those in need. Miller's view is that it is wrong to claim that all connections have equal value, but if we adopt a two-stage process, his connection theory can offer an attractive and practical alternative to helping us decide who should remedy those who need it.

In adopting a two-stage process, we also combine positive and negative duties into a coherent framework. Our first stage identifies those nations that can exercise a positive duty to remedy. At the second stage, negative duty-related factors, such as relating to different forms of responsibility, are considered. In this way, both positive and negative duties are factored into distributing remedial responsibilities.

A criticism of this theory is that it helps us assign remedial responsibilities to those who need help here and now only. It might be said that this is quite an achievement in itself given the global challenges faced. However, in only counting those states that can remedy, it risks allowing rogue states to run wild. For example, consider the case of the *evil nation* (Brooks 2011a: 199–200). Evil nation desires and attempts to create severe poverty elsewhere at every opportunity. It has causal, moral and outcome responsibility – and perhaps has drawn some benefits from its evil actions toward others, as it profits from creating misery for others. However, assume that the evil nation exhausts all its resources on its efforts to spread suffering. This leaves it with no means to provide remedy.

It seems abundantly clear that an evil nation *ought* to face consequences for its wrongful conduct. On Miller's picture, it will always be left to other states to clear up the damage caused by evil nations, and evil nations might never have a duty to remedy those they harm. This example shows that while Miller's theory is helpful at assigning global responsibilities here and now, it requires a post-remedy third stage to ensure justice is done in the long term. Perhaps evil nation cannot remedy the harm they cause others today. But there must be some means of ensuring both that steps are taken to ensure they provide redress to those harmed over time and that no further harmful conduct should arise again. While political philosophers defending ideas of positive duties, negative duties and connection theory show ways in which we might think about our duties today to help those in need, we must reflect further on how this might be sustainable and justified over the longer term, too.

## 7.5   Conclusion

Global justice is about justice beyond borders. One important distinction is between liberal nationalism and cosmopolitanism. Each marks out different ideas about the place of the individuals in the world, highlighting general duties to all as well as our special duties to those with whom we co-create a shared community with practical implications for important issues like immigration and citizenship.

When most people think about global justice, they think about the need for affluent states to provide relief to those living in severe poverty. We have examined three different views: positive duties, negative duties and connection theory. These views offer three powerful ways of justifying duties toward those distant communities. This is a contested area and readers should reflect on which they find most persuasive. Should we simply help those we can whenever we can? Or should we insist that the only ones required to provide remedy are those who contributed to causing deprivation? Or should we think about the ability to remedy alongside the weight of connections? What to do about problems for which there are natural, not human, causes? These are questions that we must decide for ourselves.

The future of global justice work is toward a more globally informed view of justice. As I have argued elsewhere, the field of global justice is insufficiently global in terms of its inputs and outlook. Most of its leading contributions are created within a specific philosophical tradition without much, if any, reference to others although the capabilities approach is an important exception (Nussbaum 2000, Sen 2009). These views developed within a bounded tradition are then applied to global issues to inform how we should think about problems and search for solutions for communities where different philosophical traditions may flourish.

We should reflect on how we might co-create an unbounded approach to global justice where we develop our philosophical approaches using resources and insights found in different traditions elsewhere. This is a journey toward making our bounded views of global justice from one tradition to be applied universally become unbounded – and developing a more *global philosophy* (or rather a more globally informed way of thinking about global justice) to address the challenges of global justice (Brooks 2013b). This is not an argument for constructing one "true" philosophy that unifies insights from across all philosophies if that were even possible, but instead about drawing on a wider range of philosophical resources to make our global perspective more genuinely global (Brooks 2013b: 262). When readers reflect on what justice means for all, we should think more about what all think justice means – and so be sensitive to our cultural contexts, assumptions and related connections.

## Further Reading

Brock, Gillian. 2009. *Global Justice: A Cosmopolitan Account*. Oxford: Oxford University Press.

Brooks, Thom, ed. 2023. *The Global Justice Reader, revised edition*. Oxford: Blackwell.

Brooks, Thom. 2023. *Global Justice: An Introduction*. Oxford: Blackwell.

Singer, Peter. 1972. "Famine, Affluence and Morality," *Philosophy and Public Affairs* 1: 229–243.

# 8

# Climate Change

## 8.1 Introduction

Our climate is ever changing. There is a broad scientific consensus that our environment is warming, and a key contributing cause is our carbon emissions. As the Intergovernmental Panel on Climate Change has made clear, the fact of climate change is unequivocal (Intergovernmental Panel on Climate Change 2019). These changes have led to melting ice caps and rising sea levels that threaten coastal communities with flooding and increasingly submerge small island nations. Climate changes have made land that was fertile become arid and extend draught to new areas. Extreme weather events, like thunderstorms and tsunamis, have become more frequent and more devastating. Climate change is happening and impacting communities across all parts of the world (Gardiner 2011). Increasingly, we see what has been described as environmental refugees fleeing their homes for safer climates to thrive in. The problems associated with climate change impact us all.

If left unchecked, climate change could bring about an environmental catastrophe endangering human lives globally. Some fear that we are getting closer to a "tipping point" that, once passed, catastrophe could become unavoidable. It is unsurprising to hear claims that we are in a climate emergency requiring urgent action in order to bring

*Political Philosophy: The Fundamentals*, First Edition. Thom Brooks.
© 2025 John Wiley & Sons Ltd. Published 2025 by John Wiley & Sons Ltd.

climate change and its associated dangers under control and provide protection for future generations so that they might flourish.

But how? This chapter critically explores the two main approaches to managing climate change. The first is *mitigation*. It seeks to mitigate climate changes through greater conservationism whereby we reduce our impact on the planet by cutting carbon emissions. Mitigation efforts can take broadly two forms that we will examine. One is the idea that we should live within a restrictive limit on consumption; another idea is that we should impose a tax on polluters that incentivizes cuts to carbon emissions while making polluters pay to help address the problems arising from emissions more broadly.

A second approach is *adaptation*. This view claims that we should seek technological advances that enable us to adapt to everchanging climatic conditions. Adaptation can take multiple forms. One is technologies that allow us to maintain similar living standards more efficiently. Another form is in ways of living that adjust to our changing conditions so that the associated harms from climate change are mitigated or otherwise avoided. Thus, if rising sea levels are an issue, we might adapt by moving communities to higher ground or creating cities afloat at sea so that any problems from higher tides are managed sustainably.

While advocates do emphasize mitigation or adaptation as a primary aim, virtually all accept that we require some measure of both as a part of any policy solution. Therefore, mitigation advocates accept that climate change is already happening and so adaptation is necessary if only to make conservation efforts easier. Likewise, adaptation proponents argue that some degree of mitigation is essential as it would lead to less significant environmental changes and so make it easier for technology to provide the necessary means we require in to adapt to a changing climate. Therefore, we do not face a choice of mitigation *or* adaptation in these debates, but rather only which, if any, we should prioritize when balanced against the other.

What all such views have in common is a shared belief that climate change is a problem that can be *solved*. In other words, it is frequently claimed that, if only we adopted the right strategy, we could achieve permanent sustainability where climate change no longer causes difficulties: we can save the planet (Hillman 2008; Sachs 2008: 11–12, 83–114, 291–295; Bloomberg and Pope 2018). As I will explain in this chapter, this view is an issue because it gets the problem wrong. It attempts to either stop the climate from changing or create the means by which these changes may not impact us, but such positions are mistaken. It is as impossible to stop the climate changing as it is to prevent the world from turning. In fact, if we managed to reduce all carbon emissions right now to zero, there is already enough carbon emissions currently in our atmosphere to continue global warming for decades (Intergovernmental Panel on Climate Change 2020). Nor has the planet required human beings to consume resources for there to have been climatic catastrophe's in the Earth's past.

Instead of seeking a sustainable and continuous forever after based on a mythical view of the problem and our ability to manipulate the climate, our focus should rather be on what I will call impermanent sustainability as a more practical and realistic end. While environmental catastrophe may be inevitable no matter our efforts, our doing nothing will only make such a future worse coming more quickly with greater force and devastating consequences. Instead, we must look at sustainability differently, buying ourselves time, doing our utmost to adapt to an endangered world and managing our climate as best we can so it can be enjoyed for generations to come. Climate change is an ever bigger challenge than many of us may think, as will be explained.

## 8.2   Mitigation

The first main approach to climate change is *mitigation*. This approach is about conservation, in seeking to conserve a sustainable future. Mitigation is where we seek out ways that we can reduce our emissions so that our impact no longer contributes to further global warming. The idea is that mitigation aims at a perpetually sustainable level of environmental impact. If we maintain lower emissions, we can stop climate change's effects and so, in essence, the problems associated with climate change are cured and cause no further concerns.

One version of the mitigation approach is the *ecological footprint*. This is a measure of the Earth's human carrying capacity; or, in other words, the maximum amount of natural resource consumption that can be safely sustained indefinitely. Mathis Wackernagel and William F. Rees claim:

> The Ecological Footprint concept is simple yet potentially comprehensive . . . It is about humanity's continuing dependence on nature and what we can do to secure Earth's capacity to support a

humane existence for all in the future. Understanding our ecological constraints will make our sustainability strategies more effective and livable (Wackernagel and Rees 1996: 3).

The ecological footprint is a tool used to compare the differential environmental impacts we have in order to address future sustainability. We calculate our target footprint size by dividing up sustainable shares of the global ecosystem equally by the number of individuals on the planet (Wackernagel 2009). This measure is our ecological footprint. The footprint "is a measure and not a space," indicating a sustainable benchmark to measure the impact individuals have on the wider ecosystem but not a carving up of any particular territory (Brooks 2021b: 17).

We then consider the actual environmental impact for individuals. We do this by comparing the actual consumption per person versus the size of our ecological footprint. This may regularly reveal gaps that show we are consuming more than our share of a sustainable footprint. This, in turn, makes clear that, unless our consumption is reduced to within the size of an *ecological* footprint, our *actual* footprint is unsustainable and may contribute to further climate change.

The ecological footprint is thought a useful device for comparing the size of a country's actual footprint with where it ought to be. Of course, countries have different populations. What we do is we multiply the number of people in their country by the size of an equal ecological footprint. This provides a measure of what that country's sustainable footprint ought to be given its population. We then compare it with its actual consumption. This provides a measurement for determining if a country's environmental impact is sustainable or not, depending on whether their actual footprint is larger than their ecologically sustainably sized footprint.

The gap between what a country's footprint is and what it should be is a benefit of this mitigation approach. It is argued that it can show us how some states may owe an *ecological debt* to others if they are living far beyond their sustainable means (Simms 2009). For instance, Singer argues:

> The average Americans, by driving a car, eating a diet rich in the products of industrialized farming, keeping cool in the summer and warm in winter, and consuming products at a hitherto unknown rate, uses more than fifteen times as much of the global atmospheric sink as the average Indian (Singer 2004: 31).

In this example, Singer uses a similar measure to the ecological footprint. He compares a sustainable share of the atmospheric sink with the actual emissions impact. A sustainable share is what the atmosphere can sustainably absorb without contributing to climatic change and its associated problems. This allows Singer to make comparative assessments of whether we are emitting beyond what the atmosphere's carrying capacity can sustainably tolerate and to identify which countries most threaten global sustainability by their emissions. In turn, this helps us understand the restrictive limits that sustainability imposes on us, the potential gap we and other countries might have to cover in order to become sustainable and a sense of the problems globally in seeking a more sustainable planet.

Two features that are crucial to determining ecological footprint size can change over time. The first is the total size of the human population. If this should go up, then an equal sustainable share of ecological space will be less. This is because we would have to divide the same ecological space by a greater number of people and so equally sized shares would be smaller when there are more people. But if the global population should drop, then an individual share will be larger because there would be fewer people with whom to split up the ecological space. So, as the world's population grows, the equal size of our ecological footprint shrinks.[1]

The second feature is the ecological space itself. If its capacity to absorb emissions increases, then we might each have a larger share – and vice versa. This point is routinely overlooked. The Earth's atmospheric sink is not constantly at the same level perpetually unless human beings create emissions. Instead, it can and does change constantly (Peng et al. 2022). This creates an additional challenge. When seeking to divide the atmospheric sink into equal shares per person, it is a fact that both the sink and the overall human population are continually changing. This does not mean that no sized footprint can be determined, but it does mean that its amount is one we must continually refresh and revise.

---

[1] Hypothetically, one might seek to increase the size of ecological footprints through war which is a perverse result. If by war the global population was reduced, then footprint sizes could be increased. It is expressly *not* my view that the ecological footprint is a problem because it might create military conflict. I do not accept that view. Of course, any such action would breach international law and be self-defeating as well as an ecological and humanitarian disaster. Nevertheless, I note the hypothetical incentive that follows from the logic that fewer people mean larger footprints (see Brooks 2021b: 26).

The ecological footprint is hailed by its supporters as a reliable measure that is fair and equitable. However, there are some criticisms raised about its use. The first is that it is unclear that requiring the same-sized footprint for all treats everyone equally, even if everyone did have the same sized share (Caney 2012: 262). This is because there will be differences in energy needs at the beginning or the end of life that may be required by individuals at those times. So, requiring the same size does not impact everyone's well-being equally. Moreover, people living in very hot or cold climates will have different energy needs than others in temperate climates. For example, the energy needs of someone in the Arctic Circle will be different than somebody else living on a tropical island. It may be that to enjoy a similar standard of living more resources are required for heating or cooling in one area than in a moderate climatic area where few such needs arise. (I can promise readers that I have noticed climatic differences when living in Connecticut versus Arizona or the United Kingdom.) Again, the same-sized footprint can impact differently the well-being of people living in different climates. An equal size footprint does not treat everyone equally.

The second concern is that equally sized footprints can treat people unfairly because it could cement the dominance of affluent states over developing countries. As I have noted elsewhere:

> An equal per capita footprint would ossify – and render more permanent – the relative global positions of the more affluent and technologically advanced countries in contrast to developing countries, which lack such infrastructure. The former would be in a much better position to make the most from their limited footprint. This would permit them to better retain their position of global privilege over less capable societies (Brooks 2021b: 23).

Affluent states are already dominant in the global economy. These countries are better able to transition to living with more limited ecological shares because they possess post-industrial advanced economies. They could leave developing nations still in the process of industrializing more permanently behind.

This concern may seem trivial to some readers. For example, it might be said in reply that perhaps insisting everyone has the same footprint-sized environmental impact does have different consequences for people living in different areas. Or that it might even restrict progress on global economic equality. Nevertheless, the response might be that these are prices worth paying for a sustainable future.[2] It is worth reflecting on what inequalities would become justifiable as a consequence of ensuring a sustainable ever-after. While I will return to consider this point more fully below, I note here that this response assumes that equal shares impacting people unequally can be a price worth paying if it did manage to create a sustainable forever after. The problem, as I will explain shortly, is it cannot ensure climate change can be controlled and managed. Thus, the price we pay does not guarantee the sustainable future we seek on its own.

A second form of mitigation is the *polluter pays principle* (Caney 2005: 752). This is the idea that polluters should pay compensation to address the harm their pollution caused. It is based on the negative duty of polluters to act in order to rectify the damage they caused. The income raised becomes compensation which is used to minimize, if not negate, environmental damage. Moreover, the principle's advocates claim that by making polluting more expensive, the high costs are believed to incentivize less consumption and reduced emissions. Thus, the polluter pays principle has two facets. Its imposed higher costs on consumption are intended to reduce emissions to a sustainable level while providing a means of taxation whereby countries can use these funds to help mitigate and adapt to the planet in a sustainable way.

The first problem is that it is unclear how much polluters should be required to pay in order for these aspirations to become a reality. Not everyone agrees, such as James Garvey:

> It is a straightforward fact that some countries have emitted more greenhouse gases – used up more of the planet's sinks, caused more climate change – than others. It's a quantifiable fact: we know something about cumulative emissions (Garvey 2008: 115).

Of course, we do have data on cumulative emissions and can confirm that some countries pollute much more than others. One issue is the data does not go back especially far, and the further back we go, the less confidence there is in the data (Brooks 2023b: 147). A second issue is that it is unclear where to set a cutoff point, such as from what period are we seeking reliable data to inform how the principle works.

---

[2] I am grateful to Fabian Freyenhagen for pushing me on this important point.

The cut-off point matters because carbon emissions are already in the atmosphere and can linger for decades. If we are to make polluters pay, then we need to know from when polluters should pay and have an idea about what they need to pay for (e.g., emissions that may last decades after they are produced).

A bigger third issue is that many polluters cannot pay because they are already dead. Emissions can linger in our atmosphere for decades. Not every polluter responsible for some share of these emissions remains alive while their pollution is still with us. If polluters must pay for their pollution, there is already much pollution caused by polluters no longer here to pay for it. Of course, it is unrealistic to expect anyone but the living pay for their pollution. But if the principle is meant to require that all polluters pay for their emissions, it is a problem that many cannot.

But suppose we could get every polluter to pay from a specified date. There is still the problem of how they might provide compensation for climate change-related harms. We can act to correct environmental damage in many ways, such as through building flood defenses or creating genetically modified crops that can adapt to changing climatic conditions. Yet, we cannot reverse or negate all of the environmental damage caused. For example, what price should polluters pay if their emissions led to an island becoming submerged or if a species became extinct? Not all changes are matters for which paid compensation can be used to correct, as some are non-compensatory goods for which no price can meaningfully provide rectification.

The polluter pays principle claims to be a negative duty requiring polluters to pay and address harm they caused. However, polluters can pollute so long as they can pay the required amount. Indeed, we might call it the "polluter can pollute as much as they can afford" principle. This would not ensure mitigation because if I can keep paying when I pollute, then I can keep polluting without limit. Thus, the polluter pays principle cannot guarantee that global emissions will be at or below a sustainable amount as it allows wealthy polluters to create unsustainable emission levels.

There is an interesting distinction that might be drawn between a *fee* and a *fine* (Sandel 2005: 93–96). This difference is based on the view that only fines are for when we do wrong. Its relevance is that, if the polluter pays principle is essentially a kind of fine, it suggests no pollution at all should happen as fines are a kind of wrong. So, our focus should be on stopping pollution and not allowing it to continue, provided polluters can afford the cost. Otherwise, if the polluter pays principle was viewed as only a kind of fee, we might tolerate polluters paying the appropriate fee whenever they polluted regardless of its effects which seems counterproductive and not what advocates of the polluter pays principle want to defend.

Carbon emissions have been described as "the greatest market failure the world has ever seen" (Stern 2009: 11). The price of goods, including oil, does not reflect the full costs to society of their production and, importantly, their use. When we pay for gasoline at the pump, the price reflects the costs of extraction, refinery, and transport to a filling station. But it does not include covering the costs to tackle the impact from emissions created from the gasoline used. If polluters are to pay for their pollution, we need to take these costs into account.

Unsurprisingly, policymakers are attracted to the polluter pays principle primarily because it provides a justificatory means by which much-needed funds can be raised and directed towards critically important environmental projects. But the price charged is supposed to lead to significant reductions in emissions if long-term sustainability is to be achieved. While higher costs can reduce use, there is no evidence it will lead to the level of reductions needed to succeed (Brooks 2021b: 41). If the polluter pays principle cannot ensure that a fine or fee will significantly slash emissions, then it does not succeed to achieving its aims.

Some polluter pays principle defenders are aware of these concerns. Caney argues that we are all under a collective world-wide duty to keep emissions under a forever sustainable level (Caney 2005: 769). Polluters are charged for their pollution, but the total amount of emissions allowed is restricted by a global cap. This may be a way of ensuring the polluter pays principle leads to a sustainable amount of emissions, as polluters cannot pay as much as they can afford to when polluting as much as they might wish. However, the work done is by setting the cap – not the amount polluters pay intended to incentivize conservation. Furthermore, if we pollute at a safe, sustainable level, then it is unclear if there is harm that must be compensated. So, while Caney might have a view about how the principle will not lead to unsustainable emission levels by imposing a cap, the principle loses its essence as a negative duty because, if the cap works, it is supposed there is no climate change-related damage caused. Thus, the way to ensure the polluter pays principle works sustainably is to render it incoherent as a principle. Instead, it would act like a tax on carbon emissions.

## 8.3   Adaptation

We need to learn to live with climate change. It is happening already. While virtually everyone accepts some combination of mitigation and adaptation is required, let us now turn to those who argue that a focus on adaptation should have priority over conservation efforts.

*Adaptation* is an approach that claims that we can address climate change best by acclimatizing ourselves to its changes. Global temperatures are rising already. If we can adapt ourselves to a future climate, then we can minimize its impact on us and maintain a sustainable future. Adaptation can take several forms, including:

- Carbon dioxide removal, such as reforestation or direct carbon capture from the atmosphere
- Greater energy efficiency
- Improved home insulation
- Investment in public services so we reduce reliance on private transport
- Increased recycling
- Use of labeling and nudges to shift common behaviors
- Improved management of sewage and waste water (Brooks 2021b: 52, Brooks 2023b: 150).

We adapt to climate change by making changes, such as investing in green technologies, increasing reliance on renewable energy, increasing energy efficiencies and using more public transport. Carbon capture, recycling, reforestation and flood defenses can all play a role in ensuring that we change in response to our changing environment. More controversially, some propose solutions like *geoengineering*. An example is using solar radiation management, whereby planes loaded with sulphate particles spray them at 65,000 ft in several thousand annual flights. This would help deflect solar radiation and create a cooling effect (Crutzen 2006). Or more conventionally, others support the use of carbon capture drawing carbon from the atmosphere to reduce its negative climatic impact.

It is clear that adaptation has huge potential and must be a part of any sustainable plan. Our choice is not *if* we adapt, but *how* we adapt given that climate changes are already under way. Harnessing greater use of renewable energy brings benefits from being a clear energy source to a source of well-paid graduate jobs. Adaptation provides us with new ways of reducing our impact on the planet that support mitigation through the use of novel technologies.

Critics point out that an overreliance on adaptation raises several concerns. The first is that adaptation puts too much faith in the benefits from future technologies that do not yet exit in order to solve potentially existential problems. For example, some argue that things can only get better as technologies re always rapidly progressing and that we can be reassured that currently unknown solutions will appear in time. Matthew Kahn argues: "in a world with billions of education ambitious individuals, the best adaptations and innovations will be pretty good" (Kahn 2010: 243). In addition, he claims: "we will save ourselves by adapting to our ever-changing circumstances . . . At the end of the day, the story will have a happy ending" (Kahn 2010: 12). The problem with this view is that if a satisfactory solution should not appear in time, the risk is we will endure a potentially avoidable environmental catastrophe than if we had chosen to mitigate and conserve instead. Such faith comes with a potentially high, even possibly fatal, cost.

Adaptation strategies can appear to be a "cheap and simple" solution to policymakers when they are anything but (Levitt and Dubner 2010: 177). For example, Bjørn Lomborg argues that "it will be far more expensive to cut $CO_2$ emissions radically than to pay the costs of adaptation to the increased temperatures" (Lomborg 1998: 318). Some estimates are that full mitigation could cost about 2% of GDP annually (Stern 2009: 54). Lomborg's argument is we should spend less on mitigation and use part of what is saved on adaptation, as he estimates the total cost of doing so would be less. The savings could then be used for other major challenges like poverty alleviation and where, in his view, such funds could be more effective (Lomborg 2008: 35, Posner and Weisbach 2010).

The problem here is with the relevant risk appetite. Suppose full mitigation is more costly and would ensure a sustainable future. If we could spend less in total (and so have additional funding to support those in severe poverty with much needed resources) and still ensure sustainability, this could be seen as simply making public funds go further and good value for money. However, Lomborg's alternative does not ensure the same likelihood of future sustainability as it relies, at least to some significant degree, on the production of new adaptive technologies that do not yet exist – and which we require for our collective future. Some might think the risk of environmental catastrophe is worth taking because they are confident it is very unlikely, but others may think that such grave risks should not be determined by as of yet unknown technologies and public policy should be mindful of taking such precautions.

Critics also highlight how adaptation is presented as making it possible that we can become sustainable without a significant impact on our lives. Dale Jamieson argues:

> Technological approaches are popular with both with politicians and with the public because they promise solutions to environmental problems without forcing us to change our values, ways of life or economic systems . . . the image of the scientist as the "can-do" guy who can solve any problem remains quite potent (Jamieson 2008: 13).

This raises the concern that if something sounds too good to be true it often is. For example, we might assume greater technological advancement would lead to better efficiencies and cut emissions. Richard Wilkinson and Kate Pickett find this is not always true. They argue:

> More power-efficient washing machines or better insulated homes will help the environment, but they also cut our bills, and that immediately means we lose some of the environmental gain by spending the saved money on something else. As cars have become more fuel-efficient we have chosen to drive further. As houses have become better insulated we have raised standards of heating, and as we put in energy-saving light bulbs the chances are that we start to think it doesn't matter so much leaving them on (Wilkinson and Pickett 2010: 223).

The evidence strongly suggests that energy efficiencies do not always lead to using less energy or less emissions. Twenty years ago, few people had cell phones. Now, most of us rely on them. They can do incredible things to make life easier while also being constantly on charge. Relatively few regularly had access to the internet or had an email account. Today, most homes do, and many of us have more than one email account. As it has become so easy to access information online, many might suppose freely used online search engines are free of any environmental impact. But that would be wrong. According to the BBC (2020), a single internet search or sent email uses little energy. But the combined global activity of both accounts for about 3.7% of global greenhouse emissions, similar to the airline industry annually. It is predicted to double by 2025 (BBC 2020). New technologies are a necessary part of creating any sustainable future, but there is reason to be cautious about what impact they can or might be expected to have.

## 8.4   Rethinking Sustainability

Mitigation and adaptation approaches are both important and present themselves as solutions to the problem of climate change. We are told that "the world now has the technologies and financial resources to stabilize climate" (Brown 2011: 198). We are reassured that "a happy ending" is possible forever if only we implemented the right combination of policies (Kahn 2010: 12). The ability to save the planet is in our power, but what we must do is decide on how to achieve it. Or so the argument goes.

The view that climate change is a problem that can be solved might be seen as a kind of *end-state solution* (Nozick 1974: 153–155). The claim is that, if the right solution is picked, that it will create a final "end-state" of climate calm that is sustainable and long-lasting (Brooks 2016d, Brooks 2020d: 241–258). This view is infused throughout the mitigating and adaptation approaches considered. It is claimed that if only we reduce our emissions enough or utilize the right technologies then we can maintain the same climatic changes forever more and overcome the current problems associated with climatic changes.

The main concern here is that this view gets the problem wrong. These solutions presuppose that if we mitigated our impact enough or adapted sufficiently, a future catastrophe can be avoidable and a sustainable, unchanging climate is possible. However, our planet has experienced several environmental catastrophic events – even before there were people around to have an impact. In other words, making our impact zero does not mean the problem of climate change is solved. As noted by Jonathan Schell:

> In this world without us, traditional evolution would indeed revive, and the procession of geological ages would resume, though without anyone around to give them names (unless in the fulness of time a new creature, perhaps some gifted fish, evolves to the point at which it can assume the task) (Schell 2020: 5).

Catastrophes can happen even if we were not here to cause them (Brooks 2016d: 127–128, Brooks 2021b: 64). For example, there have been five catastrophes already in our planet's past history. These events include ice ages, volcanic eruptions and even meteors striking the Earth, causing mass extinctions – and all millions of years before humans came along. A catastrophe-free future cannot be guaranteed. Carbon emissions can make climate change happen more rapidly and its effects more devastating, but even if we reduced our impact to zero this does not ensure the planet will be sustainable forever more.

This is a sobering analysis, but it does not suggest that we should do nothing or that our actions are futile. We need to change how we view sustainability to what I call *impermanent sustainability* (Brooks 2021b: 66). Our standard view of sustainability is that it is about creating a permanent end-state that does not change. In contrast, impermanent sustainability is a process of continual readjustment, denying any fixed mode or formula to rely on (Brooks 2023b: 153). It seeks to react to the world as it is – a world where we can never be entirely comfortably settled, as we are continually challenged to find ways of reducing our impact while improving our adaptability.

Impermanent sustainability opens up a new way of seeing climate change ethics. As I have argued before and quote at length:

> We might approach climate change from a new perspective. Our focus should not only be on how we might reduce our environmental impact, but we should extend our focus to another question: what are the normative implications of a future environmental catastrophe both foreseeable and perhaps inevitable? This different focus reinterprets climate change as a problem of management where we approach these questions in a new way. Our proposals should reconsider sustainability for a tragic world – *our* tragic world – where the choices we have are less clear cut and more sobering than the overly, and unrealistically, optimistic "solutions" already offered (Brooks 2016d: 128).

We live in an endangered world and exist in the shadow of its next future climate catastrophe. If we do not act or simply give up, then we make this future happen more quickly, with greater force and deadlier consequences for all. Doing nothing to reduce our impact and slow the pace of climatic changes can only make things worse. Action must be taken.

But some might ask what use our actions can really be if a future catastrophe may be unavoidable? One reason is that reducing our impact can make any such event less deadly and not bring it further forward. A second reason is this would help buy time to find the technologies we need to help manage our changing climate in a more sustainable way so that, when further extreme events occur, we are better placed to cope. We can develop technologies to limit the impacts if or when they arise, but this takes time which only greater mitigation can enable.

## 8.5   Conclusion

Climate change is one of humanity's greatest challenges. Political philosophers have made significant contributions to our thinking about what can and should be done. One approach is mitigation, whereby we seek to conserve and reduce our impact to some sustainable level. This approach includes advocates of the ecological footprint and the polluter pays principle. A second approach is adaptation, where our aim is to develop future technologies that will reduce the impact of climate change harms on us. Most working in this area will prioritize either mitigation or adaptation, while acknowledging some element of both is required. Together, they are thought to provide solutions to a forever after whereby climate change and its dangerous effects can be negated or brought under control and neutralized.

It has been argued that these approaches get the central problem wrong. If we rightly assume that the clear scientific consensus is correct about our cause of climate change, the rate of change, the existing impacts, and likely future consequences, we arrive at a different picture. When we look at our Earth's past, it is clear that several environmental catastrophes have happened long before there was any human beings around to cause them. There is ample evidence that climate change is getting much worse because of our activities, but reducing our impact to zero does not mean that no future climate change will occur and a future environmental catastrophe can be averted.

Some might suspect that taking action, especially at real cost and inconvenience to us all, would be a waste of time if, as is suggested, future catastrophe cannot be ruled out no matter what our best efforts. But it has been argued that a more compelling view is that we must be *more* engaged in mitigation *and* adaptation efforts to keep catastrophe in the future for as long as possible, to mitigate its impact on the planet if it happens, and to adapt ourselves to reduce its harmful impact on us. Doing nothing makes our problems worse. While the challenges of climate change are perhaps more significant than often realized, we can rise to the task with a clearer view about managing impermanent sustainability within a continuing changing climate. As I have noted elsewhere:

> Climate change justice requires each individual and every part of society contributing to that end. Only a positive engagement with grasping our reality and exploring the full range of possibilities can we rise to meet this greatest of all challenges (Brooks 2021b: 88).

Our future waits for us to write to it.

## Further Reading

Brooks, Thom. 2021. *Climate Change Ethics for an Endangered World.* London: Routledge.

Gardiner, Stephen. 2004. "Ethics and Global Climate Change," *Ethics* 114: 555–600.

Jamieson, Dale. 2008. *Ethics and the Environment.* Cambridge: Cambridge University Press.

Posner, Eric A. and David Weisbach. 2010. *Climate Change Justice.* Princeton: Princeton University Press.

# Conclusion

The Italian philosopher, historian, and politician Benedetto Croce wrote a book called *What is Living and What is Dead of the Philosophy of Hegel?* (Croce 1915). Most Hegel scholars since have concluded their studies with a comment about which parts of Hegel's philosophy still speak to us about two centuries later and which have not stood the test of time, and so have I in my work about his philosophy (Brooks 2013a, 158–161).

In this book, we have focused only on what is very much alive in *political philosophy*. The field is a continuing dialogue that can bridge across generations. Each builds off of the contributions of theorists who came before. While the circumstances may change and reference to historical events may seem opaque, the leading figures of the past speak to us today alongside our most influential contemporary philosophers. The nature and meaning of key political concepts like freedom, rights, equality, justice, democracy, punishment, global justice, and climate change have a timeless interest. To read only the historical canon misses its many invaluable connections that help us understand how we see political philosophy today. To focus on contemporary work alone fails to grasp the evolution of concepts, ideas, and applications that inform our thinking. I have never seen the history of political thought as a fundamentally different field from contemporary political philosophy. They speak to each other and to us if only we take the time to listen.

*Political Philosophy: The Fundamentals*, First Edition. Thom Brooks.
© 2025 John Wiley & Sons Ltd. Published 2025 by John Wiley & Sons Ltd.

I have not hidden my admiration of some philosophers and contributions over others. An examination of political philosophy is about exploring what is valuable to us – whether freedom, rights, equality, and more – and it can only be done honestly with integrity. Not every political philosophy or philosopher merits the same attention. Politics is about judgment, strategy, and decision-making. We approach all of this *in context*. Political thought sat on the fence is neither useful nor ornamental. It is hoped that readers can see and engage with the process of *doing* political philosophy and the excitement that comes with exploring your own views about its key concepts and their applications

Moreover, I hope you now have the tools to explore concepts, cited work, and further readings covered in these pages more substantially. That's not to say that every issue in political thought has a compelling answer. If correct views were obvious to all, we wouldn't have been debating these matters for over two millennia. Philosophers regularly disagree. This is probably inevitable. Often our dissatisfaction with the views of others can lead to innovative new ideas that address perceived shortcomings. But the main point is being able to understand the debate so you can engage and contribute. This has been my goal here.

Political philosophy is a rewarding journey that gets ever more interesting the further you dwell within it and become more familiar with it. My wish is that you feel now more at home – and can see the political in a new and refreshing spirit, within context.

# References

Aesop. 2003. *Aesop's Fables*. New York: Barnes & Nobles.

Alexander, Larry and Michael Moore. 2020. "Deontological Ethics," *Stanford Encyclopedia of Philosophy*, url: https://plato.stanford.edu/entries/ethics-deontological/ (accessed November 1, 2024).

American Law Institute. 1962. *Model Penal Code*. Philadelphia: America Law Institute.

Anderson, Elizabeth A. 1999. "What is the Point of Equality?" *Ethics* 109: 287–337.

Aristotle. 1984. *The Complete Works of Aristotle*, Volume 2, Jonathan Barnes, ed. Princeton: Princeton University Press.

Arneson, Richard. 2010. "Rawls, Responsibility and Distributive Justice," in Mark, Fleurbaey, Maurice Salles and John A. Weymark, eds, *Justice, Political Liberalism and Utilitarianism: Themes from Harsanyi and Rawls*. Cambridge: Cambridge University Press, 80–107.

Barry, Brian. 1995. "John Rawls and the Search for Stability," *Ethics* 105: 874–915.

Barry, Brian. 2001. *Culture and Equality*. Cambridge: Polity.

BBC. 2020. "Why Your Internet Habits Are Not As Clean As You Think," BBC.Com, url: https://www.bbc.com/future/article/20200305-why-your-internet-habits-are-not-as-clean-as-you-think (accessed November 1, 2024).

BBC. 2024. "UK General Election 2024 Results," BBC.Com, url: https://www.bbc.co.uk/news/election/2024/uk/results (accessed November 1, 2024).

Beccaria, Cesare. 1986. *Of Crimes and Punishments*. Indianapolis: Hackett.

Bedi, Sonu. 2009. *Rejecting Rights*. Cambridge: Cambridge University Press.

*Political Philosophy: The Fundamentals*, First Edition. Thom Brooks.
© 2025 John Wiley & Sons Ltd. Published 2025 by John Wiley & Sons Ltd.

Beitz, Charles R. 1999. *Political Theory and International Relations*, 2nd edition. Princeton: Princeton University Press.

Bentham, Jeremy and John Stuart Mill. 1987. *Utilitarianism and Other Essays*. Harmondsworth: Penguin.

Berlin, Isaiah. 1969. *Four Essays on Liberty*. Oxford: Oxford University Press.

Bingham, Tom. 2011. *The Rule of Law*. Harmondsworth: Penguin.

Blair, Tony. 2010. *A Journey*. London: Hutchinson.

Bloomberg, Michael and Carl Pope. 2018. *Climate of Hope: How Cities, Businesses and Citizens Can Save the Planet*. New York: St Martin's Griffin.

Brettschneider, Corey. 2007. *Democratic Rights: The Substance of Self-Government*. Princeton: Princeton University Press.

Breyer, Stephen. 2010. *America's Supreme Court: Making Democracy Work*. Oxford: Oxford University Press.

Brock, Gillian. 2009. *Global Justice: A Cosmopolitan Account*. Oxford: Oxford University Press.

Brooks, Thom. 2002a. "Cosmopolitanism and Distributing Responsibilities," *Critical Review of International Social and Political Philosophy* 5: 92–97.

Brooks, Thom. 2002b. "Saving the Greatest Number," *Logique et Analyse* 45: 55–59.

Brooks, Thom. 2002c. "A Defence of Sceptical Authoritarianism," *Politics* 22: 152–162.

Brooks, Thom, ed. 2005. *Rousseau and Law*. Aldershot: Ashgate.

Brooks, Thom. 2006. "Knowledge and Power in Plato's Political Thought," *International Journal of Philosophical Studies* 14: 51–77.

Brooks, Thom. 2009. "The Problem with Polygamy," *Philosophical Topics* 37: 109–122.

Brooks, Thom. 2011a. "Rethinking Remedial Responsibilities," *Ethics and Global Politics* 4: 195–202.

Brooks, Thom. 2011b. "Retribution and Capital Punishment," in Mark D. White, ed., *Retributivism: Essays on Theory and Practice*. Oxford: Oxford University Press, 232–245.

Brooks, Thom. 2012a. "James Seth on Natural Law and Legal Theory," *Collingwood and British Idealism Studies* 12: 115–132

Brooks, Thom. 2012b. "Punishment and Moral Sentiments," *Review of Metaphysics* 66: 281–293.

Brooks, Thom. 2013a. *Hegel's Political Philosophy: A Systematic Reading of the Philosophy of Right*, 2nd edition. Edinburgh: Edinburgh University Press.

Brooks, Thom. 2013b. "Philosophy Unbound: The Idea of Global Philosophy," *Metaphilosophy* 44: 254–266.

Brooks, Thom. 2014a. "A New Problem with the Capabilities Approach," *Harvard Review of Philosophy* 20: 100–106.

Brooks, Thom. 2014b. "Remedial Responsibilities Beyond Nations," *Journal of Global Ethics* 10: 156–166.

Brooks, Thom. 2015a. "The Capabilities Approach and Political Liberalism," in Thom Brooks and Martha C. Nussbaum, eds, *Rawls's Political Liberalism*. New York: Columbia University Press, 139–173.

Brooks, Thom. 2015b. "The Stakeholder Society and the Politics of Hope," *Renewal* 23(1/2): 44–54.

Brooks, Thom. 2016a. "In Defence of Punishment and the Unified Theory of Punishment: A Reply," *Criminal Law and Philosophy* 10: 629–638.

Brooks, Thom. 2016b. *Becoming British: UK Citizenship Examined*. London: Biteback.

Brooks, Thom. 2016c. "Justice as Stakeholding," in Krushil Watene and Jay Drydyk, eds, *Theorizing Justice: Critical Insights and Future Directions*. New York: Rowan and Littlefield, 111–127.

Brooks, Thom. 2016d. "How Not to Save the Planet," *Ethics, Policy and Environment* 19: 119–132.

Brooks, Thom. 2016e. "Vote Buying and Tax Cut Promises," *Theoria* 63: 20–35.

Brooks, Thom. 2017a. "Is Eating Meat Ethical?" *Think* 16: 9–13.

Brooks, Thom. 2017b. "Punitive Restoration and Restorative Justice," *Criminal Justice Ethics* 36: 122–140.

Brooks, Thom. 2017c. "Hegel on Crime and Punishment," in Thom Brooks and Sebastian Stein, eds, *Hegel's Political Philosophy: On the Normative Significance of Method and System*. Oxford: Oxford University Press, 202–221.

Brooks, Thom. 2020a. "More than Recognition: Why Stakeholding Matters for Reconciliation in Hegel's *Philosophy of Right*," *Owl of Minerva* 51: 59–86.

Brooks, Thom, ed. 2020b. *The Oxford Handbook of Global Justice*. Oxford: Oxford University Press.

Brooks, Thom. 2020c. "Capabilities, Freedom and Severe Poverty" in Thom Brooks, ed., *The Oxford Handbook of Global Justice*. Oxford: Oxford University Press, 199–213.

Brooks, Thom. 2020d. "Climate Change Ethics and the Problem of End-State Solutions," in Thom Brooks, ed., *The Oxford Handbook of Global Justice*. Oxford: Oxford University Press, 241–258.

Brooks, Thom. 2021a. *Punishment: A Critical Introduction*, 2nd edition. London: Routledge.

Brooks, Thom. 2021b. *Climate Change Ethics for an Endangered World*. London: Routledge.

Brooks, Thom, ed. 2022a. *Political Emotions: Towards a Decent Public Sphere*. Basingstoke: Palgrave Macmillan.

Brooks, Thom. 2022b. *Reforming the UK's Citizenship Test: Building Bridges, Not Barriers*. Bristol: Bristol University Press.

Brooks, Thom. 2022c. *New Arrivals: A Fair Immigration Plan for Labour*. London: Fabian Society.

Brooks, Thom. 2022d. *The Trust Factor: Essays on the Current Crisis and Hope for the Future*. London: Methuen.

Brooks, Thom, ed. 2023a. *The Global Justice Reader*, revised edition. Oxford: Blackwell.

Brooks, Thom. 2023b. *Global Justice: An Introduction*. Oxford: Blackwell.

Brooks, Thom. 2025a. "Cruel and Unusual Punishment," in Jesper Ryberg, ed., *The Oxford Handbook of the Philosophy of Punishment*. Oxford: Oxford University Press, 275–286.

Brooks, Thom. 2025b. "Republican Children," *Philosophy and Public Affairs*. 53: 37–65.

Brooks, Thom and Martha C. Nussbaum, eds. 2015. *Rawls's Political Liberalism*. New York: Columbia University Press.

Brown, Lester R. 2011. *World on the Edge: How to Prevent Environmental and Economic Collapse*. New York: W. W. Norton.

Brudner, Alan. 2009. *Punishment and Freedom: A Liberal Theory of Penal Justice*. Oxford: Oxford University Press.

Cabrera, Luis. 2020. "Global Justice and Global Citizenship," in Thom Brooks, ed., *The Oxford Handbook of Global Justice*. Oxford: Oxford University Press.

Calhoun, Cheshire. 2005. "Who's Afraid of Polygamous Marriage? Lessons for Same-Sex Marriage Advocacy from the History of Polygamy," *San Diego Law Review* 42: 1023–1042.

Caney, Simon. 2001. "Cosmopolitan Justice and Equalizing Opportunities," *Metaphilosophy* 32: 113–134.

Caney, Simon. 2005. "Cosmopolitan Justice, Responsibility, and Global Climate Change," *Leiden Journal of International Law* 18: 747–775.

Caney, Simon. 2012. "Just Emissions," *Philosophy and Public Affairs* 40: 255–300.

Carter, Ian, Mathew Kramer and Hillel Steiner, eds. 2006. *Freedom: A Philosophical Anthology*. Oxford: Blackwell.

Cicero. 1991. *On Duties*. Cambridge: Cambridge University Press.

Cohen, Gerald A. 2000. *If You're an Egalitarian, How Come You're So Rich?* Cambridge: Harvard University Press.

Cohen, Gerald A. 2008. *Rescuing Justice and Equality*. Cambridge: Harvard University Press.

Constant, Benjamin. 1988. *Political Writings*. Cambridge: Cambridge University Press.

Croce, Benedetto. 1915. *What is Living and What is Dead of the Philosophy of Hegel*, trans. Douglas Ainslie. London: Macmillan.

Crutzen, Paul J. 2006. "Albedo Enhancement by Stratospheric Sulfur Injections: A Contribution to Resolve a Policy Dilemma?" *Climatic Change* 77: 211–219.

Dahl, Robert A. 1956. *A Preface to Democratic Theory*. Chicago: University of Chicago Press.

Dahl, Robert A. 1998. *On Democracy*. New Haven: Yale University Press.

de Montesquieu, Charles. 1989. *The Spirit of the Laws*. Cambridge: Cambridge University Press.

de Tocqueville, Alexis. 1969. *Democracy in America*, J. P. Mayer, ed. New York: Anchor Books.

Dimova-Cookson, Maria. 2003. "A New Scheme of Positive and Negative Freedom," *Political Theory* 31: 508–532,

Duff, Reginald A. 2001. *Punishment, Communication and Community*. Oxford: Oxford University Press.

Dworkin, Ronald. 1978. *Taking Rights Seriously*, paperback edition. Cambridge: Harvard University Press.

Dworkin, Ronald. 2000. *Sovereign Virtue: The Theory and Practice of Equality*. Cambridge: Harvard University Press.

Easton, Susan and Christine Piper. 2005. *Sentencing and Punishment: The Quest for Justice*. Oxford: Oxford University Press.

Ellis, Anthony. 2003. "A Deterrence Theory of Punishment," *Philosophical Quarterly* 53: 337–351.

Estlund, David, ed. 2002. *Democracy*. Oxford: Blackwell.

Estlund, David M. 2008. *Democratic Authority: A Philosophical Framework*. Princeton: Princeton University Press.

Fassin, Yves. 2009. "The Stakeholder Model Refined," *Journal of Business Ethics* 84: 113–135.

Feinberg, Joel. 1970. *Doing and Deserving: Essays in the Theory of Responsibility*. Princeton: Princeton University Press.

Fichte, Johann Gottlieb. 2000. *Foundations of Natural Right*, ed. Frederick Neuhouser. Cambridge: Cambridge University Press.

Filmer, Robert. 2008. *Patriarcha and Other Writings*, ed. Johann. P. Sommerville. Cambridge: Cambridge University Press.

Fishkin, James. 1991. *Deliberative Democracy*. New Haven: Yale University Press.

Frankfurt, Harry G. 1971. "Freedom of the Will and the Concept of a Person," *Journal of Philosophy* 68: 5–20.

Freeman, Robert E. 1984. *Strategic Management: A Stakeholder Approach*. Boston: Pitman.

Freeman, Robert E., Jeffrey S. Harrison and Andrew C. Wicks. 2007. *Managing for Stakeholders: Survival, Reputation and Success*. New Haven: Yale University Press.

Gardiner, Stephen. 2004. "Ethics and Global Climate Change," *Ethics* 114: 555–600.

Gardiner, Stephen. 2011. *A Perfect Moral Storm: The Ethical Tragedy of Climate Change*. Oxford: Oxford University Press.

Garvey, James. 2008. *The Ethics of Climate Change: Right and Wrong in a Warming World*. London: Continuum.

Goodin, Robert E. 1988. "What is so Special about our Fellow Countrymen?" *Ethics* 98: 663–686.

Gould, Philip. 2011. *The Unfinished Revolution: How New Labour Changed British Politics Forever*. London: Abacus.

Green, T. H. 1986. *Lectures on the Principles of Political Obligation and Other Writings*. Cambridge: Cambridge University Press.

Gruen, Lori. 2017. "The Moral Status of Animals," *Stanford Encyclopedia of Philosophy*, url: https://plato.stanford.edu/entries/moral-animal/ (accessed November 1, 2024).

Gutmann, Amy and Dennis Thompson. 1998. *Democracy and Disagreement*. Cambridge: Harvard University Press.

Hampton, Jean. 1984. "The Moral Education Theory of Punishment," *Philosophy and Public Affairs* 13: 208–238.

Hart, Herbert L. A. 1982. *Essays on Bentham*. Oxford: Clarendon Press.

Hart, Herbert L. A. 2008. *Punishment and Responsibility: Essays in the Philosophy of Law*, 2nd edition. Oxford: Oxford University Press.

Hegel, G. W. F. 1969. *Science of Logic*, trans. Arnold V. Miller. Amherst: Humanity Books.

Hegel, G. W. F. 1990. *Elements of the Philosophy of Right*. Cambridge: Cambridge University Press.

Held, David. 2010. *Cosmopolitanism: Ideals and Realities*. Cambridge: Polity.

Hibbing, John R. and Elizabeth Theiss-Morse. 2002. *Stealth Democracy: Americans' Beliefs about How Government Should Work*. Cambridge: Cambridge University Press.

Hillman, Mayer. 2008. *How We Can Save the Planet: Preventing Global Climatic Catastrophe*. New York: St Martin's Press.

Hobbes, Thomas. 1996. *Leviathan*, ed. Richard Tuck. Cambridge: Cambridge University Press.

Hohfeld, Wesley 1919. *Fundamental Legal Conceptions as Applied in Judicial Reasoning*. New Haven: Yale University Press.

Honderich, Ted. 1969. *Punishment: The Supposed Justifications*. Harmondsworth: Penguin

Horne, Alexander. 2015. "The Role of the Lord Chancellor," *House of Commons Library Note* (SN/PC/2015).

Hume, David. 1994. "Of the Original Contract," in *Political Essays*. : Cambridge University Press, 186–201.

Hume, David. 2000. *A Treatise of Human Nature*. Oxford: Oxford University Press.

Hutton, Will. 1995. *The State We're In*. London: Jonathan Cape.

Hutton, Will. 2010. *Them and Us: Changing Britain – Why We Need a Fair Society*. London: Little, Brown.

Intergovernmental Panel on Climate Change. 2019. "Special Report on the Ocean and Cryosphere in a Changing Climate: Summary for Policymakers," url: https://www.unep.org/resources/report/ipcc-special-report-ocean-and-cryosphere-changing-climate (accessed November 1, 2024).

Intergovernmental Panel on Climate Change. 2020. *Special Report: Global Warming of 1.5°C*. Geneva: Intergovernmental Panel on Climate Change.

Jamieson, Dale. 2008. *Ethics and the Environment: An Introduction*. Cambridge: Cambridge University Press.

Johnstone, Gerry. 1988. "The Psychiatric Approach to Crime: A Sociological Analysis," *Economy and Society* 17: 317–373.

Jones, Peter. 1994. *Rights*. Basingstoke: Palgrave.

Jones, Peter. 2006. "Bearing the Consequences of Belief," *Journal of Political Philosophy* 2: 24–43.

Kahan, Dan M. 1999. "The Secret Ambition of Deterrence," *Harvard Law Review* 113: 413—500.

Kahn, Matthew. 2010. *Climatopolis: How Our Cities Will Thrive in the Hotter Future*. New York: Basic Books.

Kant, Immanuel. 1957. *Perpetual Peace*. Indianapolis: Bobbs-Merrill.

Kant, Immanuel. 1996a. *Practical Philosophy*, trans. Mary Gregor. Cambridge: Cambridge University Press,

Kant, Immanuel. 1996b. *The Metaphysics of Morals*. Cambridge: Cambridge University Press.

Kant, Immanuel. 1997. *Groundwork of the Metaphysics of Morals*, trans. Mary Gregor. Cambridge: Cambridge University Press.

Kant, Immanuel. 1998. *Critique of Pure Reason*. Cambridge: Cambridge University Press.

Knapton, Sarah. 2023. "Plants Cry Out When They Need Watering – But Humans Can't Hear Them," *Daily Telegraph* (30 March), url: https://www.telegraph.co.uk/news/2023/03/30/plants-cry-out-when-need-watering/ (accessed November 1, 2024).

Knowles, Dudley. 2001. *Political Philosophy*. London: Routledge.

Korsgaard, Christine. 1996. *The Sources of Normativity*. Cambridge: Cambridge University Press.

Kramer, Matthew H. 2001. "Do Animals and Dead People Have Legal Rights?" *Canadian Journal of Law and Jurisprudence* 14: 29–54.

Kramer, Matthew H. 2013. "Some Doubts About Alternatives to the Interest Theory of Rights," *Ethics* 123: 245–263.

Kramer, Matthew H., Nigel Simmonds and Hillel Steiner. 1998. *A Debate Over Rights*. Oxford: Clarendon Press.

Kymlicka, Will. 2002. *Contemporary Political Philosophy: An Introduction*, 2nd edition. Oxford: Oxford University Press.

Landemore, Hélène. 2020. *Open Democracy: Reinventing Popular Rule for the Twenty-First Century*. Princeton: Princeton University Press.

Larmore, Charles. 2020. *What is Political Philosophy?* Princeton: Princeton University Press.

Levitt, Steven D. and Stephen J. Dubner. 2010. *Superfreakonomics*. London: Penguin.

Locke, John. 1988. *Two Treatises of Government*. Cambridge: Cambridge University Press.

Lomborg, Bjørn. 1998. *The Skeptical Environmentalist: Measuring the Real State of the World*. Cambridge: Cambridge University Press.

Lomborg, Bjørn. 2008. *Cool It: The Skeptical Environmentalist's Guide to Global Warming*. New York: Vintage.

Mabbott, John D. 1966. *An Introduction to Ethics*. London: Hutchinson and Co.

Machiavelli, Niccolo. 1995. *The Prince and Other Political Writings*. London: Everyman.

MacKinnon, Catharine A. 1991. *Towards a Feminist Theory of the State*. Cambridge: Harvard University Press.

MacKinnon, Catharine and Andrea Dworkin, eds. 1998. *In Harm's Way: The Pornography Civil Rights Hearings*. Cambridge: Harvard University Press.

Margalit, Avishai and Joseph Raz. 1990. "National Self-Determination," *Journal of Philosophy* 87:439–461.

Markovits, Daniel. 2019. *The Meritocracy Trap*. Harmondsworth: Penguin.

Marx, Karl. 1978. "Critique of the Gotha Program," in Robert C. Tucker, ed., *The Marx-Engels Reader*. New York: Norton, 525–541.

Marx, Karl and Friedrich Engels. 1967. *The Communist Manifesto*. Harmondsworth: Penguin.

McMahan, Jeff. 1993. "Killing, Letting Die and Withdrawing Aid," *Ethics* 103: 250–279.

Mill, John Stuart. 1984. *The Collected Works of John Stuart Mill*, Volume 21. Toronto: University of Toronto Press.

Mill, John Stuart. 1986. "Speech in Favour of Capital Punishment" in Peter Singer, ed., *Applied Ethics*. Oxford: Oxford University Press, 97–104.

Mill, John Stuart. 1989. *On Liberty and Other Writings*. Cambridge: Cambridge University Press.

Mill, John Stuart. 2015. *On Liberty, Utilitarianism and Other Essays*. Oxford: Oxford University Press.

Miller, David. 1999. *Principles of Social Justice*. Oxford: Oxford University Press.

Miller, David. 2001. "Distributing Responsibilities," *Journal of Political Philosophy* 9: 453–471.

Miller, David, ed. 2006. *The Liberty Reader*. London: Paradigm.

Miller, David. 2007. *National Responsibility and Global Justice*. Oxford: Oxford University Press.

Miller, David. 2023. "Why Normative Beahviouralism Fails," *Political Studies Review* 21: 441–446.

Miscevic, Nenad. 2020. "Nationalism," *Stanford Encyclopedia of Philosophy*, url: https://plato.stanford.edu/entries/nationalism/ (accessed November 1, 2024).

Nagel, Thomas. 1986. *The View from Nowhere*. Oxford: Oxford University Press.

Norris, Pippa and Ronald Inglehart. 2018. *Cultural Backlash: Trump, Brexit and the Rise of Authoritarian-Populism*. Cambridge: Cambridge University Press.

Nozick, Robert. 1974. *Anarchy, State and Utopia*. New York: Basic Books.

Nussbaum, Martha C. 1995. "Objectification," *Philosophy and Public Affairs* 24: 249—291.

Nussbaum, Martha C. 2000. *Women and Human Development: The Capabilities Approach*. Cambridge: Cambridge University Press.

Nussbaum, Martha C. 2001. *Upheavals of Thought: The Intelligence of Emotions*. Cambridge: Cambridge University Press.

Nussbaum, Martha C. 2002. "Patriotism and Cosmopolitanism" in Joshua Cohen, ed., *For Love of Country? Debating the Limits of Patriotism*. Boston: Beacon Press, 2–17.

Nussbaum, Martha C. 2003. "Capabilities as Fundamental Entitlements: Sen and Social Justice," *Feminist Economics* 9: 33–50.

Nussbaum, Martha C. 2004. *Hiding from Humanity: Disgust, Shame and the Law*. Princeton: Princeton University Press.

Nussbaum, Martha C. 2006. *Frontiers of Justice: Disability, Nationality, Species Membership*. Cambridge: Harvard University Press.

Nussbaum, Martha C. 2008. *Liberty of Conscience: In Defense of America's Tradition of Religious Equality*. New York: Basic Books.

Nussbaum, Martha C. 2011. *Creating Capabilities: The Human Development Approach*. Cambridge: Harvard University Press.

Nussbaum, Martha C. 2013. *Political Emotions: Why Love Matters for Justice*. Cambridge: Belknap/Harvard University Press.

Nussbaum, Martha C. 2019. *The Cosmopolitan Tradition: A Noble but Flawed Ideal*. Cambridge: Harvard University Press.

O'Connor, Timothy and Christopher Franklin. 2022. "Free Will," *Stanford Encyclopedia of Philosophy*, url: https://plato.stanford.edu/entries/freewill/#NatuFreeWill (accessed November 1, 2024).

O'Flaherty, Niall. 2018. *Utilitarianism in the Age of Enlightenment: The Moral and Political Thought of William Paley*. Cambridge: Cambridge University Press.

Okin, Susan Moller. 1999. *Is Multiculturalism Bad for Women?* Princeton: Princeton University Press.

Olsson, Erik. 2022. "Coherentist Theories of Epistemic Justification," *Stanford Encyclopedia of Philosophy*, url: https://plato.stanford.edu/entries/justep-coherence/ (accessed November 1, 2024).

O'Neill, Martin. 2008. "What Should Egalitarians Believe?" *Philosophy and Public Affairs* 36: 119–156.

Orwell, George. 1954. *1984*. Harmondsworth: Penguin.

Parekh, Bhikhu. 2000. *The Future of Multi-ethnic Britain*. London: Profile.

Parekh, Bhikhu. 2006. *Rethinking Multiculturalism: Cultural Diversity and Political Theory*, 2nd edition. Basingstoke: Palgrave Macmillan.

Parekh, Bhikhu. 2008. *A New Politics of Identity: Political Principles for an Interdependent World*. Basingstoke: Palgrave Macmillan.

Parekh, Bhikhu. 2019. *Ethnocentric Political Theory: The Pursuit of Flawed Universals*. Basingstoke: Palgrave Macmillan.

Parfit, Derek. 1997. "Equality and Priority," *Ratio* 10: 202–221.

Peng, Shushi, Xin Lin, Rona L. Thompson, Yi Xi, Gang Liu, Didier Hauglustaine, Xin Lan, Benjamin Poulter, Michael Ramonet, Marielle Saunois, Yi Yin, Zhen Zhang, Bo Zheng and Philippe Ciais. 2022. "Wetland Emission and Atmospheric Sink Changes explain Methane Growth in 2020," *Nature* 612: 477–482.

Pettit, Philip. 1999. *Republicanism: A Theory of Freedom and Government*. Oxford: Oxford University Press.

Pettit, Philip. 2001. *A Theory of Freedom: From the Psychology to the Politics of Agency*. Cambridge: Polity.

Pettit, Philip. 2004. "Depoliticizing Democracy," *Ratio Juris* 17: 52–65.

Pettit, Philip. 2012. *On the People's Terms: A Republican Theory and Model of Democracy*. Cambridge: Cambridge University Press.

Plato. 1997. *Complete Works*. Indianapolis: Hackett.

Pogge, Thomas W. 2002. *World Poverty and Human Rights*. Cambridge: Polity.

Pogge, Thomas W. 2010. *Politics as Usual: What Lies Behind the Pro-Poor Rhetoric*. Cambridge: Polity.

Posner, Eric A. and David Weisbach. 2010. *Climate Change Justice*. Princeton: Princeton University Press.

*R. v. HM Coroner for Inner North London*, EWHC 857 (Admin), (2005).

Rawls, John. 1955. "Two Concepts of Rules," *Philosophical Review* LXIV: 3–32.

Rawls, John. 1996. *Political Liberalism*, paperback edition. New York: Columbia University Press.

Rawls, John. 1999. *A Theory of Justice*, revised edition. Cambridge: Harvard University Press.

Rawls, John. 2001. *Justice as Fairness: A Restatement*. Cambridge: Harvard University Press.

Raz, Joseph. 1986. *The Morality of Freedom*. Oxford: Clarendon.

Reiman, Jeffrey H. 1985. "Justice, Civilization and the Death Penalty: Answering van den Haag," *Philosophy and Public Affairs* 14: 115–148.

Rousseau, Jean-Jacques. 1997a. *The Discourses and Other Early Political Writings*. Cambridge: Cambridge University Press.

Rousseau, Jean-Jacques. 1997b. *The Social Contract and Other Later Political Writings*. Cambridge: Cambridge University Press.

Rousseau, Jean-Jacques. 2011. *The Basic Political Writings*. Indianapolis: Hackett.

Russell, Bertrand. 1925. *What I Believe*. London: Kegan Paul.

Russell, Meg. 2013. *The Contemporary House of Lords: Westminster Bicameralism Revived*. Oxford: Oxford University Press.

Russett, Bruce. 1993. *Grasping the Democratic Peace: Principles for a Post-Cold War World*. Princeton: Princeton University Press.

Sachs, Jeffrey. 2008. *Common Wealth: Economics for a Crowded Planet*. Harmondsworth: Penguin.

Sandel, Michael J. 1998. *Liberalism and the Limits of Justice*, 2nd edition. Cambridge: Cambridge University Press.

Sandel, Michael. 2005. *Public Philosophy: Essays on Morality in Politics*. Cambridge: Harvard University Press.

Sartre, Jean-Paul. 1957. *Existentialism and Human Emotions*. New York: Philosophical Library.

Sartre, Jean-Paul. 1989. *No Exit and Three Other Plays*. New York: Vintage.

Sayre-McCord, Geoff, ed. 1988. *Essays on Moral Realism*. Ithaca: Cornell University Press.

Scheffler, Samuel, ed. 1988. *Consequentialism and Its Critics*. Oxford: Oxford University Press.

Scheffler, Samuel. 2003. "What is Egalitarianism" *Philosophy and Public Affairs* 31: 3–30.

Schell, Jonathan. 2020. "Nature and Value," in Akeel Bigrami, ed., *Nature and Value*. New York: Columbia University Press, 1–12.

Schumpeter, Joseph. 1962. *Capitalism, Socialism and Democracy*. New York: Harper.

Seglow, Jonathan. 2010. "Associative Duties and Global Justice," *Journal of Moral Philosophy* 7: 54–73.

Sen, Amartya. 1995. *Inequality Reexamined*. Oxford: Oxford University Press.

Sen, Amartya. 1999. *Development as Freedom*. Oxford: Oxford University Press.

Sen, Amartya. 2009. *The Idea of Justice*. London: Allen Lane.

Sentencing Act. 2020.

Seth, James. 1898. *A Study of Ethical Principles*, 3rd edition. Edinburgh: William Blackwood and Sons.

Shapiro, Ian. 2003. *The State of Democratic Theory*. Princeton: Princeton University Press.

Sherman, Lawrence W., Heather Strang, Geoffrey Barnes, Daniel J. Woods, Sarah Bennett, Nova Inkpen, Dorothy Newbury-Birch, Meredith Rossner, Caroline Angel, Malcolm Mearns and Molly Slothower. 2015. "Twelve Experiments in Restorative Justice: The Jerry Lee Program of Randomised Trials of Restorative Justice Conferences," *Journal of Experimental Criminology* 11: 501–540.

Simhony, Avital. 1991. "On Forcing Individuals to Be Free: T. H. Green's Liberal Theory of Positive Freedom," *Political Studies* 39: 303–220.

Simhony, Avital. 2003. "T. H. Green's Community of Rights: An Essay on the Complexity of Liberalism," *Journal of Political Ideologies* 8: 269–287.

Simms, Andrew. 2009. *Ecological Debt: Global Warming and the Wealth of Nations*, 2nd edition. London: Pluto Press.

Singer, Peter. 1972. "Famine, Affluence and Morality," *Philosophy and Public Affairs* 1: 229–243.

Singer, Peter. 1979. *Practical Ethics*. Cambridge: Cambridge University Press.

Singer, Peter. 2004. *One World: The Ethics of Globalization*. New Haven: Yale University Press.

Sinnott-Armstrong, Walter. 2023. "Consequentialism," *Stanford Encyclopedia of Philosophy*, url: https://plato.stanford.edu/entries/consequentialism/ (accessed November 1, 2024).

Smart, John J. C. and Bernard Williams. 1973. *Utilitarianism: For and Against*. Cambridge: Cambridge University Press.

Smith, Adam. 2002. *The Theory of Moral Sentiments*. Cambridge: Cambridge University Press.

Sreenivasan, Gopal. 2005. "A Hybrid Theory of Claim-Rights," *Oxford Journal of Legal Studies* 25: 257–274.

*State v. Santiago (Santiago II)*, 318 Conn. 1 (2015).

Stern, Nicholas. 2009. *A Blueprint for a Safer Planet*. London: Bodley Head.

Swift, Adam. 2014. *Political Philosophy*, 3rd edition. Cambridge: Polity.

Talisse, Robert B. 2007. *A Pragmatist Philosophy of Democracy*. New York: Routledge.

Talisse, Robert B. 2009. *Democracy and Moral Conflict*. Cambridge: Cambridge University Press.

Tan, Kok-Chor. 2004. *Justice without Borders: Cosmopolitanism, Nationalism and Patriotism*. Cambridge: Cambridge University Press.

Tawney, Richard H. 1931. *Equality*. London: George Allen & Unwin.

Tetlock, Philip E. 2005. *Expert Political Judgment*, new edition. Princeton: Princeton University Press.

Thomson, Judith Jarvis. 1976. "Killing, Letting Die and the Trolley Problem," *The Monist* 59: 204–217.

*Trump v. United States*, 603 U.S. XX, 15 (2024).

Tsai, Robert L. 2019. *Practical Equality: Forging Justice in a Divided Nation.* New York: W. W. Norton.

United Nations. 1948. *Universal Declaration of Human Rights.*

United States. 1776. *Declaration of Independence*, url: https://www.archives.gov/founding-docs/declaration-transcript (accessed November 1, 2024).

United States. 1789. *Constitution*, url: https://www.archives.gov/founding-docs/constitution-transcript (accessed November 1, 2024).

Von Hirsch, Andrew, Andrew Ashworth and Julian Roberts, eds. 2009. *Principled Sentencing: Readings on Theory and Policy*, 3rd edition. Oxford: Hart.

Wackernagel, Mathis. 2009. "Methodological Advancements in Footprint Analysis," *Ecological Economics* 68: 1925–1927.

Wackernagel, Mathis and William E. Rees. 1996. *Our Ecological Footprint: Reducing Human Impact on the Earth.* Gabriola Island: New Society Publishers.

Wenar, Leif. 1995. "Political Liberalism: An Internal Critique," *Ethics* 106: 32–62.

Wenar, Leif. 2005. "The Nature of Rights," *Philosophy and Public Affairs* 33: 223–252.

White, Stuart. 2007. *Equality.* Cambridge: Polity.

Wilkinson, Richard and Pickett, Kate. 2010. *The Spirit Level: Why Equality is Better for Everyone.* Harmondsworth: Penguin.

Williams, Bernard. 1973. *Problems of the Self.* Cambridge: Cambridge University Press.

Williams, Bernard 1981. *Moral Luck.* Cambridge: Cambridge University Press.

Williams, Bernard. 1985. *Ethics and the Limits of Philosophy.* Cambridge: Harvard University Press.

Williams, Bernard. 2005. *In the Beginning was the Deed.* Princeton: Princeton University Press.

# Index

*Political Philosophy: The Fundamentals*, First Edition. Thom Brooks.
© 2025 John Wiley & Sons Ltd. Published 2025 by John Wiley & Sons Ltd.